PRAISE FOR *RADIANCE OF THE ORDINARY*

"Tara invites us into her deep intimacy with the world in all its radiant texture — joy and grief, wonder and pain, love and longing. Her writing holds both the weight and the lightness of being, and with it, the reminder that we need both. Through her words, the transcendent becomes grounded, and we're gently called home to ourselves, where the connection we yearn for has been waiting all along."

— **KATE KAVANAUGH**, host, Mind, Body, and Soil podcast

"Tara welcomes the reader in with the warmth of an outstretched hand — and one does not want to leave. Even in the depths of grief, she never leaves the reader, never loses us. Hold tight, she seems to say. Do not look away. This is important.

This is a beautiful book, true and necessary. In language that shines and shimmers, Tara shares a life lived with grace, honesty, and most of all, love. This is a book that the world needs."

— **HEATHER HEYING**, coauthor of *A Hunter-Gatherer's Guide to the 21st Century*

"This beautiful book is a new classic in the realm of farm memoirs. A gorgeous collection of essays that read like homilies, immersing the reader in the soft light of the ancient rhythms of family and farming while also offering guidance and steadying words through the harsh realities of the cycle of life. Couture's message: be strong, be productive, notice beauty. This is the farm book we needed for these times."

— **LARISSA PHILLIPS**, columnist, *The Free Press*; farmer, Honey Hollow Farm

"A rare gem sure to inspire the rooted life. Tara will not only speak to your heart and mind, but she'll awaken your subconscious with words that pierce your soul."

— **JUSTIN RHODES**, author; filmmaker; homesteader

Radiance of the Ordinary

Essays on Life, Death, and the Sinews that Bind

TARA COUTURE

CHELSEA GREEN PUBLISHING
White River Junction, Vermont
London, UK

First published in 2025 by Chelsea Green Publishing | PO Box 4529 |
White River Junction, VT 05001 | West Wing, Somerset House, Strand |
London, WC2R 1LA, UK | www.chelseagreen.com
A Division of Rizzoli International Publications, Inc. | 49 West 27th Street |
New York, NY 10001 | www.rizzoliusa.com

Copyright © 2025 by Tara Couture.
All rights reserved.

No part of this book may be transmitted or reproduced in any form by any
means without permission in writing from the publisher.

Publisher: Charles Miers
Deputy Publisher: Matthew Derr
Developmental Editor: Natalie Wallace
Copy Editor: Buzz Poole
Proofreader: Diane Durrett
Designer: Abrah Griggs
Illustrator: Maria Pace

ISBN 978-1-64502-309-8 (hardcover) | ISBN 978-1-64502-310-4 (ebook) |
ISBN 978-1-64502-311-1 (audiobook)
Library of Congress Control Number: 2025014845 (print)

Our Commitment to Green Publishing
Chelsea Green sees publishing as a tool for cultural change and ecological stewardship. We strive to align our book manufacturing practices with our editorial mission and to reduce the impact of our business enterprise in the environment. We print our books using vegetable-based inks whenever possible. This book may cost slightly more because it was printed on paper that contains recycled fiber, and we hope you'll agree that it's worth it. *Radiance of the Ordinary* was printed on paper supplied by Marquis that is made of recycled materials and other controlled sources.

Authorized EU representative for product safety and compliance
Mondadori Libri S.p.A. | www.mondadori.it
via Gian Battista Vico 42 | Milan, Italy 20123

Printed in Canada.
10 9 8 7 6 5 4 3 2 1   25 26 27 28 29

This book is dedicated to my husband, Troy.
You are my king, my man among men, my immortal beloved.
Steadfast (and then some).

And to my three daughters.
You are the radiance.

CONTENTS

PART ONE
Harvest

Sea of Wheat	3
Bison Harvest	11

PART TWO
Home

Radiance of the Ordinary	25
The Dance	31
The Making of a Milkmaid	49
Paddy	59
In My Kitchen	64
Motherhood	75
God	101
Recipes	106
Of Blood and Butterflies	117
Cutting Meat	123

PART THREE
Evermore

Hands of the King	133
Ursula	134
The Death of Our Daughter	144
Leo's Lookout	163
Little Pig in a Hut	168
Frogs	185
Salvation on Eight Hooves	191
Apple Trees	203
When I Die	209
Acknowledgments	211

PART ONE
Harvest

Sea of Wheat

Of all the places I have rested my bones, it is my bed of wheat I most remember. I remember it as I experienced it — in my small child body. That body is long gone, but there it is, resurrected, as familiar as the one that carries me now, the moment I close my eyes and go back to that place, that time. I was six years old then, with jet-black hair and big brown eyes. The old ladies and aunties at church used to gush over my long, thick eyelashes. It embarrassed me. Who would ever want long eyelashes? So I took a pair of scissors and cut them off. Then I discovered what eyelashes were for after all, and I spent the next few weeks rubbing my eyes from the irritation of the stubble.

That was the time when I was small and I lived in the country, on the corner of my grandparents' farm. There were black-capped chickadees there, singing their song to the prairie. My grandmother, a Slovak immigrant, was called Bapka, and her farmhouse kitchen was dressed in the blue-green colour of a time that's gone. She ground poppy seeds and walnuts by hand. She reached into her woodstove and brought out fresh-baked buns she topped with hand-churned, iridescent golden butter. She served plates of pierogies she had shaped, one by one, with her own fingers.

The old barn down the gravel road where my teenage boy cousins hung out was papered with pictures of naked boobs and girls in bathing suits. Threadbare, dusty sofas were striped by the bleaching, burning prairie sun that reached through those old, breezy barnwood boards. I remember buds and blooms and sweetness. Frogs serenaded me to sleep. Cicadas sang when stillness robbed motion. Geese came from, and geese left for, lands far away. Calves were born, wobbly and soft.

RADIANCE OF THE ORDINARY

Big red machines planted wheat all around us. I would wait until the wheat heads sprouted fat, milky tops, then peel them open for a snack. It was the 1970s, a time of bell-bottom jeans and Bubble Yum gum.

There was a small white church across the road from our house, plunked in the middle of a field. A looming, shimmering grain elevator with a green circle painted on the side called to me like a prairie lighthouse offering safety. Our rural school bus was full of my older cousins, who would sometimes call me to the back to sit with them. I was too young, too uncool to sit with all those teenagers, but they let me anyway. We were family. I belonged to them and they to me.

Walking into the field behind our home, the whole prairie laid out before me. Across those fields I could see the small copse of trees that lined my grandparents' driveway. My uncle lived across from their house. He worked the fields after my grandfather's death. Next to our home, another covered in asphalt siding. It belonged to Mrs. Gertchun. My sister and I used to hide in the tree line and make wild sprints for her vegetable patch when she went inside. Rumour had it that Mrs. Gertchun was one hundred years old, maybe older, but that never stopped her from appearing suddenly in her doorway, yelling and waving at us, chasing us out of her patch like the wild rodents we were. It was always worth the risk. She grew the sweetest garden peas around.

And that's all there was: the endless sea of wheat, swaying in the wind under a wide blue sky; the prairie birds; a couple of buildings; and miles of gravel roads and deep ditches. On warm days, I would walk into the wheat, skimming my fingers along the tops of the stalks, looking for just the right place to lie down. When I found it, I would walk in a circle. Around and around, from the outside in. The stillness of my world was amplified by the cicadas buzzing and the sun pulsing. I could hear the sun when I was small. It's harder to hear it now. Once satisfied with my flattened bed, I would pull a couple of heads off some standing wheat stalks as a final, fluffy touch. I would lie down, and there I would stay, drifting in and out of sleep, watching clouds in the shapes of seals and dragons overhead while I plucked wet, sweet, chewy wheat berries and ate them, one by one.

The birds would perch on the very tips of the wheat, swaying with the field. They would come and sing. My prairie chickadees sounded

— 4 —

SEA OF WHEAT

slow and hot, almost mournful. They dragged out their song, like they had all day and intended to use it up by stretching out what they had to say. "What's the rush?" Later, I learned that some birds make different sounds depending on the region they're from. Like a dialect or slang or, in this case, the perfect harmony for a still landscape.

One afternoon, I fell asleep on my hidden wheat bed. I woke to a crawling sensation in my pant leg and jumped up like a wild cat, stripping off my blue jeans and screaming, certain there was a snake in my pants. The moment I hopped up, my eyes met those of my uncle, seated in the glass cabin of the big red combine, an enormous paddle-wheel on the front, charging straight toward me. A look of terror flashed across his face. I looked up at him in that combine, unaware of the danger, fearful only of the punishment I would receive for ruining some of the wheat. I grabbed my jeans and ran all the way home. He never said a word.

Do you think it possible that a wee cricket might save a little girl's life? I do.

———

Back then, I went on the regular dump runs with my dad. I loved the dump. It was full of stories. There were dolls with missing arms, old refrigerators in pinks and aqua blues with rounded corners and protruding tummies. I would pick through layers of broken trinkets with a stick, hoping to unearth an intact treasure while my dad spoke to some old men. The dump was a world unto itself. Dead things rotted. Broken dishes that once held a family meal were scattered like constellations in the mud. Old clothes and washing machines and boots with holes in their soles found their resting places at the dump. Sometimes there were bears there, snuffling around for juicy bits. On those days, I had to sit in the truck while my dad quickly flung out our garbage.

One day, my dad and I came home from a trip to the dump in the old rusty blue Chevy to find our house on fire, smoke filling the porch. I stood in the driveway as he opened the door to the house. Flames shot out like a wild-toothed monster and engulfed him. In an instant he was gone. And then, from within that ball of fury, he slammed the door shut, and the flames were contained again. He looked back at me

RADIANCE OF THE ORDINARY

with terror in his eyes and shouted, "Tara! Run to the neighbours! Tell them to call the fire department! Go! Now!"

A neighbour on the prairie isn't like a neighbour in the city. The closest neighbour (save for old Mrs. Gertchun) was a kilometre or so away down a gravel road. When I got to the end of our long driveway, the one I ran down every morning to catch the school bus loaded with my cool older cousins, I looked back. My father was running in and out of the garage salvaging what he could. The entrance to the house was engulfed in flame — the tools and equipment in the attached garage were all he could rescue. I didn't know if I would ever see him again.

I ran. I ran and I ran and I ran. I ran with the vision of my father on fire. I ran with the weight of the world bearing down on me. Everything was up to me. I couldn't stop. That morning, I had left our two cats, Neesha and Snowball, in the house. What if they were burning? What if they were burning at that very moment because I couldn't run fast enough? I heaved and sobbed and ran as fast as I could, but I felt so slow.

When I finally reached my nearest neighbour, an alcoholic woman, she didn't believe me. She refused to call the fire department. I begged and pleaded and wailed. She slowly pulled on her boots, her two German shepherds at her side, and said, "I'll go see for myself."

She walked to my burning home. I ran ahead. When I got back to the driveway, I could see towers of flames shooting up from the back of my home, high and reaching. My father yelled, "Did she call?"

"She doesn't believe me!" I cried back.

She came into view then. He yelled some things at her. She yelled some things back and quickly turned around and went home to call the fire department.

The fire burned our home down.

My parents decided not to rebuild. My little sister and I got to go through parts of bedrooms and pick out a treasure or two. The fire hadn't quite reached the addition on the house that held our bedrooms. Our father and grandfather had built that addition only a year earlier. I still remember the smell of putrid smoke and the dampness from the water the firefighters doused our home with. I was scared by the photographs on the wall, which now showed us with bubbled-up faces. I was scared I'd find cat bones. I grabbed a bracelet and a hand-carved

— 6 —

SEA OF WHEAT

box my parents had brought back from a trip. I couldn't think of what else to take. We had to hurry. We weren't even supposed to be in there.

The fire chased us to a low-rent town house in the city. I started life at a new school that I walked to. The school bus was gone. The wheat fields and country gardens were gone. All around me were houses so densely packed that I barely saw beyond orange brick. My parents divorced a few months later. Divorce wasn't so common then, and I wasn't sure what it meant. All I knew was that one evening they took me and my little sister to Ponderosa Steakhouse for supper. They even let us eat the lollipops that came with the bill. I knew something was up. When we got home, they told us they didn't love each other anymore and they weren't going to be married anymore. I threw myself on my sister's bed. I remember looking at her bewildered face and saying, "Don't you get it?" The next morning my father was gone when I woke up. I ran through the house calling him, but he wasn't there. Why hadn't I run faster when our house was on fire?

That fire had burned and burned and left a charred ring around all I had known, all I had ever wanted. A home, a family, a bed of wheat to sleep on — all of it ashes. I was still small, but I was big enough to shoulder the burdens of adults. And big enough to know I wasn't home.

———

I spent the next many years of my life trying to find the peace and belonging I knew in the wheat fields. I dreamt of the prairie birds and their mournful tune, but in the waking hours it eluded me. In the city I would climb trees, the biggest and tallest I could find, and I would cry in their limbs or watch the little people below, detached in my secret world. I would go down to the riverbed and light fires. I would stay out playing marbles until the streetlights came on. I became a bit of a marble shark. Every game I played was for "keepsies," and it was always high stakes — jumbos and the coveted crocks. It was all or nothing.

I started to smoke. I got beat up by a gang of girls. I was lonely. I missed my dad. I took it out on my little sister. I had a tumultuous relationship with my mother. I was desperate to grow up and get out and answer the hunger inside of me. I tried out private Catholic school. I tried out public high school. I got kicked out of school. I partied and drank and

— 7 —

RADIANCE OF THE ORDINARY

searched for something I didn't understand. I dated angry boys and bad boys — any boy who seemed disturbed enough to be interesting.

Living in my second apartment (after having been kicked out of the first for a party in which some guys set off the fire extinguishers), I found myself with no money. I started working at a truck stop on the Trans-Canada Highway with my auntie, who had been working there for decades. She was a kind, good-hearted woman, and she could tell a joke as salty as a sailor. She would sit down with the long-haul truckers at three in the morning, smoking, swearing, laughing, and telling jokes. They all loved her.

All night I would peel hard-boiled eggs and mix enormous bowls of tuna salad to make into sandwiches. When the truckers came in, smelling of diesel and exhaustion, I would fry them up a burger. The restaurant called them "nips." There was the "cheese nip," the "fully loaded nip," and the "big nip." "Nip" as in "nipple" wasn't a thing back then. I wonder if they've changed the name since.

And then, having been christened into the world of rough, down-to-earth, working-class fellas, it was only reasonable that I accepted a proposal to join the army. I had no money and no long-term prospects. I drank and partied away every dollar I earned. My second apartment was evicting me. What did I have to lose?

So, at eighteen, I joined the army. They put us all into a Hercules aircraft — no windows, no seats save some webbing strapped to poles, and every last wire and pump exposed. Nothing like the commercial jets that soothe our fears of mechanical failure by hiding any sign of mechanical anything. The door closed, and the feelings and sounds told us we were air-bound. When that giant rear end opened again, a group of pissed off looking soldiers stood before us, yelling and cursing and demanding we "get your shit together!" Rucksacks were thrown all over the tarmac. Dust blew everywhere. It looked like a deserted airfield with no signs of life. We could have been anywhere, but we were in the middle of nowhere Saskatchewan, and I was about to have my whole world disassembled piece by piece.

I slept in a metal bunk bed in the military. I slept on the benches in the backs of trucks with dust so thick we had to wrap scarves around our faces to breathe. I slept in mud wallows. I slept in concrete bunkers.

— 8 —

SEA OF WHEAT

I slept wherever I could when the moment arose, but I found no rest. I left one place and went to another, and then another. The military shuffled me to where they wanted me. They told me what they wanted me to do. They gave me what they wanted me to have and trained me to be what they wanted me to be. And I did it all. I was in the top of all my courses. I was given awards for fitness. I won a frozen turkey for marksmanship at the Thanksgiving range competition. I taught recruits. I manned the command post. I adapted.

I was also charged for being AWOL because I was too drunk to set my alarm. I got lost with a few friends and ended up off-roading on an artillery range, coming dangerously close to being obliterated. I got into fights. I pushed my body when it said, "no more." I learned how to be all of the things I was supposed to be, but the rebellion would never settle. In those worrisome moments of stillness, when things were quiet, that old ache would resurface. I missed something. Always missing something but never knowing exactly what.

———

Eventually I left the military. I fell in love with a man. I had my first beautiful baby and then another and then another. Girls, all of them. Chubby, substantial little babies who instantly transformed my world. For them I could be more than what I could muster for myself alone. But my husband, Troy, was still married to the military, too, and so we continued moving from home to home. Everything was transitory. Nothing was permanent. In every house we lived, even the military rental housing, I took care to make it feel calm and welcoming. I didn't have control over much, but a peaceful environment was within my capacity.

Every time we moved, one of our first priorities was to find our farmers. My mother brought me up eating real food. She had no faith in the margarine everyone was starting to use back then. She scoffed at the sweet, sugary cereals that graced my friends' tables. I was green with envy when I went to sleepovers and got to pick whatever soda I wanted to drink from the shelves in their basements. We ate chips and candy, and in the morning, we had frozen waffles drowning in syrup that was mostly high-fructose corn syrup. My breakfasts at home

— 9 —

consisted of eggs or homemade muffins or nutty whole-grain porridge with (disappointingly) real maple syrup. Over the years, my yearning for junk food gave way to an appreciation for the real food I had grown up eating — food that set the foundation for how I would feed and nourish my own family.

So, whenever we moved, locating those farmers who would feed our growing family was as important as setting up our utilities and switching our drivers' licenses. Our farmers provided our family with raw milks and cheeses, beautiful golden-yolked eggs, butter, sweet garden produce, berries, and autumn apples. We bought bison and pork, beef and chicken. In one place we lived, an emu farmer provided us with enormous eggs, maroon-coloured meat, and wondrous fat.

During one of those early years, when our young family was blooming, we went to an open farm day at one of the farms where we bought our meat. It was the end of the day, and the sun was setting a glowing red on the prairie horizon. Our kids had climbed the big round hay bales, and then skipped across the tops of them, laughing and evading the cracks that threatened to swallow them whole. Troy and I were enjoying the peace of the moment — little-girl laughter bouncing off barnwood boards, frogs calling one another from the ditches — when suddenly I heard it. That bird. The bird of my wheat-bed serenades. The chickadee of the prairie clan. It never left. It knew its home. It was there, and so was I.

I looked at Troy and said, "This is what I want. This is what I've been looking for."

Bison Harvest

I sat in the front of a flatbed rig, wedged between two cattle ranchers, Richard and his burly brother-in-law, Moe. The smell of diesel filled the entire cab as we traversed the endless prairie in search of a bison herd that might have been anywhere in Richard's thousands of acres. I listened as the two men discussed the possibilities. We climbed subtle inclines in the landscape, sure that at each crest we would look out on the herd. These bison lived like their ancestors who had once dotted these grasslands, roaming. Herds of antelope resting in the morning sun sat upright at our appearance, then bounded away. Red-tailed hawks flew overhead. Deer scattered across the prairie. But there were no bison to be seen. A part of me was relieved. No bison meant I was off the hook. I didn't have to witness anything. For when we found the bison, the ranchers would select the one that was to be harvested. They would kill it.

———

I had first met Richard, his spirited wife Kathy, and their bison years earlier, when Troy's military posting landed us in Alberta — land of Canada's cowboys and prairies and, a short drive away, the Canadian Rockies. As with all of our military moves, the first thing we did upon arrival was sort out where we would get our food. That "where" was always a farm.

Like many young people, I had been chased into a stint of vegetarianism by my introduction to the horrors of industrial farming practices. When my immune system began to break down and my muscle slid off into a heap on the floor, I had the good fortune of meeting an incredible healer who, to my dismay at the time, told me I needed to reintroduce sourdough bread with butter, eggs and bacon, and drippy roasts and potatoes, all of which I had liberated myself from during my vegetarian enlightenment. I thought her mad.

I got sicker.

I thought her worth reconsidering.

I brought those foods back into my diet and I thrived. Not long after, I found myself in a crowded hall listening to a presentation by a gal named Sally Fallon Morell. She spoke about the traditional foods our species has thrived on for generations and what our modern, industrialized, processed diets have done to us. I already knew what she spoke of to be true for myself, but here was the science and common sense behind it. What Sally shared with us that day solidified our family's direction; our commitment to buying all of our food directly from farmers was made then and there. And wouldn't you know it, this fine fella Richard, a cattle and bison farmer raising his animals solely on the native shortgrass prairie, just happened to be in that crowd. We met. We talked. Troy and I made a date to visit his farm and see what he was up to.

That first tour of Richard and Kathy's farm was followed by many more. They became "our farmers." Every year we purchased our beef, bison, lamb, and chickens from them in the fall. It's in the fall when farmers harvest grains, produce, and even (I'd argue *especially*) animals, if they're following the rhythms of nature. It's in the fall, after a spring and summer of fattening on sweet pasture grasses and other forages, that animals are at their healthiest, fattest, and highest nutrient density. We've come to expect meat or lettuce any time of the year, but there's a dishonesty in that. That's what grocery stores do best — they erase the seasons and the natural scarcity with the illusion of consistent abundance. Nothing is asked of us, other than our dollars. We are not asked to economize, to preserve, or to use the entirety of an animal. We don't even know all of the good bits that are supposed to come with our choice cuts, never mind when it's the best time to harvest an animal. It's just another way that, at least in the West, we humans have become more separated from the natural world. Our food carries a signature, a message that speaks to our body of time and season and place. When

— 12 —

BISON HARVEST

none of those things align with what we're currently experiencing in the world, there can only be incongruence. But more on that later. Let's get back to Richard. I like it there, with him, best.

Richard soon became one of my dearest friends. One of my earliest memories of him is from an open farm day he and Kathy hosted — the same day my prairie bird called me home. There was a tremendous spread of food roasting over fire and bubbling away in cast-iron cauldrons. There must have been close to a hundred people there. Parents with young children, like ours, gravitated to the baby lambs and calves that would nibble delicately on little outstretched fingers. The dairy cow, friendly ambassador on behalf of the more aloof beef cattle, came to make the rounds as any good representative must. At one point, Richard gathered us all to go visit the chickens. He had a tub of something in his arms.

As we walked, he spoke to us about how chickens are raised today — how they are "vegetarian fed," to their detriment. He told us about the marketing fallacies of such campaigns; how keeping a chicken inside and feeding them soy not only makes *them* sicker, but us, too. By the time we arrived at the chickens, hundreds of them fenced in a field, he had most of us convinced. For those who were still doubting, he had in his arms his coup de grâce.

"Hey, guys!" And there was that playful smile of delight that would spread across his face when he was about to really pull one off on someone. "Guys! Who here thinks chickens are vegetarians?" A couple brave souls raised their hands a few inches high. "Okay — watch this!" And with that, Richard reached into the tub he was carrying and threw the ground meat trim and organs into the air above the chickens. A great sprinkling of bloody raw flesh rained down on those birds, and we, the captive audience, watched in disbelief as they went absolutely wild. We observed the transformation of placid, clucking chickens into rabid, carnivorous dinosaurs. One would grab a morsel and run, the others in hot pursuit. They would squawk and fight, running with their dangling bits to find a place of refuge in which to eat their bounty. Wings flapped, chickens jumped in the air and slammed their chests against one another. The frenzy lasted mere minutes, and the ground was pecked clean.

— 13 —

Nope. Chickens are not vegetarians.

Over the years, I started going to Richard and Kathy's farm for more than just meat. I went to learn. I went to hang out with one of my favourite humans in all the land. I went to work. I went to find the sweet, bone-weary fatigue that slides over your body when you lay yourself to rest after a long day of physical labour in the outdoors. Richard and I shared books and authors and new ideas we had heard. We talked philosophy and Wendell Berry, for who could separate the two? We talked about food and mental illness and the anger in our society, for who could separate the three? I remember a book about finding the best steak in the world and what it would take to make it. I wrote to the author, boldly proclaiming, "I know where you would find that steak — come to Alberta with me!"

It wasn't all lessons and deep conversation, though. Richard was a prankster, always up for some fun. After a day of castrating calves, I made the mistake of betting against him while we were moving some wayward cow and calf at night. I was sure he had misread her tag number. He, of course, knew he hadn't. The next day, I found myself eating raw calf testicles with a chaser of tequila, my brazen confidence trumped by a rancher who truly knew his cows.

He delighted in telling stories of his pranks, from the time he rigged up a ghost on a wire to hover over the prairie for his kids on Halloween to others that I dare not mention. He had a boy's heart in that big man's body. He could be vulnerable and confused by cruelty, and he would sometimes express fury over what humans were doing to the Earth. And he was the most dedicated, capable man I had ever called "friend."

But of all that I came to know about Richard, there remained a riddle I could not solve. How could a man so deeply connected to nature, a man so dedicated to doing what is right over what is easy or pleasurable, aim a rifle at the head of one of his animals and pull the trigger? How could he kill?

I tried to overlook it. I tried to push away the thought. I convinced myself that because he grew up doing it, something was calloused and hard in him. That's how he did it. It was automatic, drilled in at a young age when he couldn't yet contemplate the significance of such things. Right, yes: that's how.

BISON HARVEST

And yet, something niggled me about that story.

One of the greatest lessons I've come to learn is how enormous the distinction is between an animal loaded onto a trailer and taken to an abattoir to be killed and an animal chewing its cud under the sunbeams when, suddenly, *bang!* Not a single moment of awareness or fear or stress. I understood that then and I understand it even more fully now. I can recognize the distinction in the flavour and energy of the meat. My family, and all of Richard's other customers, benefitted from a man who pulled the trigger so we didn't have to. But my gratitude for Richard bearing that heavy load was mixed with bewilderment.

"How do you do it?" I asked him.

"It must be done," he said.

"Can I come?"

I barely believed the words as they escaped my lips. Yeah, right. I couldn't. I knew I couldn't.

———

I'm not sure everyone would have been as afraid to witness death as I was when I volunteered that day. From the time I was a little girl, I was plagued by fears of death. Plagued, truly. Whenever my mother left for an evening, I would stand on the electric baseboard heater under my window watching for her return, sure it would never come to pass. She would most certainly die, and I would most certainly be all alone. I had rituals in my prayers that I thought would safeguard me and my family from dying. I was certain I would never live to be an adult. Everywhere, and in everything, death was imminent. The deep, black, everlasting nothingness. That's where I was headed.

What a wretched design life was! To have and do and be and then, all of a sudden, in a moment, die. As I got older and stopped begging my mother to stay home, I kept that fear of death, only I kept it so well buried that I never much thought of it. Instead, I behaved as if I would live forever. I was careless and reckless and wild. Death was not welcome in my life. I had mastered that fear, kept it at bay by ignoring it. Like an annoying friend, death would soon get the hint when it received little attention.

— 15 —

RADIANCE OF THE ORDINARY

But something had become dislodged when I met Richard. That fascinating, rarefied human who would stop dead in his tracks to witness the simplest of nature's offerings at his boots. A prairie crocus. A loyal dog. A universe of microcosmic life in the tiny puddle of rain pooled in a cow's hoofprint. Nothing would escape him — not a sunset, not a rain shower, not an owl on its perch, not an antelope on a faraway horizon. He took it all in, the abundant beauty and the abundant heartache of what we were doing to it all. He was a man built of salt and earth — real. I needed to know how he possessed both this wonderment and the ability to take an animal's life. I wanted to understand what he had and why I couldn't find it. And in order to do that, I knew I had to say "yes" to the things he did. I didn't know where I was going, but I trusted him to show me. I wanted to know, to really know, what he held to be true. Unbeknownst to me at the time, Richard had become my mentor, a guide in my life to places and ideas I had never known.

Through the time I spent with Richard and his family, it became apparent to me that my understanding of nature was a superficial gloss. I cognitively accepted that there was a "circle of life," but I only wanted to participate in parts of it. Give me the baby ducklings but keep the decay and decomposition, if you please. Observing Richard's dedication to wholeness, his own preferences aside, made me realize how my perspective was infantile. Maybe in the holes, in the gaps, in the parts avoided, was the treasure all along.

"We have to face our shadows." We've all heard something along those lines. I live by it, now more than ever. Then, in those conversations with Richard, I decided for the first time that I would excavate death from beneath the avalanche of tactics I used to keep it buried; I would let it out into the light of day. If I were to have my own farm one day, it would be a farm that was governed by nature. I would only raise animals if it was me who killed and butchered them. It was a sincere commitment, and to make it, I knew I would have to first face death.

———

We had been driving for close to an hour when we finally came upon the bison, the entire herd, lounging in a valley. Calves with their mothers,

BISON HARVEST

young bulls and heifers mingling with the elders. Off to the side stood a strapping young bull. He had been pushed out — the main bull saw to that. One didn't have to look hard for the leader of the pack. He stood dead centre and proud to the herd. As the mothers turned to hide their calves and stepped back, he stepped forward, thick with power and steady with purpose. What a majestic beast he was.

We shut off the truck and got out. A light wind and the occasional prairie bird call were the only sounds. It was just me and the two ranchers. I stood quietly, trying to take my mind off what we were there to do. I looked — marvelled — at those men's hands, as thick as grizzly paws from decades of lifting, hoisting, pulling, heaving, ripping, grasping, and wrestling, yet gentle enough to softly caress the small of their beloved wives' backs.

We stood there, under that blazing prairie sun, looking at the bison. The men were pointing out different animals, evaluating them as potential candidates for the day's harvest. I listened and watched and tried to see what they were seeing, but I knew nothing about measuring the "finish" of an animal. That wouldn't come until years later.

All I could hear was the pounding of my heart as Richard showed me which one it would be. I stepped a few feet back from him as he leaned over the front of his truck hood and took aim. The bison weren't far from us. That was important. I knew that after he shot the animal, we would rush to her so he could sever the arteries connected to her heart. She would be brain dead, but the heart would continue to pump blood out of her body and into the prairie soil, the earth swallowing her lifeblood. I wanted to close my eyes. I wanted to turn around. I didn't want to see an animal in pain or her herd wild with fury or fear. I told myself, once again, that I couldn't do it. How could anyone look at such a majestic creature and kill it? It was a perversion, a wrong, an injustice incapable of correction. I decided right there that what I had learned was that humans are a deranged lot. To look through the scope of a rifle at something so profoundly beautiful and pull the trigger? Unfathomable.

And there, from within the deep layers of my fear, something more powerful commanded, "Do not close your eyes."

Bang!

— 17 —

RADIANCE OF THE ORDINARY

The shot rang out and the animal collapsed to the ground. My ears and eyes couldn't decipher a gap in time between the two. A sound; a collapse. Instantaneous. The other bison jumped back, looking bewildered, but they didn't run. Richard ran to the collapsed animal and cut a slit in her chest that allowed him to sever the arteries. A great gush of blood poured out. I stood behind him. The bison stood around. I stepped closer.

I touched her then. Touched her and prayed as her eye stared, unflinching, at the blue sky. The last thing she saw — her blue sky. The silence was so deep I could hear my heart beating. The powerful breaths of the bison exhaled into the space between us.

Something found me then, on that vast prairie. It entered me, swirled and danced, moved like a sweet, soft wind through the thick wool of the bison and the strands of my own hair. There was no dark force, heavy and thick, sucking away the brilliance of a life. There was no shrinking or ending or contraction. Instead, I felt an opening, an expansion of space. An unknown portal revealing itself with an invitation to enter. I couldn't measure the offering, and I understood logic to be the wrong tool. The material world receded. Spirit expanded. Here was a place I at once understood. I belonged. All was well. Life was transforming. It was holy. It was sacred. It was Divine perfection and the enormity of it all could only be met with humility.

My hand was still on the bison. I looked down at her again and knew her body was empty. She wasn't in it anymore. I could see her more clearly in the spaces between and beyond us. I began to weep. How glorious she had been, animated with a powerful life force, and now . . . she was not. It was heartbreaking, but there was something more, something surprising. I was overwhelmed with joy. In an instant, I felt an assurance and clarity the likes of which my Catholic school teachers could never deliver. That bison was dead, but death wasn't what I had been told it was. I'm not suggesting the bison went up to bison heaven and roamed about for all eternity. I have no idea where that bison went. But I knew she was a part, always, of the whole. Her death, all of death, feeding the life that will one day feed death again.

She wasn't in her body anymore. A body left behind to nourish us, as the life that had been moved on. Wherever she went, that beautiful

— 18 —

BISON HARVEST

animal, she carried on her mighty back the turmoil of a young girl and the confusion of a young woman. She left, in her wake, utter, untouchable peace.

———

And then it was over. The physical world, held back by our collective trance, would be contained no more. The sound of hawks crying overhead and rustling unease among the herd ushered us back into our brains and the tasks that now had to be completed: connecting chains to her rear legs; running the winch to hoist up her body; securing her body on the bed of the truck. As we drove away, I looked in the sideview mirror. The bison were following the truck. I turned around and watched as the whole herd trotted quickly behind us. They were staying with their herdmate. I was heartbroken. I didn't want it to be true that they cared, that they held emotion, that they were bonded to this dead animal. But neither did I want to be a girl who tucked things away in dark corners anymore. I had to acknowledge and sort through the deep ache I felt alongside my sense of joy and wonder.

The ending of a life, the power of that moment, is generously saturated with both pain and elation. That is the truth. It was the first time I realized honesty lies in opening up to the duality of life. I could hold myself open to pain and love in the same moment. Both could be real at once. That had to be true because they were both there, tumbling around wildly in my heart.

I forced myself to watch the herd just as I had forced myself to witness the death of that bison only moments earlier. What was she to them? A daughter? A friend? She was part of their herd, their collective, that much was certain. She had her place in their hierarchy. I didn't need to make up a human story to satisfy my unknowing. Whatever it is that holds meaning for an animal, for those bison, she was part of that. She had purpose, and she belonged, in some bison way.

We headed back to the farm, where we hung the bison carcass outside and began to gut and skin it under the purifying sun. Cheemo, the comedic husky, took no time to find us in the field. He squeezed himself between my calves and set to work plucking the eye from the carcass. A husky knows where his nutrition comes from. I was surprised by my reaction to the visceral act of burying my fingers in the woolly hide and pulling it back as my knife slid cleanly between it and the flesh below. It was primal and connecting, something remembered by the ghosts lingering in my bones. We talked as we went, laughing, telling stories. Marvelling. Marvelling. Marvelling.

After the hide fell to the ground, Richard slid his knife down the soft underbelly of the animal, unwrapping a most miraculous gift. Inside, a treasure chest full of the deep, shiny liver, as clear and bright as a ruby; golden suet wrapped around glistening, loaded kidneys; a powerful heart as beautiful and red as a spring poppy. Richard pulled out these riches, holding them before my eyes. One by one, each turned over, illuminated by sunbeams. The deep yellow fat glowed on that still prairie, where the lonesome call of black-capped chickadees rang out and a red-tailed hawk soared high overhead, watching.

The fret and worry were gone. My hands were covered in blood. My clothes were covered in blood. And because of that blood, running over and into my skin, that animal was now and forever a part of me. A gift so monumental I never could have understood then how dramatically it would alter my life.

When our afternoon of skinning, gutting, splitting, and then finally hanging the cleaned carcass in the meat cooler was over, we made the rounds for evening chores. There was life that had to be fed and watered and moved and closed in from predators, and it depended on us. Then, a hot shower washed away the soil that had blown into my hair and the blood that had dried in the folds of my skin. And finally, finally, a long, luxurious supper of bison hump roast with roasted garden vegetables swimming in raw Jersey butter, and a vanilla custard made with farm eggs and that same Jersey's milk.

There is nothing sweeter, no meal more delicious, no shower more luxurious than the ones that come after a day of hard work. Pleasure earned is the only real pleasure worth having. When exhaustion and emotional upheaval and hunger culminate into a whirling dervish of discomfort, you know you are only moments away from something delicious. So, make it delicious. What an opportunity!

I laid down in Richard's spare room that evening, silent save the coyotes howling right outside my window. They would feast, too.

BISON HARVEST

I couldn't sleep. I was buzzing with pleasure and relief and revelations. All those years, afraid of death, and there I was, suspended in that coyote cacophony, realizing I was free at last. I was euphoric. I thought of the bison following the truck carrying the body of one of their own, and I felt deep sadness. And I was aware, again, that I was capable of holding conflicting emotions simultaneously. It never was true, what society had taught me up until then. One thing didn't have to be wrong for another to be right. And furthermore, I knew that my pain or discomfort did not determine the rightness of a thing. It was so much more layered and complicated than that. It was too much to decipher in the moments before I fell into a deep slumber, but those thoughts would return. They would return again and again.

———

I expected to come away from my first experience harvesting an animal steeled and hardened. I would have the skills needed to do the dastardly deeds on my own farm. A necessary evil. What actually happened is that I came away cracked open in extraordinary ways. It was as if all the years I had lived up to that day were a jumble of experiences, thoughts, and ideas stored in my pockets. I could roll them around between my fingers, but I could never make much sense of them. They loaded me down and jingled incessantly, but the map legend that deciphered those symbols was missing. I couldn't anticipate that the bison harvest would be the legend that put it all together. I knew then that I knew nothing much at all. There were no words or lessons or definitions for my experience. None were needed. I was touched, and I was healed.

That day opened me up to the false narrative around the dichotomies of life. It opened me up to profound truths. And in those truths lived both light and dark, sweet and bitter. It's not that one exists so the other must, too, but that one exists *for* the other, *in* the other. Together, one and the same. Joy in pain and pain so that joy may live. All parts in a symphony so brilliantly played that it's only possible to discern which instrument is playing what if we really concentrate. But why concentrate? Why tease apart anything when we can know them more fully together? Why not be swept away with the melody of the whole?

RADIANCE OF THE ORDINARY

I used to chuckle at Richard and how his Alberta accent caused him to say some words in an odd way. One of them was "beautiful," which he pronounced "beauty-full." But he was right all along. Too lazily, and without really opening to it, we say something is beautiful. Richard took care with that word. He didn't let it roll off his tongue and fall away. He would point at something in the sky or perched on a fence post, and he would say, "Look at that, Tara, isn't it beauty-full?" He was right. He was right about everything. It is all so beauty-full.

PART TWO
Home

Radiance of the Ordinary

So it was that to buy our first farm we had to agree to purchase the home — a terrible 1960s kit house made of orange brick, vinyl, linoleum, and every other plastic you can think of — for the land and not the house. We would have a farm, a beautiful farm, with two hundred acres of lush, rolling fields of grasses and wildflowers. There was an underground aquifer that erupted between two boulders and ran, tumbling down softened rocks until it disappeared again into the earth. Wildflowers swayed around large ponds that migrating ducks thought worthy of resting in for a time. Deep in the woods, an enormous mound built of carefully placed rocks, clearly arranged by human hands, held the bones of something (or someone).

We filled that farm with the majestically horned Highland cattle of my dreams. We had Jersey and Guernsey milk cows and then added some old Canadiennes from a friend who had kept a closed herd for decades. We had the powerful, black, gentlemanly bull I had yearned for over the last many years of dreaming my farm dreams. We raised heritage breeds of pigs and chickens and turkeys. We bred them and sold them. We had an acre garden filled with all the open-pollinated seed varieties I had worked with on other farms. There was abundance, and there were endless hours of work.

We gutted the house and made it livable. It was "fine for now." It was, after all, all about the farm, not the house. We were used to living in houses made by and for others. We were used to decorating and applying new paint to spruce up things a bit. We were used to quietly and continuously anticipating the end of a time in one house and the inevitable move to another. But here, on this land, maybe we could build a good house one day. We would stay for the land and remind ourselves to appreciate what couldn't be replaced.

We spent five years on that farm. Every day, from dawn until dark, we worked. We built fences and livestock structures, we cut hay and stacked hay and fed hay. We rotated our animals on grass every single day. We ran water lines and carried water buckets. We built new things and tore down dilapidated structures. We cleaned out old barns for weeks, filling eighteen-foot-long refuse bins again and again with broken glass, rotting old clothes, smashed fluorescent bulbs, and every bit of household waste the previous owner couldn't burn. He didn't believe in the dump — "too expensive" — so he filled his land and his barns instead.

I loved that land, and it came to know me. But it was distant, too. Traumatized, maybe. Soulless, for certain. It was strange that, having no intention of moving ever again, I found myself pulling up real estate listings one day while Troy and our youngest daughter, Mila, drove to the dump. It's only now, seeing those words, "while Troy and our youngest daughter, Mila, drove to the dump," that I am aware of the weaving together of two pieces of the same cloth. It was after a trip to the dump, decades earlier, when my father and I came home and found our house burning. Decades later, while Troy and Mila were at the dump, I found home again.

I called Troy and excitedly told him about an incredible-looking farm I had found just over an hour away. I read to him the realtor's words. I explained what the pictures looked like. It had a farmhouse, a real, stone foundation farmhouse that was 170 or so years old. Maybe it was falling apart in real life. Maybe it was caving in and crumbling, but couldn't we go look at it? I had a feeling, a strong intuition. We're supposed to have this house, I told him. As uncharacteristic as my actions may have been, it was his that were more so. He's a logical sort of fella, steered by common sense and facts. But we had been together a good many years by then, and we had both learned, through many trials and tribulations,

— 26 —

RADIANCE OF THE ORDINARY

how his sound logic is best mixed with my intuition. He turned the truck around, part way to the dump, and came home. "I've never heard you like this," he said. "Call the realtor and see if we can go look at it."

Look at it we did, that very afternoon.

As we approached that unknown farm, the map indicated that we should turn onto a side road. At the corner of that road was a sign that read, "Radiance of the Ordinary," with an arrow pointing in the direction of our destination. I looked at that sign, stunned.

Years earlier, I had been perusing a used bookstore. The best kind of used bookstore, filled with books from the floor to the ceiling, some crammed under the bottom shelves, resting on the floor. Great, weaving columns of books leaned against shelves sagging with the weight of obscure titles and passions, all rescued from oblivion. I found a book slid on top of the others on a shelf. I pulled it out and was immediately stopped dead in my tracks by its title: *Radiance of the Ordinary*. Imagine, I remember thinking, devising a better string of four simple words to guide us through life? The book turned out to be about rural Japan, but I bought it for the title alone.

So, when that road sign popped up, I knew wherever it was we were going, it was to be our home. I knew it without a doubt.

As we drove down the side road, I made Troy stop in front of an oddly shaped building painted silver. Out front was a hand-lettered sign. "Radiance of the Ordinary" was a little business selling homemade brooms, custom furniture, and yurts, housed in an old cheese factory from the mid-1800s. Maybe, long ago, the people who lived in the house we were visiting had delivered their milk to this very cheese factory. And still, both buildings stood strong.

The moment we stepped into the house, we felt something profound. It was beyond the aesthetics or the square footage. There was something transcending the tiny, dark kitchen and the homely addition. The house wanted us. The house had been waiting for us.

For almost two hundred years, this home had held families. They came to this farm, and they cleared it of rocks, which are still mounded in enormous piles scattered throughout the forests and grasses. They built a small barn and carved their initials in the hand-hewn

— 27 —

beams. They took some of the rocks they had plucked from the soil and formed them into the foundation of the house. This house was home to families who loved it, were loved in it, were loved by it. It was shelter and warmth. The house could hold her people because she was anointed as home.

Nothing makes sense from there. Another family, from Toronto, wanted the home as a weekend getaway. There was a bidding war. We didn't even have the money or approved mortgage to buy it, but we did anyway. We won the bidding war and arranged the financing and made a pretty penny on our first farm because of our years of toiling to improve it. We moved that whole farm to our new land. We filled trailer after trailer with cows and pigs. We loaded our movable rabbit and chicken houses onto flatbeds and transported our flocks. One night they went to bed as usual; the next morning they woke up to a new universe. Everyone looked confused.

We walked through the hallways of our new home bewildered. It was a long, cool sip of water, and we had no idea how parched we had been. This home delighted in us. When we put in windows to let in the sunshine, she sparkled. When we painted the tired walls, she smiled. We sanded her floors and oiled them, and they are soft beneath my feet. We warmed her with wood and filled her bones with the real and the worn. There is nothing plastic here. No varnishes or coating, no laminate or vinyl. My home understands who she is and loves us through her authenticity.

The materials here hold echoes of lives past. Antique farm tables and wool, sheepskins, and furs. There are old ceramics and crocks, tarnished brass and copper lanterns. Our world is lit with beeswax candles and oil lamps. Old, nubby linen lines decrepit, creaky stairs. Our furniture is solid wood because it's old, and that's how furniture was made back then. It's taken me decades to collect these old things with which to surround ourselves. All of it loved and used by others, filling our home with the resonance of their love held therein. Our home is full of the spirit. Human hands touched and crafted what is here, not machines. I've lived in machine houses, and they never were home.

RADIANCE OF THE ORDINARY

But this is home. The home that was here all along. The home that sat waiting for me to move through what I must, to learn what I had to, so I would recognize her the instant she was shown to me. I am held. Our family is held. These walls hold peace and love. I work with her to create this sanctuary. An escape from the madness, silence from the bickering — we are untouchable here. This is home, and I can rest. There is nowhere to go. There is nothing to find. Here, I can be still and listen to God. I can grow into my life.

I recently read a book that told the story of Laura Ingalls Wilder and the complicated, often antagonistic relationship she had with her daughter. As a grown woman, Laura was proud and pleased of the home she was finally able to create with her husband, Almanzo. He built their home, carefully hewing beams from the trees he felled in their forest. He collected endless stones to build their gorgeous fireplace chimney and hearth. After a lifetime of moving, Laura was finally home. Their daughter, Rose, had different ideas. She built them another house, loaded with the latest technology, like electricity and plumbing, and moved them into it. They stayed as long as they had to in appreciation of the outrageous amount of money she had spent on it, but the moment they could, they returned to their handmade home next door.

I wouldn't leave this humble little farmhouse for all the riches in the world. I understand why Laura and Almanzo returned to their home. It was *their home*. When they weren't in their home, they were in a house, waiting. When they returned home, they were at peace again.

At seven years old, I left the only home I ever really knew, her bones burnt and plastic sheets covering the gashes that revealed her guts. I had lived in houses before that one, and I lived in endless houses after. Today, I am home again. I hope my old home, eventually rebuilt by another family, is loved. I still love it, and I think that matters.

I'm writing this in the darkness of an early winter morning. The fires I started in the woodstoves have calmed into glowing embers. My old Great Dane, Louis, is snoring, curled up around the kitchen cookstove. He's more of an enormous cat than a dog. The beeswax pillar candles, thicker than an arm, are burning next to me. Their

RADIANCE OF THE ORDINARY

wicks remind me it's time for a trim by flickering and sputtering in their pools of melted wax. I shorten them with my brass scissors and the flames return to their peaceful glow. My whole home conspires with me to share these words. I can be me because I am held here, safely tucked into my life.

The Dance

Our dance together. Him and me. Me and him. Both of us wound up in something bigger than either of us alone. The floorboards beneath our feet are worn and rutted with our steps. He holds me. I hang on. I wrap myself around him and feel his spine beneath my fingers. My face nestles in his neck, and I smell him.

We dance and dance; all these years we have danced. He moves and I move around him. I take a step, and he illuminates my way. When our children were small, I spent most of my days alone, but when he returned from faraway adventures and the drudgery of providing for a family, we danced then, too. Sometimes it was harder to find our steps. Finding ourselves uncoordinated, we would bicker.

"You're on my toes!"

"You won't let me lead!"

But we would try again and again until we figured out the steps and the rhythm of us.

There are no small children anymore. Now two are grown women, full and vibrant. Now one lives in the heavens, full and mysterious. The music is quieter, but it's to our liking. The floor is all ours. Nary a toy in sight to trip us up. Sometimes it feels too big. The walls, no longer needing to absorb the sounds of three children playing or three teenagers fighting, have grown lazy. Everything echoes. On second thought, maybe the walls aren't lazy. Maybe they're full and they can't take anymore.

Hurried mornings and hockey schedules and rowing regattas are faraway memories. It's our time now. After loss and grief and incomprehensible heartbreak, we find ourselves here. Still together. Still in awe of every nook and cranny, every bend and bone of each other's bodies. We sit on the couch together, and instinctively my leg folds under his and his arm slides over this part and I shift further down into that part. Those rutted paths so familiar. When we're there, we're home. I hardly know where I end and he starts. He would say the same. So tightly sewn together we can't even see the stitches.

On this dark winter morning we wake together. All our lives we've woken together. Gone to sleep together. When he was in the army, I woke with him if only to be the first face he saw, sending him off into the metal and thrashing with a kiss and a hug and the fortitude of home. That loyalty remains, all these decades later. "Steadfast" — that was the word we chose for our marriage many years ago. Steadfast despite all obstacles. Steadfast carries us when we've had enough and reinforces us when we're weary.

It's five o'clock and we start our day with a naked hug. The air is bristly in this old farmhouse, but I am in my lover's arms. The whole world is still asleep, and we have it all to ourselves. This is what we choose to do with our time. We hold each other. Then we move. Then we slip on our pyjamas and wool slippers and head down the creaky wooden stairs to the kitchen. He goes directly to the woodstove in the living room and gets the fire started. I go to the cookstove in the kitchen and do the same. The silence of the house fills with the popping and crackling sounds of wood aflame.

Louis hears the woodstove and scratches on the backside of the door from his bedroom. Our old Great Dane has been around long enough to know the dance. He's figured out his own way to take part. I open his door and give him his good morning pets. He walks straight to the living room where he takes up residence beside the woodstove. His bones seek out the penetrating heat of fire. Often, he will lie before the fire and stare quietly into the flame. I don't know what he's thinking about, but I know he's at peace.

When my cookstove is hot, I put on the kettle. While the kettle heats, I grind the coffee beans. There are no lights on yet. We are mindful of the dark, keeping the inside of our home in alignment with the outside. So, we move by the shadowy light of oil lamps and candles. It's all warm and silent save the shuffling of our woolen slippers on

THE DANCE

the wood floors. He is warming our mugs with scorching hot water. Years ago, I read a little French cookbook wherein the author spoke of the indignity of pouring tea or coffee into a cold cup and serving it to one's company. Well, we certainly don't want any such indignities on a morning like this. Since I read that all those years ago, every cup that holds a hot beverage in our home is first christened with hot water. I wonder how I ever survived before I learned this trick.

The water is boiling, and I pour it over the coffee beans while he gets the cream. There is no fresh cream for us in winter. We leave our milk cows to rest now. It's too cold to ask more of them. Instead, we leave them the same as nature would leave a mother ruminant cow. Let them use their energy for heat and a warming layer of fat. Besides, they are on hay now, the dried grasses of summer. Their milk is lower in nutrition and flavour. We'd rather wait for the sweet abundance of spring. But we've squirrelled away a few jars of last summer's cream for special moments, and this morning, we've decided, is worthy of thawed summer cream. Not because of anything on the calendar, just because we have been judicious in our cream usage, and there's plenty to keep us until our cows have their calves again. It is a morning made special thanks to that rarified cream.

Sourdough bread is toasted and slathered with liver pâté. Eggs are poached. A jar of summer peaches is opened and poured into bowls, topped with a heap of homemade yogurt. Some moose sausage from Tory's successful hunt snuggles up to the eggs.

Into the black coffee the dollops of slightly warmed cream go, and together we walk in a procession to the living room — him and me followed by our Border Collie, Tinder, who surely and definitively follows closely behind. Tinder, the little black-and-white dog with the brown eyebrows, is the spark that gets everything going around here. The tractor moves because he wills it. The turkeys shuffle around the barnyard because he makes it so. The postal delivery truck drives in and reverses out because of his talents. He has confidence where some may question its validity. The only thing he has given up on are the barn cats. Barn cats care little for his self-esteem, and they use his every attempt to get within their vicinity as an opportunity to thump him over the nose or give him a swipe with their claws. But the barn cats are a distant memory this morning as he successfully herds his humans to

— 33 —

their spots on the couch. When we get there, he lies down at our feet. Surely, in his mind, he is holding us in our places.

I light more beeswax candles. The oil lamp creates an orbit of light that includes us. The winter chickadees and blue jays are still sleeping, wrapped in their feathers for warmth. There is no noise at all except the crackling fires and the slow snoring of Louis, wrapped around the hearth like a cat. We fall into our places and our limbs start to find their way all on their own. His leg over mine, my other over his. A foot tucked into a lower back, an arm resting over a knee. I couldn't say what goes where. It's all automatic, each bit thinking for itself, finding its true north, and then all is right. It's comfortable. It's peaceful. Everything where it should be.

We eat our beautiful food and savour our strong coffee, and then we read together. Every now and then he says, "Listen to this," and I put down my book and listen. Then we talk about it for a while. Sometimes we stare off into the fire with Louis, contemplating an idea or dreaming up a new adventure. We stay like that until the sky is tinted with the halo of the rising sun. I get up and he gets up and we blow out candles and wind down the oil lamp. It's time to go outside. Time to do our part to welcome the dawning of the new day, the rising of the life-giving sun.

We walk to the summer kitchen at the back of our house. It's cooler in here, and the cold air trapped in our jackets give us a brisk welcome. I grab the rolled-up sheepskin. We head outside, where we are immediately greeted by two of the barn cats who also know this dance. They follow us into the orchard where we have the only view of the rising sun through our encircling forest. All around us, forest, but there, in the orchard, a little break between the sumacs and cherry trees, facing directly east. I unroll the sheepskin and lay it on the ground. I hold on to him to balance me while I take off my boots. He does the same. We stand, grounding to the frozen earth through wool and snow as we wait for the sun to appear. Three more barn cats come yawning and stretching out of the barn. Each cat vies for our attention. We pick them up, one by one, as the others knead the sheepskin at our feet. Sometimes there's silence, punctuated by the purring of exuberant cats. Sometimes we talk. But this isn't the time to discuss the day's tasks and business. This is a time of prayer and gratitude. We are here! Alive! The whole cluster of barn

THE DANCE

cats purr in unison, each one with their own unique purr. Some deep and guttural, others riding high in their throats. All of them serenading the morning sun. How wondrous this world! Little cats tuning our hearts to the small miracles in a day. Reminding us to look for them.

We pray with our eyes set on the sun's golden eye. We set our intentions for who we will be on this fine day. And after, we slip on our boots again, shake out our sheepskin, and trudge through the snow back home. I can smell the woodsmoke in the air. I look at our home and wonder, "Who are the lucky people who get to live there?" We go inside and shake ourselves off. Our morning is set. It's time for breakfast and chores and a day full of life's demands. But we go into it reinforced. We go into it with joy and calm. The world can have us now, at least as much as we're willing to give.

———

It's all lovely, yes? It's as lovely as we've crafted it to be. And as much as I'd like to leave us there, cozied up by the hearth, I cannot. As romantic as the soft days of this country life may sound, they are only soft because of the hard days. There's nothing wrong with romance — I quite like it myself — but to only show that side of things is dishonest, and it's important to identify that dishonesty wherever it exists, especially in this time, in this world, where we are inundated with images of endless pleasures. Where our culture sells us on the idea that hard work is beneath us, or out of reach. Where entertainment is our highest calling. That strife and disappointment are wrong, frustration something to run from, discomfort something to avoid at all costs. None of these things are true, and they keep us locked in a perpetual chase with no fulfilling destination. They are romance as a gloss, a thin veneer of gauze and plastic roses meant to keep us eating without ever being satiated. And because of that, I need to pull us out of that warm wintery nest of pleasures and into the reality of what makes it so profoundly and deliciously pleasurable — and that reality is work. Hard and demanding work.

The pleasure is earned through our labours. The slowness of winter comes after seasons of exertion. But spring will always come again. Spring demands the awakening of life. From the trees to the flowers, the hawks to the snakes, it is a time to wake up and get moving.

— 35 —

RADIANCE OF THE ORDINARY

Spring demands we earn our keep. We leave behind the fires and the long, leisurely mornings where darkness conspires with time to hold us in the shelter of our home for a little longer. Spring bustles and blooms and fleets and prances, shaking her mane wildly, covering us all in her dew and rains. She insists we get out of bed and get on with our days.

When I was a little girl, I always felt lucky to spend a night with my grandma and grandpa. My grandpa, a joyful, hard-working French-Canadian carpenter, would come into our room when it was still dark and snapping with cold, singing, "Good morning to you, we're all in our places with sunshine-y faces!" The song was unending, his voice cheerful and insistent. We grumbled and tried to hide under our sheets, but it was no use. Spring is just like my grandpa. Or maybe he, like her.

In the spring, buds and babies and blooms. From dormancy, we move into a speed of growth impossible to capture. Skeletal trees burst with life, from buds to unfurling leaves in a seeming instant. Birds return, chattering and chirping, singing and twirling, long before the sun finds its way into our windows. The mourning doves and whip-poorwills sing throughout the night, joining the mating frogs.

We spend our days outside now. All day every day. There is much to do. Our muscles grow sore, our lazy psyches shocked by such demands. "Where's winter! We want winter!" cry our sleepy bones, but winter is gone and spring will have none of that talk. It's time to work! Our milk cows have their calves, and soon we find ourselves sharing milk, which means sharing milking duties. The calves, of course, have a much easier go of it than us. Our big, clumsy hands are no match for their sucking prowess when it comes to getting that luscious, creamy spring milk, but we endeavour nonetheless. We share milk with the calves. It's always our goal to raise healthy animals, improving the genetic pool of our little herd year by year. That means babies stay with their moms. It makes for calmer, happier cows and vibrant little calves that grow into calmer, happier cows.

Whatever we do, we try to follow along with the way nature has designed things. The folly of the human is to always think he can outsmart the brilliance of our Creator. We prefer to emulate what's already been figured out by a force much brighter than our puny little minds. Our animals spend the entirety of their lives under the same

— 36 —

THE DANCE

skies they gazed upon when they were born. They're adapted to our stifling summers and our frigid winters. They graze the fields and the forests of our little farm. They eat thousands of species of forage, not just one type of grass. They eat leaves and shrubs, wild herbs and medicinal plants. They eat legumes and wildflowers. And in their meat, the profound nutrition from all of those wondrous compounds, too varied and numerous to ever really know.

Our ducks' lives revolve around their pond and the fields around it. They live with bossy geese who, like the ducks, lay their eggs year round but collect them every spring, hiding them from raiding humans until, when they've determined it's time, they start to sit on those eggs. Soon enough, the pond is filled with little balls of fluff, all dutifully following their mamas like clouds. Our chickens and turkeys, too, lay their eggs of Easter egg blue, dark chocolate brown, light caramel brown, and even olive green, all year round, but on one special spring day, they decide it's time to sit on those eggs and refuse to get off. Sure enough, one morning I will go into the chicken house and hear a little peep, and then another.

And that is when my favourite sound in all the world commences: the sound a new mother makes to her babe. It's a specific sound, unique to every type of animal, but uniformly one of connection and security. A new mama cow makes the most buttery, low, guttural moan to her calf. It can sound worried as she watches her calf struggling to stand on its wobbly feet for the first time, falling again and again. It can sound reassuring as the calf calls out, having lost sight of its mother. It's an "I'm here. This is me. I'm your mother" sound. It's beautiful and it's tender.

Mother hens have their own sound — a small chicken rumble from their breast. They peck around, showing their chicks where to find the water. They alert their babes to food, calling them with that excited noise that brings the little ones running. Geese banter back and forth. The ducks imprint their ducklings with their duck mama call. All of the animals, in their own ways, quickly and strongly bond with their babes. There's always an odd mama here and there that has some trouble, but that, too, is the way things go.

Our pigs wallow in mud puddles they've dug out to their specifications. They use their powerful noses to dig into the earth to find the roots and shoots of the things they love best. They need to be moved around.

RADIANCE OF THE ORDINARY

The sheep, too, need new electric fencing reels strung every day. And so it is, from the time the grass has grown enough to turn the animals out on it, we start our days outside, collapsing electric fence sections and stringing up new ones. When it's raining, we are still out there. When the heat is oppressive and the humidity is suffocating, we are still out there.

Spring is when we earn our keep. Garden beds must be amended with compost and weeded and planted. Milking must be done every day, and with that the making of cheeses and butter and cultured dairy products — enough for a year of eating. Fruit and nut trees are fed with the life-giving compost we have made from the manure and bedding of our farm animals. It's the time when Troy fires up the sawmill and starts milling us boards and beams for the projects that need be done while the earth remains unfrozen. Every year we designate one project "the big one" for the year. A bunch of small ones will squeeze their way in beside it, but the big one is the one deemed mandatory, and we commit ourselves to it no matter how strong the desire to nap in the hammock.

Last year our big project was a poured concrete root cellar, a thing of my dreams. For years we were creative with how we stored our fall harvest. We stored our food in clamps (essentially holes in the ground), in makeshift meat-hanging cellars, in our storm cellar, and even in the cold corners of our basement. We had put in our time. Finally, after a few decades of patiently waiting, we were able to build my root cellar. Dug into the earth, it has a natural granite floor, and its poured concrete walls and ceiling are adorned with boulders and big rocks we collected from our farm. The roof is planted in the same grasses as the fields around it. Inside are shelves full of my preserves, ferments, cheeses, and meats. There are baskets of autumn root vegetables like turnips, potatoes, and carrots, and there are jars of freeze-dried and solar-dehydrated foods. Sometimes I sit in there and admire the bounty, appreciating it all the more knowing what it took to fill those shelves.

And spring is where the "knowing what it took to fill those shelves" part is just beginning. We plant and prune and feed. New babes and new life of all sorts require more attention and time. Freedom to come and go from the farm is limited. We are needed here. Things are happening and we're responsible. We interfere as little as possible, but

THE DANCE

when my favourite milk cow, now fourteen years old, is about to have her calf, I am going to be present to make sure all goes well. That's just part of the deal.

Spring, of course, gives way to summer. The sun, our life-giving sun, can feel oppressive at times. We soak up every bit of her we can, stripping down to only what's necessary for any given task, but she can be a bit much on those hot, hot days. On those days, the ones heavy with heat, it feels like the whole world is hiding, only the cicadas still awake. The cows hide in the shade of the trees, chewing their cud. They'll only come out early in the day and once the sun has started its downward journey. The chickens pant, lying splayed out in their dust wallows hidden below the enormous old crab apple tree. Our dogs pant incessantly and scratch at the door of the house, hoping to find a cool floor to spread out on. But there's no escape for us.

In summer, I spend my days tending the garden, collecting whatever is ripe — summer squashes of all ilk, sweet green peas, flowers of all sorts — and bringing them into my old farmhouse to ferment and preserve. Throughout the seasons I forage the wilds, too, looking for the plants we use as food and medicine so I can prepare them for whatever their use will be. It's during these months, from spring to summer and on into fall, when we grow, harvest, prepare, and preserve all of the food we will eat over the coming year.

Sauerkraut and pickles bubble away in enormous crocks. Homemade vinegars, wines, and ciders bubble away in dark corners of the cold cellar. My kitchen is overrun with hundreds and hundreds of glass jars, all at some stage of readiness for the endless procession of jams, jellies, fruits, chutneys, sauces, and pickles I prepare. Cheeses age and herbs are salted down for preservation. All the troops are called into action during the autumn harvest. The solar dehydrator, used all summer long for edible flowers and foraged plants, now holds the last of the season's herbs and foraged mushrooms. Our five freezers are filled to the brim with beef, lamb, goose, turkey, rabbit, venison, moose, and old roosters and hens. There are bones and organs and rendered fat, every last bit of every animal honoured and used. We do it all ourselves. Every animal born is raised, harvested, and butchered by us. Root vegetables are dug and preserved in our root cellar. Wood

— 39 —

RADIANCE OF THE ORDINARY

is piled near the house. Cattle are moved up to the barnyard from the forests they've been living in all summer. Winter housing is prepared for all the critters. Hay is stacked. The hatches are battened down. A full year's worth of food packaged and preserved. We race toward the completion of endless tasks knowing we will never quite get there before winter arrives with her calling card.

We work to earn the slowness of winter again.

———

There was a time when my perspective on the struggles and frustrations in life aligned with the dominant narrative of the day — that they were something to be avoided, and, when that didn't work, something to get through as quickly as possible so I could return to the good stuff. In there was the dichotomy I unknowingly built into my days: when things were "good," I was "good." When things went astray — when I was outside in −30°C temperatures, messing around with a piece of metal fencing my cows knocked down — I was "bad." That was me, a little boat at sea, heaved about by every wave that came.

I didn't suddenly wake up a Zen master, unaffected by frustrations. I went through a trial of some of the most condensed and profound frustrations in my life and was forced, in the valley of death, to either pick a different route or stay where I was, reacting in the same ways, until I soured and puckered and wilted away. That was at the first farm we bought. I decided I didn't want to pucker after all.

We bought our first farm in 2012. For years before that, I had been working and learning on farms all over Canada. As we moved around and found the farmers who would feed us for a time, I also begged them to let me be their farmhand. I sanitized bottles with our raw milk farmers. I moved cattle with our beef farmers. I fed hay and weeded endless gardens and planted tiny little seeds. I shoveled more manure than I care to remember.

We were struggling for cash back then. I was staying home with our three young daughters, working only a few appointments each week as a nutritionist. Troy was still an infantry officer, gone most of the time. I spent my days driving to farms for our food, shuttling our daughters about, going on adventures in nature, and sitting on the floor at our

THE DANCE

local libraries reading books on farming. I knew how to rotationally graze cattle before I even had a cow.

So, when we finally bought our first farm, after years and years of saving and searching and waiting, we were ready. It was going to be hard work, but, by golly, it would be a dream come true! And it *was* a dream come true, but it was also truly and completely trial by fire. Five years of endless turmoil, eating our suppers at eleven o'clock at night, fixing crumbling infrastructure, and embarking on projects that demanded all of our time, money, and attention. There were frozen pipes that burst, a contaminated well, a house with mould, barns with stray electrical current that would zap you if you dared touch the metal support beams inside, water pipes that had to be laid to move water over two hundred acres, buildings to build and fencing to erect. We planted thousands of trees. And our marriage was on the cusp of ruin.

Years earlier, Troy had gone back to university to become a medical doctor. It was a trying time for our family, especially for him, as he navigated a return to school with "kids" half his age. He took on an enormous workload of classes and grueling residency requirements, all the while being a devoted family man. These were the years preceding the jump into the purchase of our first farm. We went into that new life with years of fatigue wrapped around our ankles.

In all our time together, the relationship I shared with Troy had been the one steady, untouchable thing I could hold fast to. One day on that first farm, in the midst of mind-numbing exhaustion, I looked up from the row of carrots I was thinning and watched Troy as he worked. He looked miserable. We had been locked into that unyielding pace, moving through life focused only upon meeting demands. Our lists of to-dos were never-ending, and we were acting like victims, slaves, to . . . to what? To decisions we had made.

"Are we going to be okay?" I asked.

"What do you mean?"

"Is our marriage going to survive?"

I wanted his automatic reassurance, something he had always given me without a thought. I wanted his, "Of course! How could you ask such a thing!?" But that's not what he said. He stopped weeding, looked up at me, and said, simply, "I don't know."

— 41 —

I could hardly believe what I was hearing. It could not be. I immediately categorized this news as "bad." Who wouldn't? It was bad. I might have even felt sorry for myself for a time. But bigger and louder than my sorrow was my fury at feeling victimized by my circumstances — circumstances we had willingly created.

"No," I decided. "That cannot be. Our marriage is not up for grabs." And I meant it. Whatever had to go would go. I had made a vow to this man, and I wouldn't let anything usurp that.

That day not only saved our marriage but brought us through to today, where this man has become not only my best friend, but my co-conspirator in building the life we want to live. We — Tara and Troy, just a gal and a fella — are alright as two separate people, but it's the us, the we, that is the great, beautiful, fragrant, and unfolding blossom of our lives. Without that day in the garden, we never would have gotten here, to this enduring marriage that would soon, although we didn't know it then, come to face a devastation we never would have taken a second to imagine — the death of our child.

It was through those five years of toil, with joy and happy moments woven through, of course, that we solidified what was important to us, what we valued, and how we would choose to live our lives as designed by us. When we knew our relationship, one we thought beyond reproach, was starving, we started to look at the sources of its malnourishment. Date nights weren't going to cut it. We needed to act, and not just say, our marriage — our family — mattered.

But how could we do such a thing? The logistical hurdles quickly fill a mind that dreads the unknowns of change. Oh, the excuses we give ourselves. How could we change? We knew we wanted to grow and raise our own food, but could we do that without the demands of making a profit? If we downsized to a new farm, what of all the work we had put into this farm we loved? How could we ever get that back? Wouldn't picking up and moving just mean the same thing somewhere else? Same shit, different pile and all that jazz? We felt stuck. Beholden to the behemoth consuming us.

What I've come to learn is that I don't need to have the perfect answer for every worry that pops into my head. Answers have nothing to do with action. I need only make a decision and move in that direction.

THE DANCE

I conspire with my Creator, and I have utter faith that when I walk in the direction I've decided upon, the trees will clear and the path will unfold before me. It happens every time. Now, it's automatic. I decide and I go and whaddya know? The answers work themselves out. It's no surprise at all, but it still elicits my awe and abundant gratitude.

Our path out came via a new farm, half the size of the other. Everything shifted. We downsized to the number of animals we needed to feed and nourish ourselves. We planted an orchard with dozens of trees instead of the thousands we had planted at our first farm to create windrows across wide expanses of the windblown fields. We planted a garden with food enough for us. We stopped breeding pigs, and we got rid of our goats. It doesn't mean there wasn't work to do, but work is not a bad thing when you find the sweet spot. We had learned the difference between work and burnout. Yes, we work, but in every day we build in time for pleasure.

Those pleasures are simple enough, but they're the integral moments of a life. I can't tell you what Troy and I were working on last summer, but I can tell you it was a scorching hot day. When I found our milk cow panting in the tree line, I hauled out the garden hose to spray her down. I had come into the house and made us some ice cream. Some of our cow Bea's fresh raw cream mixed with ten or so egg yolks, vanilla powder, and a little splash of maple syrup. I rang the house bell (yes, still a useful tool in these parts), and Troy came in, drenched in sweat. We stripped off our clothes and ran naked to our cow trough hot tub (filled with icy well water in the summer months). We jumped in, whooping and hollering at the shock of the cold. We sat in there for as long as we could stand it, then ran back to the house. Only we didn't know the FedEx driver was around the corner, waiting at our front door. I'm glad Troy is a faster runner than I am. The delay gave me time to divert.

We took the next hour to sit (now dressed and suitably presentable) with big bowls of ice cream on our porch. We love that porch. While we ate, we watched two diligent phoebes patrolling the apple tree in front of us, gulping up little worms and aphids and tirelessly delivering them to the nest above.

It was such a pleasant moment, but no more pleasant than the one we shared the day before, drinking icy, fermented milkweed cordials

— 43 —

RADIANCE OF THE ORDINARY

in the same spots. On that evening, we were sitting on that porch again, mesmerized by the fireflies putting on a show all around us. Our exclusive performance, brought to us by the miracles of a loving God who put us here at this time to witness them. True pleasure. If we had sat there all day, lazy and slovenly, we would have felt restless and irritable, but we worked hard all day and came to rest with gratitude.

We never would have gotten here, to this place, had it not been for those years of struggle, learning what comes of a relationship from neglect. Maybe it's just us and our stubborn-minded tendencies, but our learning comes through living. I never have been one to listen to the warnings of others. One thing might be true for one person, but life is about variables, I say, and that same thing might not be true for me. This has kept me in good stead, but it can be a tough way to learn. It opens up endless avenues that most wouldn't venture down. The longer I live, though, the quicker I pick up on what is happening in any given moment. I no longer need hindsight to answer my questions – I can sense when I am being shown a new lesson or when a deficiency in my thinking and behaviour is being illuminated for me to consider and correct. It's a gift developed from a consistent practice of self-reflection.

I no longer look to Troy to fill in my blanks. I did that in the early part of our marriage. When things went wrong, my mission was to assign blame. I grew up with this practice. Something broke or something went astray, and it was immediate blame. That was the answer. Who needed to carry the guilty cargo of responsibility? When something accidentally fell and broke, the disappointment and wrath were projected at the person whose clumsy fingers were holding it at the time. When we depend on others to say or do the right thing, to fill holes they don't even know about, they will inevitably fail us, and we use that failure to obscure our own wounds. It never gets anyone anywhere. There is no truly lasting joy that comes from being right, no growing closeness with another person, but we do it all the time. We're more comfortable laying blame on a flesh and blood person than we are in facing and calming our own emotions. The problem is the cost of that temporary high – that release valve of accusation. And that cost is the formidable wedge that grows between two people. A wedge is not what I wanted in my marriage.

THE DANCE

I tried to figure out — *we* tried to figure out — how to hold up our marriage as the thing that it was supposed to be: a sacred union, a sum greater than its parts. The thing that kept coming up for us, in our bickering and strife, was humility. Humility doesn't need to be right. Humility doesn't make demands of someone. Humility has me turn inward instead of assessing the failures of my love. He is my love. And if that's so, what can I do in my life, who can I be, in return?

I was thinking about this one day while I was picking my way through the forest. The self-heal was in full bloom — so, too, the Indian pipe — and I was wandering off the worn trails of our woods onto the secret trails I share with the white-tailed deer, two loyal farm dogs, a menagerie of barn cats, some forest-dwelling bovine, and the occasional black bear. None of us are telling where they are. But that day I was feeling a little blue. Maybe I didn't sleep well. Maybe I had eaten something that didn't agree with me the day before. Maybe I was just grumpy. I was walking along, annoyed with myself, and then I got to thinking about Troy and how he was rushed and curt that morning. And then I got to thinking about how he had been rushed and curt a little too much lately. And then I realized that he didn't really seem to appreciate my nice meal the day before. Oh, sure, he said, "Thank you, it's delicious," but he was somewhere else. Where was our closeness? Why did he feel so distant, and why does everyone feel so distant, and do my children even *like* me? And what am I doing with this life anyway? What is the point, and . . .

You get the picture. Before long, not even cognizant of where my mind was taking me, I was in a whirling tornado of pitiful thoughts. What could I say to Troy to get him to hear me, to understand me? And then, as sure as the knocks of the ravens above, a strong, clear voice filled me: "Be love."

It stopped me dead in my tracks. Be love. Not be loving. Be love — wholly and without expectation. Instead of looking to others to fill me with what I wanted, I could be what I wanted. I could give more of what I wanted for myself. It sounds simple enough, but my muscles needed practice. I am a nurturing person by nature, but to be love, especially when I wanted to receive, was a struggle. And when I considered why that was, I realized that my perspective came from a place deep inside of me, small and selfish. I didn't like that. I didn't want to be that kind of person. How easy it should be to give our love, fully and without reservation, to those we love. What slight could ever erase true love? What inadequacy could ever require us to withhold?

Being love is the antidote to loneliness. It is the connector when we feel disconnected. And that, too, has been a great pleasure in my life. Even during the most harried situation, I am bestowed with the power to be love. The marvel of it all is that the more I have worked to be the person I want to be, the more intimacy and love has filled my life. That never happened when I was making demands on others' shortcomings.

———

This year, Troy and I are building a cordwood, wood-burning sauna together — a project for our health and our joy. We're also going to dig out an old-fashioned well in the forest in a spot that already bubbles up clear crisp water for most of the year and, curiously, is surrounded by cut rocks — a clue and a love note left by humans long gone. I imagine that first sip of water after days of digging into the earth with the hot sun on our backs. Our muscles, sore. Our will waning. But, oh! That first sip! No water from the turning of a tap can ever match what will come from the depths of the earth, revealed by our hard labour.

It all sounds lovely (admittedly, it's our kind of lovely) because it is lovely, but built into every lovely thing is the sacrifice of energy and efforts to get there. *And that is what makes it so.* We could pay someone to dig the holes and put up the fence and build us a sauna. And in the equation built using pure reason, most would look at finances as the key component. But finances are a weak measure of happiness and a strong governor of possibilities.

I once read there's a certain amount of money that is known to bring a sense of calm, and after that threshold is met, accumulating more and more does nothing to increase our well-being. I've come to understand that as true. In my life, there were times when I had to make twenty dollars stretch over a week to buy food. There were times when I could only put a couple of dollars in my gas tank. Those times were not characterized by calm. Now, decades into this adult life, we're okay. We could be a lot better off financially if Troy joined

— 46 —

THE DANCE

the marching ranks into full-time work and if I dedicated my time to online courses and consulting, but then we'd have more money and a lot less of the life we've spent shaping. I would have a lot less time to watch my granddaughter grow. A lot fewer surprise encounters with snapping turtles on my trail and their newly hatched babies.

Have you ever seen a newly hatched snapping turtle baby?

Every year, a dinosaur of a snapping turtle visits the front steps of our home. She's surely sixty to seventy years old. Maybe we share a birthday. She comes in the spring and goes directly to the corner between the stairs and the house, tucked behind a clump of flowers. I've given up on the flower bed; she arrives, waves around her powerful legs in the soil, and ruins it all anyway. Besides, what flower is more wondrous than an old, craggy turtle with green moss growing on her scarred and chipped shell, laying her precious eggs at the foot of your home? She stays there for a few days, lying in her soil depression. I peek at her regularly. You would never even see her if you didn't know where to look. After a few days, she will be gone. Her little eggs impossible to see.

She will never know if her efforts were successful. She will never be rewarded for the pilgrimage she makes from her marshy home, across fields and gravel roads. I wonder how far she has to come to get to our house. And why this house? Maybe when this house was built, one of the children found a young snapping turtle and made it his pet. Maybe the turtle and the child spent their sunny days together while the adults collected fieldstones to set into mortar for the foundation of their house. Our house for now. And maybe that turtle, the ancestor — the great-great-grandmother of our turtle. A long line of dinosaurs passing on the message: "Here is safe."

I'm going with that. I'm going with the invisible threads between long-ago humans and turtles and the baptism of this house with the wisdom of ancient mothers.

Whatever it was and continues to be, last year was the first year I finally saw the first turtle baby after it had just hatched. I had tried to spot them for many years, but I failed every time. I was sure a racoon or skunk, eager to dine on such a juicy morsel, had made it before I did, but I'm not so sure anymore. Last year, I was sweeping the front

— 47 —

walkway with my corn broom when I noticed that the piece of dirt I was about to brush away was moving. When I bent down to get a closer look I saw the most miraculous little creature — truly a miniature snapping turtle, identical in every way to its mother, save for the moss and the scarred shell of a long life.

I picked it up and felt its tiny, soft claws patter along my arms and hands. When a baby bird is born it looks nothing like a bird. I suppose it's obvious when we see it in a nest and use our imagination, but still, there's a long way to go. Same thing with a human baby. (Thank God adults aren't stretched out versions of babies, but babies are pretty darn cute at their scale.) All sorts of animals are like that, from rabbit kits to goslings. But others come into this world showing us exactly what they'll look like all grown up, no imagination needed. Deer are like that. Our calves, too. Reptiles of all sorts. And that little turtle, as perfect as can be, already full of intention and purpose. That tiny turtle was hellbent on getting to wherever the echoes in its tiny turtle bones were telling it to go. I let him go and watched as he made his way. Onward ho!

There is no way to put a value on such a thing — on all those years of watching that devoted mama, who sometimes walked right past me as I was bent over in the garden, giving me a little warning snap to leave her alone while she completed her work. The watching. The connection to turtles and humans of old. The stories I get to live in brought to me from unknowable places. A baby turtle, fresh with life, in the palm of my hand. There's no material thing that can fill me, no satisfaction so whole and delicious as taking up my place in the natural world. I am a part of these little miracles, as loved and as precious. I was created with love, an integral piece of this magnificent whole, this dance of seasons and pain and pleasure and work and play.

I could work for big dollars instead of big life, but then who would watch the barn swallows dive and collect the wild mushrooms from the forest? Who would notice the baby turtle on a mission to join his calling life?

The Making of a Milkmaid

To make good butter — or rather, sublime butter — we must start with the cow. Actually, that's not accurate. It doesn't start with the cow at all. It starts with the soil and the universes of conspiring little creatures that live within it, feeding the plants the cow will eat. If the soil is poor, the plants will be poor, and the poor cow will be poor, too. But that's enough to know for now — let's start with the cow.

If ever there was a bovine version of Loki, the god of mischief, Clementine was it. She was my first milk cow. A beautifully built, straight-backed, wide-jawed, doe-eyed bombshell of a Jersey. She had an udder like a heifer, tight and round, with nice milking teats. One doesn't understand the significance of a nicely shaped teat until they endeavour to hand milk a cow. A little too small — what I call "belly button teats" — and the milker must whittle their hand grip down to a thumb and a finger or two. Cramps and complaining are sure to ensue. Unfortunately, those belly button teats have been bred into modern-day cows so they accommodate a machine rather than the mouths of their babes. A little too big and the newborn calves will struggle to wrap their mouths around them. No, Clementine was, like Baby Bear's porridge, just right.

She produced so much butterfat that she was the envy of her barnyard pals. Her wonderful, thick cream was the source of so many of our delicious summer creations, from homemade ice cream to sweet summer butter to whipped cream for anointing sweet, drippy summer fruit. I'm sure I heard the whispers of her envious herdmates: "Sigh... some cows have all the luck."

Only nobody, human or quadruped, knew our little secret. They had no idea what went on behind closed barn doors. Clementine, practically perfect in every way, was a diabolical, impatient, naughty, stubborn, argumentative lass put on planet Earth to teach me a thing or two. Of that I am certain.

Milking Clementine started off romantically enough. She had a beautiful little butterscotch calf that she doted on, but she still had too much milk. We desperately wanted to start training our own little oxen team, so we adopted a second butterscotch calf, previously destined for the veal industry. He was too small to go in a trailer by himself, so we brought the new calf home in the backseat of our car, wrapped up in a feedbag with only his head poking out. The two calves were instant friends, and Clementine was very accommodating. She let the interloper milk from her immediately. All was copacetic.

And then milking time came.

To milk a cow as we milk a cow, you must first bring the cow to her milking stall. We begin by giving the cow a gentle rubdown, a nice massage if you will, with some lovely warm water — that is, if they're clean. But some cows aren't clean. Some cows have a penchant for taking a poop and then lying in it, and when they come into the milking stall, the horror of what you must attend to before you can even get to the milking part confronts you in all its caked-on glory. These cows tend to be the same ones that come in looking like they rolled in wet mud hours ago. Where they found the wet mud is a mystery that often goes unsolved. And still, there they are, filthy. These "dirty cows" are not hard to pick out. Look at any herd of lovely cows in a large field of rich, sweet grasses, all bucolic and shiny, and my money is that somewhere in that herd, if you look closely enough, will be "the one." Always gotta be one.

And here I'll give credit where credit is due. As challenging as Clementine would soon prove to be, she was too proud to lower herself to "dirty cow" status, no matter how insistent she was on making my morning milking with her pure hell on Earth. Along with her beautiful milk, being a clean cow is about all I'm willing to offer in Clementine's good name.

Morning milking time saw me walking into the barn with my stainless steel pails and a bucket of warm water and rags. I would always bring two milking pails. You will soon understand why. In the barn

THE MAKING OF A MILKMAID

was another large stainless steel container with a lid that could hold gallons of milk or, in its place, the dreamy aspirations of a failed milking session. I would then head to the top of the hill behind the barn and call Clementine: "Cooooooooome Bosssssssss."

There's a certain character to the calling of a cow. I've heard different farmers use different words, but that long, drawn-out call with its particular inflections is remarkably similar from farmer to farmer, place to place. The first time I was shown how to call a cow I thought I was being pranked. Richard and I were moving his cows from one field to another, and he said, "Tara, call the cows." I looked at him with a "how dumb do you think I am" smirk. He insisted he wasn't kidding, but I didn't bite. I wasn't going to be the joke at the evening dinner table (again). So he called them. He showed me the tone and the long drawing out of the words, and I watched in amazement as the cattle herd came running, bellowing with anticipation.

I once watched a video of a woman dressed in gauze and angel wings using her remarkable voice to sing a call to the "coos," and out they popped from the mist like spring crocus shoots. Nowhere to be seen one minute, then suddenly encircling her in magnificent numbers, staring with their big, curious, wanting eyes.

I didn't stand on the hill in my flowing dress, nor did I sing an ancient Gaelic song, but I would have if I could have. Instead, I stuck with the rugged call Richard taught me and that my cows came to know as mine. I called my cow, and my cow, so sweet and eager, popped her head up from whatever blade of grass she was interested in, took one look at me, and came running. Across the valleys, over the hills, disappearing and then reappearing bigger and bigger as she got closer. I would stand there and laugh as her udder swung from side to side. Surely, I would think, today will be different.

When she reached me, Clementine would run right by, straight into the open barn, down the length of one wall and into the doorway to the stalls. She would go right into her stall, first one on the left, and stand, shifting about impatiently, as I attached a thin chain to her collar. Then she got what she had come for. I wish I could say it was me, and perhaps we can pretend it was if we imagine that I were a few scoops of alfalfa. It was all about the alfalfa.

— 51 —

RADIANCE OF THE ORDINARY

I would clean off her udder and the milking would start. Clementine, happily munching away, would recognize this as her moment to take an enormous poop. Every single time. You can tell when a cow is about to pee or poop; they sort of hunch up their backs and adjust their footing while their tails rise. Must keep themselves clean while they poop on their humans, you know. These signals give the exasperated milkmaid time to grab the milk pails and back up, if she's paying attention. With Clementine, I had to always pay attention.

A poop in the milking stall delays things for a hand milker. I've seen dairies with an electric wire running the length of the milking stalls so that if the cows start to hunch their backs, they get a zap. It limits the peeing and pooping to keep things cleaner. That's not happening here. So, when the inevitable occurs, it means cleaning up the wooden floorboards and any other victim of poop splashes before starting the milking over. It's not so unusual that a cow will have a poop or a pee while miking. Some never, ever do — God bless them — but here and there it is to be expected. But this was not Clementine. Clementine loved her morning poop in the milking stall. She loved it so much she would even do it twice. And then, for good measure, she would have a pee or two as well.

Sometimes a cow will poop when they're stressed. Let us not waste a single second thinking Clementine was stressed. She was habitual and determined, not stressed. She was happy and calm as can be. She was in her favourite place, munching on alfalfa as the sun rose and the songbirds sang their morning serenade, fully enjoying her reign of terror over her hapless milkmaid.

Finally, once Clementine was cleaned, and sometimes cleaned again, the milking would recommence. I would milk and Clementine would stand glassy-eyed and relaxed. I would squeeze and release, squeeze and release, filling the barn with a rhythmic sound as streams of milk hit the metal pail, until there was enough milk to change the tone. The pool of frothy white milk grew. It was lovely. Me and this beautiful cow, this incredible beast of such power and grace. I would sit on my wooden stool, my head pushed into her side where a little nook, maybe designed just for a human head, welcomed me. I could hear her breathing, my head rising and lowering with her body. As I marvelled

THE MAKING OF A MILKMAID

at the rightness of, and the connection I felt to, such a moment with such a beautiful animal, she would lift up her leg just then and slam her hoof into the milking pail as fast as a rattlesnake bite. Sometimes, when she calculated just right, her hoof would go directly in. Most times the pail would spill, or else her hoof would flick in enough dirt and grime to make the whole pail undrinkable.

A legion of barn cats always came running when it was time to milk Clementine. I think they drank more milk from her, the hoof-in-the-pail milk rejects, than we did. I would have to stop milking and either clean up the spilled milk or pour out the dirty milk into enamel pie plates for the cats and chickens, then retrieve my second, clean milk pail to start again.

Then, Clementine would remember another of her superpowers. If she whipped her tail just right, she could evoke a yell or a grumble from me. She was a talent with that tail. My elderly neighbour taught me how to tie it up and out of the way so she would be able to swing the base of her tail without those fine little leathery hairs on the bottom reaching my face or, worst of all, my eyeballs. This only infuriated Clementine more, and she took to shifting from foot to foot to foot, threatening to knock over my pail with every movement. I released her tail and learned to quickly turn my head. Usually, it wasn't so bad. She'd catch the side of my head rather than my eyeballs. Usually.

And so it went with every milking: poop, pee, kick, whip, leg shift, knock over pail, poop, kick, leg shift, whip, whip, kick, kick, pee, knock over pail.

I learned quite quickly to never take my eyes off her legs. I knew by a telltale twitch in a muscle what she was planning next. It was a wordless game of one-upmanship. Could she get her foot in the pail, or would I block her with my forearm and move the pail, saving the precious milk, just in the nick of time?

Our miking session over, I poured the milk into the milk can, grabbed a handful of alfalfa as a little reward (even when no reward was due), and brushed Clementine. And here is where, before my very eyes, she returned from her demonic possession and inhabited that lovely, gentle bovine body of hers again. As I brushed her, I would talk to her, and she would stand as still as a statue, purring if you use your

RADIANCE OF THE ORDINARY

imagination. She closed her eyes and stretched out her powerful neck in absolute bliss when I brushed her brisket; wiggled her bum when I scratched her tail head. She had nowhere in the world better to be.

I, on the other hand, was wound tighter than a wildcat, but I had to keep it together. This was milking, or so I thought. And this was my beloved, bucolic animal. I brushed and scratched and rubbed her. In a relationship with such an extraordinary creature, in that quiet peaceful moment, it's nigh impossible to remain stressed out and frazzled. Not if you really are in that moment. Sure, you can bring the rest of your life with you, but then what's the point of moments changing at all? In that old barn with sunbeams bursting through the cracks in the walls and barn swallows swooping in — back and forth and back and forth, feeding their demanding little babies — warm, sweet-smelling gusts of air from Clementine's big, glossy black nose, I figured the perils and frustrations of milking were all worth it.

When I was done, I would go to the large doors, built to accommodate Belgian horses, and fumble with the rusty latch. Clementine, knowing this part of the routine well — the part where I opened the door and she returned to her herd and her babies in the fields — would linger behind me. One day, as I was opening the gate, I could feel her getting closer, but I was busy swinging my arm over the bottom part of the Dutch door and didn't take precautions. I should have taken precautions. She was impatient to get outside, and I was oblivious. She stood behind me and swung her enormous head. Unfortunately, on top of that enormous head were a fine set of beautiful, symmetrical horns that caught me in the back. She wasn't charging me or trying to ramrod me. She was just swinging her head, as an impatient cow will, and I, caught up in my task, wasn't paying attention.

I whipped around in horror and yelled at her. She looked at me, all nonchalant. If a cow could shrug, that's what she would have done. "You snooze, you lose, sister."

I was black and blue for a few weeks, but I wasn't gored. She wasn't an aggressive cow; she was a demanding one. And on that day, she taught me a valuable lesson — one that I still carry with me: You can never be solidly sure of any animal. They all must be treated with healthy respect for their power. To this day, when I am with any of

THE MAKING OF A MILKMAID

our farm animals, I am relaxed and happy, but I'm also cognizant of body language, where I'm putting myself and where they're putting themselves. I watch for hooves and heads, beaks and talons. It becomes second nature over time. Clementine taught me that.

But oh, how I loved her! When I went to the field to move the cows, her neck would snap up at my sound and she would come charging across the grasses to me. Just to me. It was scratches she was after and it was scratches she got. We would sit there in that lovely pasture full of sweet grasses and wildflowers and shoot the shit about the miserable milking of the morning. "How come it's always so bad?" I'd ask, and she, with her big pools of brown, liquid-love eyeballs would assure me, "Tomorrow will be better."

Tomorrow was never better.

One especially dastardly milking morning, Troy came into the barn to see how things were going. Clementine had just taken her second morning crap, and I had run out of clean milking pails and washing-up water. He found me — that poor man — sobbing in frustration. "She hates me! She really, really hates me!" After talking me down from the ledge, he suggested I call Richard, who had milked cows all his life. Richard would know what to do. Richard could help me.

I called Richard later that afternoon. I expected some tips and tricks to turn Clementine from a rogue milker into a pleasant milker. What I got instead was hysterical laughter and an awakening. "Oh, Tara," Richard said, "you got yourself a helluva cow!" The more I told of her antics, the more Richard laughed. He was like that — man did he delight in such things. But he was laughing at the cow, not at my follies. It had never once crossed my mind that maybe it was the cow, not me. Never had I thought, "Maybe, if I had a different cow, milking would be different."

"But what do I do with this cow?" I pleaded.

"I don't know. Try singing to her," he offered.

And that's how it started — the singing. As usual, we started our morning ritual — all aboard the USS *Hellacious* — and she readied her bowels, bladder, hooves, and legs for the festivities. Only on this day, I started singing. At first, Clementine seemed confused. Her ears pricked back, and she listened, forgetting about that second milking poop she

— 55 —

so loved. I continued to sing, watching her. I sang and sang, every song I could think of. I sang my old childhood songs from elementary school. I sang "Frère Jacques" and old gospel songs and Fleetwood Mac and "The Logical Song" by Supertramp. She was intrigued. She was still! I kept singing. Then, clueing in, I suppose, on the fact that the songs were different tempos and tones, she began to do the bovine version of fast-forwarding or skipping what was on offer, only the button she pushed was me and the finger she used was her hoof.

If I delayed between songs, trying to think of another — kick.

If I sang a song that had pauses between lines — kick.

If I sang a song she otherwise didn't appreciate — kick.

When I started to lose steam and ideas for songs, I threw in the classic, "You Are My Sunshine." Ha! Sunshine she was not! But something odd happened. Clementine's whole body relaxed. She didn't move an inch. Even her whipping tail remained still. I was astonished. I kept singing it, every verse. I knew them all, because my grandpa used to sing it to me when I was little. When I was really lucky, he would open the top drawer of his dresser and pull out a glass cup that held his harmonica, soaking in whisky so the wooden reeds wouldn't dry out. I loved it when he played for me. I loved watching how it slid over his lips, how his chest billowed in and out, and how his strong, dark hands, thick with a lifetime of hard work, opened and closed and danced all about that shiny instrument.

Apparently, Clementine liked it, too. When I tried to switch to another song, she kicked me again. Her body stiffened; she shifted. I went back to "You Are My Sunshine," and the magic ensued. It was as good as any siren song sung by the enchanted ones of the dark forest. She was transfixed. As long as the band played on, all was well. A gap in the music, perhaps an attempt to sing something, anything, different, and Clementine would immediately express her displeasure.

There were days when madness knocked on my mind's door from the incessant singing of "You Are My Sunshine." The repetition made a rut in my brain so deep that the song came rolling in all day long. I'd be weeding the garden and it would pop up. I would be filling a watering trough and there again it would come, taunting my sanity. I would see Clementine, and like a Pavlovian response, "The other night dear,

THE MAKING OF A MILKMAID

as I lay sleeping, I dreamt I held you in my arms" would echo through my synapses.

That was the cost of doing business with Clementine. What I didn't know at the time was how important that cow was to the making of me. She, as Richard had said, was a "helluva cow." Quite. Clementine never minced words, even if she never used them. She was my teacher par excellence. As I've gotten older, I've realized that when God made me, a few shakes too many of stubborn may have fallen into the mix. I learn from doing. I learn from failing. I don't learn so well from people telling me things. In hindsight, I can see that Clementine had my number. It takes one to know one.

Like the trainer from *Rocky*, Clementine taught me every move a cow could make. She put me through my paces. She drilled me and tested me. She brought me to the brink of milkmaid hell. And still, she delivered milk that filled the jar halfway up with golden, silky cream. Still, when I went into my kitchen and pulled down my butter churn and wound it around and around, the sunshine she ate appeared as fat golden globules — the wondrous butter that would nourish us. She rewarded us. Clementine taught me how the making of good butter required the making of a good milkmaid.

When autumn came, we stopped milking Clementine, as we do with all of our cows. Their energy then is best used to put fat and thick coats on their bodies in preparation for our frigid winters. We can do without milk for a time. Over the following years, Clementine had more calves and nursed them alone. I never milked her again. Instead, I purchased a couple of Canadienne milk cows from a friend. Both of them stood as still as soldiers when they were milked — professionals, the pair. I suppose I was done with my lessons. I didn't need them anymore.

Since those days of horror and revelation, we've had a handful of milk cows nourish us, our farm, and their babes.

We had Daisy, a tall Guernsey who had no moo. We had sweet Anja, the subordinate sidekick to Zaide, who always slept curled beside her calves no matter how big they got, horns at the ready for any creature that dare threaten her family. We had beautiful Mischa, a sable-coloured brown Swiss, daughter of Ursula, the best milk cow

— 57 —

RADIANCE OF THE ORDINARY

of all. And there have been more. We have all of their names painted on signs above our milking stanchion. An honouring of the beautiful beasts that nourish and teach us.

Today we are milking Bea and Dolly. Bea is the heart of our farm. Beautiful Bea, the steady and the stable. I cannot imagine this farm without her, but I know it will be one day. Until then, I will enjoy every interaction I have with her. She is the most wonderful mother in all the cow land. She's also a worrywart. When the other cattle, especially the rambunctious young steers and heifers, get in their moods and begin their maniacal antics, running and bucking and smashing into each other in exuberant play, there is Bea, standing off to the side, making her low, guttural moan of concern. She stares pleadingly at me: "Don't you see what these maniacs are up to? Do something!"

It doesn't matter where I am around the farmyard; when I hear that sound, I know Bea feels it is in my best interest to know about whatever is happening. She's a bit of a tattletale, yes, but who in the world doesn't love an old tattletale cow?

Milking Bea is a breeze. Every day, like clockwork, she walks herself to the milking stanchion and waits for me to arrive. I open the gate and she walks in, calm and content. She happily, dare I say *thoughtfully*, chews on her alfalfa while I milk her. Never does she lift a leg; never does she use her tail as a weapon. She seems to enjoy being milked as much as we enjoy the beautiful, rich, golden milk she shares.

As for Dolly, this is her first year with a calf. She had a lovely roan-and-white fella we dubbed Mugwort. Dolly is a quiet Jersey, sweet, with a moo more whisper than call. She stands patiently while I milk her, happy to chew her alfalfa while her calf plays in the field in front of her. I like her. She's sweet and easy. I appreciate that, having earned my way with the toughest drill sergeant I've ever known — Clementine, bestower of hard knocks and life lessons. Under the stormy skies, she really was my sunshine.

Paddy

One fine morning, I found two of my apricot-feathered ducks sitting on a nest together. They tend to do that, my ducks. When they see a fellow duck crowning her lofty throne of downy feathers and eggs, another decides it seems like a good idea. But they don't divide and claim. They share in the duties and then share in the raising of those tiny little creatures. When I get too close they huff and puff and hiss, inflating their feathers with the steamy loft of their fury to make themselves look bigger. But if I press on, they will run away.

Apparently, one of the local skunks pressed on. Just as the eggs were starting to hatch, the skunk found the mother ducks. The ducks, having to make the Sophie's choice between their living ducklings and the eggs below them, headed to the safety of the pond with their ducklings scrambling behind them. The skunk loaded up his coffers with whatever he could carry and went home to feast on his bounty. But first he stopped for a snack or two. I had interrupted his successful morning marauding.

Around the duck house, there were eggs and traces of eggs leading beyond the fence and into the forest. Some were half eaten, others were recoverable, but there was one in the mix, lying just outside of the nest, that looked as if it had been cracked open by the occupant inside. But something didn't quite work out right. Small pieces of the shell were missing, and the membrane below it was dry and leathery. The little duckling must have been trying to work his way out when it either ran out of steam or found itself hindered in some other way.

I examined the egg, expecting there would be nothing much to do in the way of saving the creature, but I noticed something almost

RADIANCE OF THE ORDINARY

imperceptible at first glance. The little, black-feathered duckling inside was breathing. I could see a moving, sticky mound expanding and contracting through the cracks and breaks in the egg. If he were to live, he would have to get out of the egg, only the egg's slippery, malleable membrane and the duckling's moist feathers had all dried up into a cementing glue. I couldn't peel the egg off of the duckling. That's a job he needs to be able to do on his own. It's part of the process of that little thing fighting itself into the world. But there was no way this duck was getting out of its jam without me.

I watched him for a long while, deciding which route to take. Around here, we rarely intervene with nature. We trust in her wisdom and respect her decisions, but as farmers we are also committed to doing what we can to preserve viable life. It has nothing to do with economics and everything to do with our care and affection for our animals. It may seem puzzling to some, considering that one day I will eat my steer, to see how much effort and care we put in when he is rejected by his mother or hurts his hoof and needs diligent care. "Why bother?" some may ask.

We live in a symbiotic relationship with our animals. We deeply respect them, and we hold affection for them as we come to know them over the years. One day, they will die and their bodies will feed us. That is a gift of such magnitude that the very least we can do is offer our energy and time to ensure their lives are to their liking. A cow can wander the fields and snack on alfalfa. A duck can build her own nest of down and dried grasses, shaping it as she thinks fit. A sow can roam about, grabbing mouthfuls of straw to build her own nest into which she will birth and nurse her tiny little piglets. This is our sacred duty.

Still, we must also remain grounded in common sense. When an animal is infertile or aggressive or otherwise problematic, we remember we must serve the whole of our farm organism, not the sentimentality of our hearts. There are always tough decisions to be made around a little farm or homestead. Especially given our small size, we work very closely with our animals. There is no place for a mean, powerful cow or a big tom turkey with murder on his mind.

But the breathing little being in the leathery membrane of his cage? Well, it was worth a shot in my estimation. I brought the broken orb

PADDY

inside the house and moistened it with a cloth soaked in warm water. Maybe, if I moistened what should have been moist, the little duckling would be able to complete his journey and get out of that egg. But it was worse than I thought. The membrane had dried into a hardened crust on the duckling's body. I had to moisten it by sprinkling water over the exposed membrane. Bit by bit, I moistened and moistened, waited, and moistened some more.

The duckling began to shift and then chirp and then shift some more. A tiny little piece of eggshell fell away and revealed a tiny black beak that opened and called and breathed with relief. I couldn't see his eyes or make out what was what, but there was his bill, open and calling and breathing. I couldn't believe it. That little fella might just make it out after all! It took almost two hours for that determined duckling to make his way into the world. And wouldn't you know it, the very first thing he saw, the creature he would imprint upon, was me.

From then on out, everywhere I went, Paddy followed. When I cooked in the kitchen, Paddy ran behind my legs chirping wildly, trying to keep up with his mother's toes. (Or were the toes his mother? I was never quite sure.) When I showered, Paddy yelled for me to hurry up. When I did morning chores, I had to slip Paddy into the pouch of my hoodie. That was his favourite spot, tucked in nice and warm with only his head peeking out to see what we were up to. In the garden, Paddy zoomed around, always chirping his worried chirp when he didn't see me or hear me for thirty seconds.

Whenever I was out of sight, Paddy would screech, as if shouting, "Mom! Mom!"

I would reply, "Chirp chirp, chirp chirp," which meant "Yes, Paddy, I'm here."

And he would rush over to me before wandering off again a few seconds later, which started the maniacal calling and reassuring cycle all over again.

In the house, the sweet sound of Paddy's little webbed feet slapping the hardwood floors was constant. He moved with confidence, around or over Louis, who watched him with confusion, and Tinder, who took great delight in herding the little fella under tables and into other rooms. Paddy went along with the herding until he was forced too far

— 61 —

RADIANCE OF THE ORDINARY

away from mama, at which time I was summoned to rescue him by his high-pitched, panicked calls. And then I would mutter, "Chirp chirp, chirp chirp," with less enthusiasm every day.

Mostly, Paddy pooped as ducks do. He would take three steps and spurt his liquid duck poop. They don't show you that on the adorable Instagram videos. They don't show the human running after the duckling with old towels and a spray bottle. Everywhere Paddy went there was poop. Despite my initial failure at reintroducing Paddy to the duck flock, which by then had forty new ducklings of their own to assimilate, I knew I had to make it happen. He was getting bigger and I more frustrated with the demands and needs of such a vulnerable little thing. I had to get the ducks to accept him.

It wasn't easy. My earlier attempts had been abject failures, but this time I was committed. Incessant poop cleaning will do that for you. I brought Paddy to the pond and he jumped right in. The other ducks swam over to him, curious about this interloper, and Paddy put on his turbo propellers and zoomed over to where I was, hastily lifting his whole body out of the water and making for the safety of my rubber boots.

And so it went, day after day. These odd creatures, quacking and swimming about the pond, confused and scared him. He wanted nothing to do with them. But I persisted with the daily visitations, a few minutes at a time. And then one day, rather than ignoring him, a handful of ducklings swam over to him and offered, in their duckling way, that he could hang out with them if he wanted to. They were going to the pond edge, the cool place to hang, where they buried their little bills to snack on juicy bugs and the minerals of the earth. I suppose he thought that sounded like fun, because he followed along.

I stopped going to the duck pond then. I wished little Paddy godspeed and removed myself from his view. As far as he knew, mom was no longer. I'm not sure how he felt about that. But in my absence, his survival necessitated bonding with the other strange creatures in his midst. A few weeks later, Troy, who was doing the duck chores, told me he couldn't even tell which one was Paddy anymore. I could tell, as I watched with binoculars from afar. I could see him there, happily swimming with his duckling pals, learning the duckling ways.

PADDY

When I called the ducks out of the pond and locked them up at night in their house, out of reach from predators, they came in a huddle, rushing to get past my boots. But there was always one duck, a drake in fact, who would saunter past me nonplussed. Of course, it was Paddy. He had grown a fine, white feathered bowtie on his chest as his fluff was replaced by feathers. A first-class gentleman. He didn't need me anymore, and that, I suppose, is how it's supposed to be.

In My Kitchen

I have had many kitchens in my life. Most of them were make-do's. Old kitchens with melamine countertops. Kitchens where the butcher-block top of the dishwasher on wheels was my only cutting surface. Kitchens with peeling up linoleum and peeling down paint. All of them utilitarian in the military style of utilitarian or gaudy in the 1980s builder style of gaudy.

None of those kitchens fit me. They were shaped wrong. They were too tight in some places and baggy in others. Their materials itched. They were akin to today's fast fashion clothing — meant to do the job without really getting at the soul of the matter. Any wall will accept a few cupboards screwed into it. A sink can be plunked into any room with a floor that will take a hole. That's still not a kitchen.

I wonder what percentage of my life has been spent in a kitchen. Many years ago, exasperated by the shoebox kitchen in one of our military rental houses, I flung myself into Troy's arms and begged, "Please just promise me one day I will have a kitchen of my own!" He promised, and he came through. It took many, many years, but that man's word is good.

When the day finally arrived for me to renovate the kitchen of our 170-year-old farm home, I knew what I wanted to do. I had spent the prerequisite decades of my life becoming intimately familiar with all the ways a kitchen can go wrong. I knew that the kitchen really is the heart of a home. It's the fiery, beating centre — the place from which good things come. From my kitchen, the nourishment that allows us to go into the world, whole and sound in body and mind, able to meet what's out there for us on any given day. A kitchen has to rise to its purpose.

IN MY KITCHEN

My dream kitchen, which I now lovingly own, is made of natural materials. There is a warm resonance that pulses from natural materials that's missing in the plastics and polymers of synthetics. I don't wear synthetic clothing, and I wouldn't dress this fine lady of a home in it either. My kitchen is a place where real food, nourishing food, is honoured and prepared. There is no margarine here, no artificial, manmade concoctions. There was no need to carve out a space for a microwave: I've never owned one. But I did need a place to put my cast-iron pots and old wooden spoons. I've collected those over my lifetime. They are my tools of the trade.

In this era of addictions and distractions, I have heard the words "food is not love" spoken often. *Oh, but food is love. Real food. Real love.* It is true that we can't fill the hungry voids in our souls with items meant to drown but not quench. But real food, what I call "God's food" as opposed to "man's food," is love when it is consecrated with our intention and attention. That is the role of the cook in the kitchen — the blessed transmuter of food into loving nourishment.

There was a time when food didn't come with a possibility to heal or harm. Food was just food. That time was just a short while ago. There were no adulterated foods. There were no grocery stores with endless aisles of ready-to-go and microwavable and instant. There was just food, and everyone needed some skill in preparing it lest they die. We are the same creatures as those humans were, only now we have to make choices every day around our food. Will we eat the stuff of commerce or the beautiful foods of Creation? It's a battle for your dollars, and more than your waistline is at stake.

I was almost fifty years old when I finally got the kitchen of my dreams. It's not the kitchen of other people's dreams, perhaps, but it is uniquely and wholly mine. The floors are planks of white oak, left as white oak instead of covered with varnish. That was important to me. We walk around barefoot all summer, wool slippers in winter. I want to feel the soft wood under my toes. Let our movements wear marks into the open grain of the tree that once lived. The cabinets were built for me by a local cabinetmaker. They're made of real wood and put in the places that facilitate my dance in the kitchen. In the centre, a large island made from a shopkeeper's counter that I bought years ago from

— 65 —

an antique dealer. It sat in my living room for a few years, waiting for its debut. I use it every day, multiple times a day. The ghosts of those who have used it, touched it, filled it with its scars and marks, work alongside me. At Christmas it's covered with roasted goose, homemade charcuterie and cheeses, summer's preserved fruits, and all the other delights from our place in this world. In the summer it overflows with the jars I fill with fermented vegetables and the fruits of my garden and the canning concoctions I put up for the year.

In the corner of my kitchen is a small window that swings inward. When I was a little girl, I loved watching Saturday morning cartoons. In those cartoons, a dastardly hobo or a naughty cat would watch from the bushes as a woman in a dress, high heels, and apron put a steaming hot pie on a window ledge to cool. Does anyone have window ledges on which to cool their homemade pies anymore? I do. Now, I do. I had a fine young window-maker man build me a window that came with a ledge. It opens with a little brass latch, and it is made of old glass with soldered, diamond-shaped pieces running across the front. It's a small thing. Nobody notices it, but it delights me. In the summer it remains open, with a direct line of sight to our enormous old apple tree that bustles with life. From the rustling, heavily laden apple branches to the baby chipmunks to the nesting phoebes, that little window frames them all. And so far, no hobos or naughty cats have shown up to thieve my cooling vittles (though one day I did have an unexpected visit from our old orange tomcat, who thought the kitchen window the most efficient way to deliver his offering of a dead field mouse).

My walls are covered in lime plaster and limestone that inhales and exhales, filling the space around us with charge and calm. A wood cookstove illuminates our cold mornings with the dancing light of the flames across the walls and ceilings. It's a favourite place for Louis, our ageing Great Dane, to curl up. It never ceases to amaze me how tiny a ball my little "house pony" can curl up into. His sweet mumbling and deep breathing a part of this peaceful kitchen, too.

Big windows let the beauty of the seasons find us inside these walls. Plants hang from windowsills and line up anywhere a sunbeam streams in. The outdoor plants, too, are strategically planted at the base of the windows to attract all manner of butterfly and bird. Last year a diligent

IN MY KITCHEN

little hummingbird came every morning at six o'clock sharp. We would hear him before we saw him. A little revved up motor, zigging and zagging his sound all around us until he finally came into our line of sight. Our morning gift. I hope he returns.

There is more to my kitchen. A little corner cubby that my husband sometimes sits in, sipping on a wild, homemade soda, keeping me company while I cook. Sometimes, in the middle of the day, we find each other in our secret little corner. Maybe we have a cup of tea and read awhile. In the warmer months, we head out the back kitchen door and sit outside while things heat up in the house. That door was also built by my talented window-door-maker. He's a young fella from Ireland, where he apprenticed under skilled joiners to learn the art of traditional window and door building. A few years ago, when the original doors on our house started to get wobbly and drafty, he took them to his shop and did some magical stuff and returned them. Nary a drop of glue or strange plastic bits. Only wood and craftsmanship. He built us the kitchen door that brings us outside to our screened-in porch. And that is a wondrous place to be.

The porch becomes part of our inner ecosystem in the warmer months. The doors and windows stay open. The chattering and goings on of the outside world are welcomed in. Summertime brings a great deal of work. That is the time of building projects, fencing, repairs, and moving animals about. The work is endless and exhausting, and it brings with it that deep-bone sweetness of vibrating pleasure the moment you stop. There's nothing quite like the release of the body after hours of labour. In our case, a midday break, a little afternoon delight, is mandated. That, too, happens in the screened-in porch.

My kitchen is all those things. The heart of my living home, thumping rhythmically, steady and calm. It's reassuring. It's solid. It's love.

A few years after my kitchen was completed, I realized it had become increasingly challenging to find space during the hustle and bustle of summer's bounty. It's also awfully hot, bubbling three pots of chutneys and fruit butters and cheeses on a stove while making lunch. So, I added on a summer kitchen to the back of our home, just as in days gone by. We outfitted it with an enormous cast-iron sink we rescued from the side of the road years ago, as well as my enormous

RADIANCE OF THE ORDINARY

supply of canning jars and butter churns. Now, when the cow's milk is flowing and the garden and orchard are overflowing, I need not sacrifice the space I use to prepare our daily food. The summer kitchen comes to the rescue.

I never feel richer than when I am in my root cellar, surveying the shelves of our bounty. All the work to grow and raise and prepare that food transformed into glistening gems of magenta, deep ruby reds, radiating yellows and oranges just like the sun itself, deep olive greens, shining umbers and earthy browns. Yes, that's when I feel most proud, most grateful for the pleasures and demands of our efforts. The work of our lives made manifest.

That bounty comes from the unfathomable beauty of Creation into and through the earth. Things grow under the warmth of the sun and the calls of the moon. Celestial bodies pull and push. The winds touch, the rains kiss, and the birds and the frogs sing life into existence. And things grow some more. Flowers form and then open. Tiny little fruits build themselves out of the wondrous imagination of some Great Being who saw it fit to shape a baby's little bum cheeks into the same shape and roundness as an apple. I can only laugh with unencumbered joy at the brilliance of it all!

In everything, a miracle. A peach with fuzzy skin and the sweet, dripping juiciness of summer's elation. The very sun captured within its flesh. We eat them until our tummies ache every summer. And then I can them in only a tiny bit of honey syrup. There's no need for sugar with peaches so fine, and I'm not sure where cane sugar even grows here in North America. No, I'll stick with honey. I'm quite certain a bee touched my peaches a time or two. Bees and other pollinators that tickled their flowers when they were still a tree's dream. They know each other. Yes, honey is right.

Come winter, those jars of peaches in my root cellar will make a surprise appearance in my kitchen whenever I sense the short, dark days could use an infusion of sunbeams. We'll eat them with a meal of a fatty, drippy beef roast, let's say a bone-in blade roast, because a.) all roasts should be bone-in if we give a hoot about flavour and texture and b.) a jar of peaches should be accompanied by my favourite type of beef roast. So, we've eaten our lovely meal of braised beef roast

IN MY KITCHEN

with some goose or duck fat–roasted potatoes and pickled asparagus. Afterward, like the belle of the ball, a little bowl of peaches makes its grand entrance with an exuberant gust of the fragrant, sweet smells of summer. Everyone turns their heads! Who could resist?

Yes, that is love. Love of the offerings we have been so graciously given. Love of our place and of our most honourable role of capturing such gifts and transforming them into our own offerings for the humans we love. Anointing the already sacred with a touch of ourselves. It's a sacred honour.

I grew up hearing otherwise. I grew up hearing that women must be "liberated" from the kitchen. We had to be liberated from many things, apparently. Liberated from caring for our children. Liberated from homemaking. Liberated from marriage. All of it leading, quite nicely, to "liberation" from our homes so we could be chained to the workforce.

What that looked like, at least through my eyes, was that I had little choice at all. A woman's value was in not being in the kitchen. My value was assessed by my education and my career. I could stay home with my children, but I sure didn't carry the clout of someone who impressed at the dinner party with her lofty-sounding job.

I see more and more young women choosing otherwise today. Families willing to sacrifice the objects of our modern day — the big houses and fancy cars — for a quality of life centred around the simpler pleasures. A home-centred life orbiting around their families. It's challenging to make that choice, but no more challenging than spending our days driving to and from work, giving our hours and days and years to someone else. Everything has a cost; we just have to figure out what we're willing to pay.

My husband and I made the decision, decades ago, that there was irreplaceable value in my contribution as a homemaker. I still like the union of those words, "home maker." To make a house a home — my, what a role to play in the lives of the people we love most of all! I am ever grateful to him for seeing my efforts and acknowledging them, daily, even now. I am equally grateful that he went out into the world, into high-risk and highly stressful work environments — that he took that on for his family so we could live in an environment of peace and harmony, with routines and structures built for us, by us. So we could

— 69 —

RADIANCE OF THE ORDINARY

live nourished even when the dollars were meagre. I thank him for this daily, too. Together, we've been able to create something that brings our lives meaning.

My contribution to my family brings me meaning as well. Through my hands passes the cream that I transform into butter. With my experience, I can bring joy to the people who share meals with me at my table. I'm a piece of what God had in mind when he came up with the beautiful food that nourishes us. I am in union with Creation and my beautiful people. Our food is unadulterated. It is not the simulacrum of corporations. I will not open my mouth and accept their facsimiles into my body, and I will not offer such things to the people I love.

I want honest food. Read food. Meat that bleeds. Raw milk from the udder of a plump cow whom I watched as she grazed in the meadow, barn swallows swooping around her. Her body making the milk at that very moment. The milk that would bring us cream when I plunged the pail into the frigidly cold waters of our deep well. The cream that I would skim off and make into butter. The butter we smother on that roasted meat. Give me cheeses coagulated with the enzymes of a calf's stomach and the wild yeasts of old wooden cheese moulds instead of the sanitized laboratory sachets and plastic forms.

Give me my unadulterated life! Raw and messy and whole.

We douse the meat in chemicals to make it look vibrant and fresh, then wrap it in cellophane. We wash the eggs and dip them in chlorine to rid them of the gift of a feather from the soft underbelly of the mother hen. We remove all traces of connection — a leaf, hair, bones, hide, crumbs of soil. And in every little thing wiped away, so too the wiping of our awareness. *Nothing here has died for us. No need to think of such things.* And the blessings, like the clumps of earth that once clung to that carrot, are washed away.

Real food, left intact, demands our humility. Our eggs are warm in my hand when I take them from the nesting boxes. I can't deny the link — there was a body here, moments ago. That sweet chicken or duck, sitting in this box, called by the urges of her body to lay this egg. This perfect orb. A shell with its precious treasure inside. Like a clam, but different. Sometimes there's poop on these eggs. Sometimes a duck or a turkey or a chicken decides that the time is right, they aren't going

— 70 —

anywhere, you can't have their eggs! It's spring, and their bodies tell them it's time to sit on those eggs and do their own homemaking. The forces of the heavens conspire with some unknown, untouchable part of them to make babies. And so, we back off and watch as they do their miraculous thing. That such a small, seemingly insignificant creature can tap so instinctively into some preprogrammed part of their psyche demands humility, too.

––––

One day, when Troy was still in medical school, we went on a farm tour at a local friend's biodynamic farm. We walked through the fields, listening as our friend explained how biodynamics understands the farm as a living whole. It's an intricate, interrelated whole — a system with each component reliant on the vitality of the next. The ponds and forests, the grasslands and animals; they are like the organs and lifeblood of our bodies. There is respiration and digestion, exhalation and inhalation, circulation. Each piece fits into the next. For this reason, we can't just pluck out a piece here and there without affecting the whole. There can be no monocropping of broccoli without the fertility of animals. We can't grow seas of soy without the trees and the chickens and the sheep. Well, obviously we can do these things, but the cost we pay for ignoring the whole are evident in the soil and, as it must go, in us.

Troy stood contemplating, then said, "There's absolutely no difference between the body and the Earth." Perhaps deciding that he had come up with a pretty good model, God made one and then overlaid that model on the other. We are woven into each other with purpose and intention. I am fed and held and nourished by this Earth. There is no separation other than that which is manufactured, and that is something of which to be suspicious. Anything that keeps us from knowing our place in this world should be understood as a wedge between us and the bountiful gifts we have been given.

Modern allopathic medicine is not much different than the other vehicles of the profiteers. Everything is dissected into parts. A kidney problem requires a nephrologist. A chronic sinus infection demands an ear, nose, and throat specialist. A whole, living system chopped up into its mechanical parts. Nature and us alike.

— 71 —

RADIANCE OF THE ORDINARY

These days, there is so much talk about saving the Earth. The climate, the climate, the climate! The Earth is not the climate. I imagine someone defining me as my fingernails, my fingernails, my fingernails! I wonder how much of it can be boiled down to the fact that the climate can be measured and profited from and how much of it is simply because our beautiful Mother Earth is a stranger to most. Their food comes from packages, their heat from a vent. They live in plastic and drive around in plastic and wear plastic, and they want to do something because their plastic boxes tell them to — to switch their lightbulbs and pay more taxes and the climate will be fixed.

That is not how we fix anything. We don't have to fix anything because we can't fix anything. Nature is just as that little hen, built with a knowing. She knows what to do. We just need to stop with the interruptions. We need to live in unison with her. We are designed as a part of this beautiful place. We are not a plague on this Earth. We are here as active participants, loving partners in a relationship of mutual satisfaction. Her windswept apple blossoms pouring from the skies are there for us, too. She loves to be admired. Creation delights in our awareness and hallelujahs!

The more we know the world as she was created, the more in love we fall. To know her is to love her. And the more in love we fall with this world, the more we find ourselves. We find ourselves through our connection. The same intelligence connecting us all. We see the illusion of separation with clarity. I am interwoven with the dragonfly and the oak leaf. I drink the cold sap from the maple tree and my blood becomes something different. I am a soul in a body built from this Earth. All of life into death so that I may live. It's mind-blowing when we pause long enough to shake off the dulling of separation — that lie we're all soaked in.

Threads and cells and hair and fur and mycelium and plasma and sap. The sun, the moon, the skin, our pupils, the soil, roots, and water. Brilliance, even in the infinitesimal. This great, heavy tapestry woven with our ancestors, the heavens, miracles, grief, laughter, and gut-wrenching wails. A baby cradled in its mother's arms or carried by the scruff of its neck in its mother's mouth. A baby laid in a nest woven of dried grasses, looped over the tiniest of lilac branches. A baby laid on

IN MY KITCHEN

the underside of a leaf with hope and faith. A call for life answered. Spider webs and blowing cattails, owl calls and wolf howls, the voices of children, the sighs of lovers. Peaches and golden summer butter. You and me. All of everything together.

A tiny seed holding a secret life. Bursting open under the whisper of instructions imbedded within. A proclamation of life! A thin string growing into a root. Growing into an umbilical cord. Roots and limbs spreading until life reaches for the source of life. And the sun feeds us all, plant and animal. Alchemy that starts in the mysterious unknown and ends with the communion of our forks.

All of it ends and begins again in my kitchen.

Imagine having ever believed such a thing was a burden.

I once had a reader on my newsletter comment that she didn't follow me for discussion about food. She wanted me to stick to other topics. Fair enough. I understand how people arrive at a place where they believe there are categories to life, to people. We go to the psychiatrist when there's a problem with our thinking. Everything we need, from a plumber to an electrician, serves a categorical purpose. Sometimes we even use the people in our lives that way. We want them to "stick to their lane." *Be what I need from you.*

But that's not honest. People will do that, offer you that, if there's a benefit to them. Instagram is full of them, millions of people making reels in the formulaic way to please the algorithms. A little jaunty, inspiring music to stir the spirits for a moment while luscious images give us a dopamine hit of perfection. A sip of pleasure from simply looking at a blue screen. Everyone, from the people who make it to the people who consume it, gets that one piece they need from another.

But food is not a sidekick to the other things I talk about. It's not an addendum to the discussions of love and death and living an authentic, sovereign life. It is impossible to remove that element — that which builds our bodies and minds — and expect to find peace and harmony within ourselves. I cannot be me if I remove the piece that feeds the body I live in. If I eat the pseudo-foods of commerce, I become the pseudo-human of commerce. I am dulled and depressed. A doppelgänger incapable of living with the clear eyes and heart I want to live with.

— 73 —

RADIANCE OF THE ORDINARY

We speak of macros and vitamins, and we watch the scale for clues about whether what we consume is working for us. It's all so paltry compared to the robust messages we are given every day. I cannot fully witness the miracles of this wondrous life if I am not sound in body and mind. The brilliant tiny flowers poking their heads out of a dusty, grey ditch are a blur as I walk by when I am physically clouded. Fake foods are a shroud. They obscure us from brilliance. They limit us from our potential.

In my kitchen, I want to honour the gifts God has given me. I take what we have been given and transform it into something delicious, something infused with the love of my heart and hands. In my kitchen, I am in my sacred place. I am a small part in a chain of life. I create offerings to the health of people I love. The food I make with care and reverence is food that will allow them to live in health. Clear eyes, sound mind, loving heart. Whoever it is they are here to be, I want to see it. I want their strength and conviction. I want them to be steady and resilient. Food is the foundation. Without it, everything else is harder to reach.

Motherhood

There's an old mother pine that lives in our forest. She has an enormous, thick trunk and a base carpeted with her fallen limbs. Each year, she reaches higher, puts what's left of her into the needles that sprout so high up, my eyes only see them as clouds of green. As she has grown, the winds have blown her soft, resinous branches until they snapped and fell to the ground. Ice has coated her brittle bones and laid heavy until even the slightest breeze was too much for her to bear.

Most of the branches that grew out from her body to collect the sunlight have broken away. It's only her now. The pinecones that carried the seeds of life, that which she has put her whole life force into feeding and growing, are gone. She is now only an enormous, scarred trunk with only a few paltry branches, still reaching for sunlight, at the very, very tip of her existence.

It's not enough. There's not enough of those soft green needles to feed her life. She's too old now. Her reserves are low. Still, she does what she must. She continues on as she always has. She takes what is left of her and offers it in sacrifice to life. Life feeding life.

I spend a good deal of time with this tree. Sometimes I sit at her base, my back against her solid strength, and listen. Sometimes I hug her and we weep together, her sap oozing from what was, my tears falling for what was. We understand each other. She comforts and teaches me. She is the grandmother who no longer lives in my world. She is my aching heart, my lonesome mother hips with nothing to carry.

There was a time when the tiniest of hands used to reach for mine. Those little hands, so soft and vulnerable, searching for the reassurance and connection of mine. Such a simple thing that would happen many times a day, but now, so far away, it feels like a dream. Were those little round creatures really here? Where did they go? When you ask that question seriously, people look at you like you're a little nutty.

"Where did they go? They grew up."

True enough. But it doesn't answer the question. We grow into other things, yes. The infant turns into the baby. The baby into the toddler. The toddler into the child. So it goes. One version of us folded into another. It's sensible and necessary; life rolls on. We might sometimes pull out a picture and fondly remember when our children were babes, but it's not until later, in the stillness of our own unfolding story, that the enormity and speed of our life becomes clear.

You grow and grow. You feed your limbs and spread your roots. You are solid and dependable, nurturing and trustworthy. You know your task. You are a mother. I am a mother. Firmly rooted but vulnerable to the whims of the winds and the storms of the skies. And then, one day, there is only the smallest collection of branches at the very top, just enough.

Life grows bigger. And then, life grows smaller.

––––

I had three beautiful little girls once. Three daughters, all with big brown eyes and sweet buttery skin. My first daughter, Tyra, was born when I was in my early twenties. I was still more wild than tamed, more determined and stubborn than refined by expectations of who I should be. But that all changed when she came into my life, round and perfect. She was over nine pounds, and I was in over my head.

I had no one to show me how to breastfeed. The nurses in the hospital told me to feed formula, "so much easier." My doctor told me to feed formula, "nutritionally complete and no fear of deficiencies." It was my first deep initiation into motherhood. I decided then and there to trust myself over authority. I was young and inexperienced, clueless and all alone. I had no idea what I was doing. But somehow that baby girl thrived. She grew. She learned to smile. She lit up my whole life. She needed me and I was determined to grow into someone worthy of that need.

The limbs of who I was before motherhood fell away. They sat at my base, nourishing the soil that fed the universe of life that fed

MOTHERHOOD

my hungry roots, those nutrients going back into me, into who I was growing to be: a mother. A mother as only I could be. I didn't know what that meant, how to be what my daughter needed from me, but I knew what I didn't want to be.

And my dark-eyed Tyra grew and grew. She was effervescent! Curious and funny. Resilient and fiery. Brave and ready for any new challenge or opportunity that fell in her path. And I grew with her. I watched and learned as she left behind the round softness for the strong, lean bones of adolescence. There was nothing to do as a mother but to witness her transformation, again and again, as she shed the little girl I was so madly in love with, had grown so good at mothering, and became someone else. Childhood into adulthood riddled with little deaths. Each version of us lying on the forest floor.

I had two more babies after her. Two more little girls, and each one got a different mommy than their oldest sister. I had learned. I had grown to trust myself and my decisions around the health and raising of my children. There was no internet then. No mother or aunties to sit beside me at my obscure army base and show me the ways. I had to learn through trial and error. I had to build my own momminess. A cobbled together version from my own life experience, from the behaviours and tactics of the moms around me to a chance encounter I had with a great author, Barbara Coloroso, and simply living life with my children. What felt incredibly lonely and insurmountable at the time turned out to be one of the greatest gifts of my life. In that loneliness, in that absolute unknowing, I was able to become the mother I was meant to be. I figured it out.

Tyra had her first set of vaccinations at four months old, later than normal at the time because we were in transition, moving to a military base across the country where her father was posted. She had a terrible reaction to that first set of vaccines. I didn't know what was going on. She had been fine that morning before we went to see the doctor for her shots, but later that evening she was screaming and wailing in a way I had never heard her scream before. I was alone and exhausted and tried everything that came to mind. Finally, realizing there was something going on that was beyond me, I took her to the hospital.

They admitted her that evening and set up a cot in her room so I could stay with her and nurse her. I didn't know a soul in that small military town. I had nobody to call. I just stayed there with my baby, rocking her as she screamed and screamed. I cried and cried. They told me it was a fever. But I knew it was something more. I didn't associate it with her vaccinations earlier that day because such a possibility wasn't even on my radar.

I brought her into my little cot to nurse her. She vomited shortly thereafter, and a big, burly nurse came in, just as I was sitting up to clean us up. My baby was red with sweat and screaming and my milk was all over both of us. The nurse snapped, "Your milk is sour! Look at it all curdled! She's going to need formula or she'll end up on an IV!"

I was so ashamed. My milk was sour! Was that why my baby was so sick? I had endured excruciating pain when I first started nursing my baby. With no one there to guide me, no books to consult or YouTube videos to give me clues, I had just put her on my breast and let her suck. I knew nothing about latching and how to hold her. I knew nothing at all. I ended up with cracked, bleeding nipples and outrageous pain every time she nursed. I cried at every feeding time. Fortunately, by the miracle of another mother, I had found La Leche League and went to their meetings, where kind women showed me how to effectively latch my baby onto my breast. After that, breastfeeding was a walk in the park. Only now, this miserable nurse was telling me my milk was sour. Nobody had ever even mentioned that possibility to me, and here I was, the source of my baby's illness.

But there was that quiet voice inside me. The one that thought it simply untrue that I was making my baby sick. Why, then, did she want to nurse so much? How could milk curdle in my body? Why would my body do such a thing without me even noticing or having any health issues? None of it made sense. Even if I didn't have the education or maturity to question the nurse's declarations, I didn't buy them either.

I spent the rest of that night walking my crying baby up and down the halls until the nurse told me to go back into our room. I then walked in circles in our room. I was terrified something very serious was happening. When I asked a different nurse why my daughter would scream like this, she replied, "Babies scream when they're sick sometimes. We're still not certain what's wrong, but we need to bring down that fever."

MOTHERHOOD

Early in the still dark of the next morning, the grump-ass nurse came huffing and puffing into the room. My baby had fallen into a fitful sleep, and I was beside her, delirious with exhaustion.

"Your baby is burning up and you make her hotter against you!" she exclaimed.

"It's the only way she's comforted."

"If you don't leave her in her crib, we're going to remove the cot."

She reached for my baby, startling her out of her sleep. The crying commenced. She then laid my baby on her back, in the crib, and proceeded to pour a paper cup of liquid medication into her mouth. Still only four months old, and knowing only the sucking tactic to get liquid down her throat, she started choking on the liquid.

"You're choking her! She's choking!" I came up behind the nurse, watching in horror as she manhandled my sick child.

"Mom! You need to step away!" she shouted, using her enormous behind as a defensive block to keep me from reaching my child.

The nurse was dribbling in liquid and then pinching my baby's lips together so she couldn't spit it out as she simultaneously used her forearms to keep my child from turning her head. I didn't know what she was giving her and I didn't know why.

What could I do? I pushed the nurse away, which, unfortunately, also happened to be into the wall, and I picked up my baby as she spewed medication, hollered, and gasped.

"You are out of line, Mom. You are out of control!" the retreating nurse bellowed.

It was one of the most miserable moments of my young life. I didn't know what would happen next. Today, I'm certain, what would happen next is a security guard showing up. Maybe even child services. Maybe they'd accuse me of disallowing treatment of my child or think me unfit to parent. But that wasn't the zeitgeist over thirty years ago. Then, even me, a twenty-one-year-old lone mother, had some authority, had a say in her child's health. But I was desperate to get out of that hospital.

I was relieved when the nurse finished her shift and was replaced by a fresh and friendly group of nurses.

"I hear your baby hasn't been able to keep down any medications or her milk," one of those fresh and friendly nurses said.

— 79 —

RADIANCE OF THE ORDINARY

"She's nursed twice this morning and she kept it down."

"That's good news."

"I want to go home."

"The doctor will be in shortly to look her over and make that decision."

The doctor did come in, hours later. By then I was so desperate to go home that I asked him to discharge us the moment he entered the room. He was a kind man, very tall and lean, and decades older than me. He was slow and methodical with an air of capable kindness. He let me hold my baby while he looked at her. I liked him.

"It's interesting that your daughter was vaccinated yesterday morning," he said.

"Why is that interesting?" I asked, still oblivious to any connection.

After looking at her chart and giving her a once-over, he stood up and asked what I was going to do if he let us go home. I told him we'd take a bath together and snuggle in our bed and I'd nurse her and try to sleep. I suppose that was good enough for him because he discharged us. But before he left, he looked solemnly into my face and said, "If I were you, I wouldn't vaccinate this baby again."

All I could say in my shocked stupor was, "Oh."

What kind of doctor would do something as irresponsible as condemn my daughter to certain death by telling me not to vaccinate her? I left the hospital with a mountain of questions tumbling around in my mind. Was he suggesting her recent vaccinations had something to do with those wild cries and her illness? Could a vaccination do that?

Days later, I found myself at the library, but they didn't have any books on vaccinations beyond what to give your child and when. I ended up flipping through the yellow pages of the nearest city, two hours away. I was looking for bookstores and writing down the numbers on a pad of paper. I called them all asking if they had books about vaccinations. "You might want to try Babbling Brook Books," one of the voices at one of those numbers offered. Maybe it wasn't "Babbling Brook." Maybe it was "Whispering Meadow Books" or "Singing Rocks Books" or something like that. Whatever it was, it was pretty hippie sounding. But I drove the two hours and bought two books on vaccines, plus a package of macrobiotic plum candy. One of the books listed each type of vaccine followed by its pros and cons. The other book shared

— 80 —

MOTHERHOOD

the concerns around vaccination that I had never been privy to. It was eye-opening, and a pivotal moment in my life as a mother.

I am, to this day, grateful for that old battle-axe nurse who showed me the mother lion living within me by instinct. An instinct I learned to trust and take confidence in and that protected and served me and my children and my family innumerable times. And I am most grateful to that kind doctor. Surely, he no longer roams this planet, but my daughter and her daughter do because of his generous, open mind.

I never did have Tyra vaccinated again. I never had any of my children vaccinated. Those two books opened up a world of exploration and education for me. I subscribed to newsletters and joined parent groups. Everything then was done by mail and in-person meetings. It was an effort, but one that ensured a robust education I doubt I would have gotten by reading some internet bullet points. I heard from other parents whose children were injured by vaccines; they knew all about "that scream," that primal, animal shriek of a child whose body is being damaged before our eyes. Some recover. Some are forever changed.

That effervescent little baby has grown into a beautiful, vibrant young woman with her own little bubbly babe. I may have been insecure as a young mother, but through the challenges I was given, I developed an authentic confidence. I got comfortable with difficulty early on in my life. It doesn't mean that I liked it or looked for it. But I was around it often enough that I came to understand how lessons unfolded in those moments, even if it would take hindsight to decipher them. I don't lean on hindsight much anymore.

When I made the decision that vaccinating my baby again was simply too big of a risk, it meant I had to make other decisions to go with it. We ate a pretty standard diet back then. No fast or processed food — I at least had the sense to cook all of our food from scratch, but it was the typical grocery store fare of conventional meats and dairy and grains. I didn't even know what "organic" was back then. But when I learned about vaccinations, I also learned about immunity, health, and other ways to support our immunity and health. I took some homeopathy courses in the basement of the military community centre. I found farmers to buy nourishing food from.

— 81 —

RADIANCE OF THE ORDINARY

I found a little health food store in town owned by a wonderful man from Germany. We became friends. He taught me about tissue salts and real food and the perils of Western medicine. His parents owned the bakery next door that sold traditional organic sourdough spelt bread. He told me to eat it with lots of butter on top and with eggs and sausage. I listened to him. All of these paths opened up to me, a whole new world of health and direction — I became a nutritionist — all because I had the tenacity and courage to follow my instinct. But, mostly, it was because I had the open heart and mind to meet life as it came.

It has remained that way. Year after year. Limb after limb. All of my babies brought with them profound, and often painful, lessons. I grew. They grew. And then, one day, I noticed they no longer needed my limbs at all. They were their own trees, reaching through my branches for their own light to feed on. Understanding their need to grow, I have sacrificed the limbs that were shading them.

That's the hardest part of all.

———

Once I had a bustling family of five. We always lived in a peaceful home, something I think of as the most important element in a home. But there were always voices and ideas and projects and classes and worries. So many little offshoots to occupy my mind and efforts — the work of raising a family. Raising good people who one day, if you've done it right, will head out into the world and make their own decisions, their own offerings, their own contributions.

I don't remember hearing words like "self-esteem" when I was young. I didn't hear them when my first two children were young. But by the time our third daughter was born, it seemed an ever-present drumbeat. Where once kids just did a thing and life went on, suddenly a "good job!" was always thrown in. For every nose blown and every toy shared. It seemed we needed to identify and reward what was once a given, with its own consequence as feedback. Destructive behaviour brought unfavourable consequences. Behaviour that was generous and polite or open and kind brought more rewarding consequences. Whatever it was, there wasn't a need for a hovering parent to label it all.

— 82 —

MOTHERHOOD

"Good job!"

"You shared that toy so well!"

"Do you think Sally might want her toy back?"

Yes, Sally wants her toy back, that's why she's crying and reaching for it.

I recently witnessed a little girl, five or so years old, take another child's toy. The bereft child asked for her toy back, but the other child refused to return it. Hostilities escalated quickly with both children crying. That's the normal part. What astounded me was when the mother of the toy-grabber pleaded with the other child to let her daughter keep the toy. "Next time you see us, I'll bring you two new toys! How's that?" I was gobsmacked when the other mother joined in. "Did you hear that? You'll get two toys next time!" The little girl wasn't having it; she wanted her toy back. She didn't get it. The mother of the wee thief quickly left with her smug daughter squeezing her new stolen toy.

What are the lessons being taught to these children? Why didn't the one mother simply say, "No, that's Mary's toy and you'll need to give it back to her now." And why didn't the other mother reinforce the same? It's weak, spineless parenting that results in children having expectations that do not align with the realities of life.

"Self-esteem" recently became the all-important marker of successful parenting. Suddenly the onus was on parents to boost their children's confidence with cheery pep talks. But what parents ended up doing was keeping the hard stuff about life away from their children. Parents became their children's shields and fan clubs all in one.

I don't know about you, but I can receive a hundred compliments and one insult and it's that insult that burrows in. We're designed that way, exquisitely sensitive to that which threatens our connection with the collective. Sometimes those insults are simply cruel, and we're left to dismantle them into their component parts and do what we must to chuck them in the trash. Other times, there's some validity, some stringing truth, built in. Either way, it behooves us to look them over to make sure there's not something useful in there. There's nothing life-threatening in a critique or an insult, even if it feels that way.

But children raised with only praise and protection from a dangerous world grow up seeing a dangerous world from which they need to

— 83 —

RADIANCE OF THE ORDINARY

be protected. They lean into the comfortable and the buffered, sensing their inability to take on the hard stuff. Instead of being guided on how to meet hardships and challenges head-on and discovering qualities within themselves that they didn't know possible, they're kept from them altogether — their strengths and undiscovered abilities darkened in the shadow of their parents' shields.

We recently had a sweet and curious five-year-old girl over at the farm. It's fun to have young energy around. There's a large blackcap raspberry bush by our front door that I leave to grow wild so couriers and our mailman and other visitors can stop on the way up to our door and have a little summer snack of sweet, sun-warmed berries. On the day of the little girl's visit, the bush was heavy with the shrub's fat gems. She noticed them right away and stood before them at eye level, aware that the bush had thorns.

"Daddy, you pick them."

Her father encouraged her to pick them and picked a couple for himself to entice her to join in on the sweet feast.

She refused. "Too prickly!"

She dug in her heels as her father tried to cajole her. She wanted berries, but she wouldn't pick them.

Here's where I would have shrugged and walked away when my kids were small. I'd give them the space to figure out how to get berries without getting pricked by a thorn. At five years old, that's reasonable. Yes, you'll probably get a sting or two. I still do when I'm not paying attention or simply can't resist a big, fat berry deep in the centre, but isn't there learning there too? A sting to remind us: not like that. And for the effort and risk: the reward.

Her mother came and picked a handful of berries and poured them into her daughter's cupped hands. No risk. No work. Just reward.

It's this avoidance of hardship, of work, of toil and struggle that disallows for the development of authentic confidence. And it's this same approach we take to everything in today's culture. We want "good vibes only," thinking that's how to get good vibes only. We want light without dark. Youth without age. We want pleasure and fun without hardship and challenges. We want life without death. And we actually think that we can get it! We are so busy shutting off half of our lives,

— 84 —

MOTHERHOOD

running from lessons and truths, that we've ended up in some semi-reality. A world of diversions and distractions from meaning. It's no wonder that we're seeing people using virtual reality headsets to pull themselves ever further from the real world. Because, as it turns out, the real world is full of hard things. And for someone who knows little of their potential and resilience, it's no place to be at all. How do we call on fortitude when we've never met it before?

Parenting is tough stuff. Toughest of all is watching as your children struggle. Stepping in is always easier than stepping back. Disciplining is always tougher than allowing. Implementing appropriate consequences is the pits. Who wants to listen to a child crying or throwing a tantrum in public, or deal with a sullen teenager who didn't get their way? Not me. But parenting isn't about what I want. It's a beautiful, loving union, but it's also learning to grow outside of our limitations. It's the adults, as well as the children, learning what we're capable of and what's expected of us. And maybe, in the end, you have children with the confidence and resolve needed to head into the world knowing who they are. And maybe that goes well. Maybe they make their own babies one day and you get to see them parenting as you parented them, and you might just feel a little bit good about that.

And maybe you don't. Maybe life has different plans for you and for them, and you must accept that, too, because life is surrender and surrender is acceptance. There is grace in that, too. You teach your children to navigate their hearts toward gratitude instead of injustice. And if you have taught them well, you have only been able to do so by living it.

Be that role model for your children. Let them absorb your confidence and assuredness. Be their leader, their trusted guide, their loving mama and papa. Love them enough to offer them discipline and structure so they can be challenged in the warmth of your home before heading out into the big, big world. Let them figure out for themselves that they got what it takes.

———

When our Tyra told us she was planning to have her baby at home, I was happy for her. I figured her home birth would involve a midwife and her husband. Perhaps a doula for extra support. Maybe that's what she was thinking initially, but as she read all manner of books and other resources, her ideas around pregnancy and birth evolved. She found some books about birthing written before it was considered solely the domain of doctors delivering babies. By golly, those doctors sure do deliver a lot of babies! I remember correcting my doctor, who kept using that phrase with me. "You're not delivering the baby, I am. But I appreciate your support all the same."

I suppose stuff like that rubs off on a kid. If not directly, then most definitely in spirit. All of my daughters are curious, seekers like me, but most assuredly they are their own people with their own ideas and passions. I'm proud of the women they've become. And I'm awed by their fearlessness. They all left home after high school and forged their own paths, travelling around the world working on farms, one as a nanny in Europe. They hustled, often creating their own way to earn money, including making custom dresses while going through college or sewing costumes for the film industry. Today, our second born, Ella, has a wonderful small business creating the most beautiful, truly clean beauty products from plants she grows and forages and the animal fats from our farm and a friend's farm. She researches and experiments endlessly when she's not in her office as an acupuncturist, carving stones into chubby angels or making handmade lace. Tyra is raising her daughter and putting herself through school to be a homeopath. Our conversations are always lively and fascinating as she educates me on whatever new pursuit she's immersed in.

Throughout their years of figuring out what they've wanted to do, they've never stopped learning. When we talk, I'm energized by what we share. I, too, am constantly hungry for knowledge. I, too, want to learn and evolve. I had to remind myself of that when Tyra let us know she would be having her baby without any outside assistance at all. She would be at home without a midwife.

I was shocked. I hadn't heard of anyone having ever done that. To her credit, I suppose she must have figured we would be worried. She talked to me and Troy about what she had learned, was learning. She pointed us to resources and books. She listened to our worries and our opinions, but she held firm. We recognized that our concerns were

MOTHERHOOD

based on what we knew, the things we had experienced, and that we may not have the full story. In fact, it was possible that what we knew to be true may not have been true at all.

If I am open to the possible, I'm open to the possible. Listening does not mean agreeing. I listened to Tyra. She is my daughter, my first born. I believe in her intelligence and have never ceased being awed by her tenacity. My daughters are courageous, and that's not something I ever want to dampen for the comforts of my worried mama's heart. I wouldn't dream of such a thing. But it's hard — hard on my end at least. There have been many times, confronted with a decision or path our daughters have chosen, when Troy and I have "known" it's the wrong one or "known" we had a better plan, but we let them take it on and deal with their own consequences. It doesn't mean we sit mute when they tell us things, it just means we share what we think, and they take it or leave it. They're respectful of our opinions, but they remain driven by the courage and passions of their own hearts.

I don't think courage is a trait we can instill in our children with words. In fact, I don't think many traits are instilled with words. Our kids are watching us. They see us taking on things. They watch how we act with overbearing, toxic relationships and wayward school officials. They absorb the behaviour we display. But it's not only that; they're absorbing a way of life. If there is peace in the home, they live with centring around peace. If there is yelling and drama, they become accustomed to the dopamine hits of fight or flight. When their parents are loving to one another, displaying affection and respect, they look for that in their relationships. And when we stand for the things that are important in our lives, they understand there are things worth standing for.

People talk about raising children, but nobody ever told Troy and me about how tough it would be to adapt to parenting an adult. How did that work? Was there an age when we just started doing things differently? We had no idea. All we had were our experiences of being parented poorly as adults ourselves. It doesn't mean we weren't loved. As we unfolded into our adult lives, our parents never unfolded into their new roles. Some of them remained where they were, parenting a child who no longer existed. The tactics that worked when we were kids, ones of manipulation to bend the will to the favours of the parent, just didn't work as smoothly. The distance created in the roles of child and authoritarian made us feel resentful and unheard. There was no interest in who we had become as adults. No questions about what we were learning or what we were passionate about. No questions at all. Only suppositions and the offering of a relationship that remained stuck in the past and demanded in its interactions dormancy and submission to control.

That's all we knew when we entered into relationships with our daughters as they moved from children to teenagers to young women. We used what we *didn't* want as a model to build something better. It's been that model, of using what we *didn't* want, to build something in lieu of knowing exactly what we're actually building. That has been the guiding principle Troy and I have used all of our married lives. It's easy to identify what works swimmingly, but sometimes, most of the time for us, we don't have those models to emulate in our own lives. We didn't know what a healthy marriage looked like, at least not the type of "healthy" marriage we wanted. I couldn't have told you all those decades ago where Troy and I would end up or what our relationship would even look like. We were different people then. I was a young woman built of feminist ideas I didn't even know were there. He was a young man contained and controlled by authority of all ilk. We fell in love and then used the next many years to move away from the things that hurt and damaged us and toward the things that brought us joy and closer together.

I wouldn't have known, and probably would have been horrified back then to have been told, that where we would end up in our marriage is in a place not far off from where my grandparents started out. Over the years we've shed ideas around what's acceptable in our marriage. We've devoted ourselves to each other, and this Us that is bigger and more beautiful than either of us individually. That's not to say we are not individuals with our own passions and pursuits. Because that's just as important. There is no thriving, growing Us if there is no thriving, evolving Tara and Troy. We bring into our marriage each of us, the best of what we can muster. And that best for us just so happens to fit quite nicely with the traditional roles of man and woman, husband and wife.

MOTHERHOOD

Somehow, we fell for the idea that a woman is strongest and at her powerful best when she's emulating the roles of a man. I remember the women of the 1980s in their power suits, shoulder pads galore, the bigger the better, all jacked up to take on the world of men. It went from a desire for some to being co-opted by governments that saw the potential of a whole new demographic to tax. Women were liberated from the kitchen and their snotty-nosed children. There would be corporations to feed us and minimum-wage workers to raise our children. Buried in the messaging was the idea that it was futile and demeaning for a woman to nourish and care for her children. That didn't escape me. I knew, growing up, that I had to find a career. Staying home with my children was never an option. Those were ideas from the past. I was a woman and a woman was liberated! My schools and my teachers and the whole world around me told me so. The young women don't need to be convinced of this anymore. They are dripping in the messaging around what makes them worthy: good jobs, good pay, status. What I learned is now a fact of life for them, like language and breathing.

When they were done with the women, they found the men, who were still out there being men. And if women are to be more like men in order to elevate themselves, it would only make sense to raise the value of a man by demanding he leave those brutish, manly qualities behind in order to claim a softer, more feminine demeanour. A man is at his sensitive, most connected best when he's emulating the qualities of the feminine.

Only a woman doesn't really want an emasculated man. And a man doesn't really want an aggressive, masculine woman. Not really. Nobody wants to be in competition with a partner or potential partner, but here we are. Men claim their worth through "allyship" with women; women boss around their men and then bemoan how weak they are. It doesn't work and I don't think it's meant to work. Simply, there are forces in this world with no intention of giving us models of respectful, loving, thriving relationships. There's no benefit there for the machine. The machine is fed by the things that cause our humanity and fulfilment to diminish. The machine rumbles and rolls along in search of production, consumption, and profits. It's just the way it

— 89 —

RADIANCE OF THE ORDINARY

is. But I am not a cog, and I am not going to blindly follow the line into the hopper.

Troy is power and might and an open, loving heart. His most tender parts are safe with me. I am awed by his steadfast solidity. When, in a house full of hormonal women who, at times, could become as noisy as alarmed hens, clucking about one thing or another, he would stand solid in the centre. He was, and remains, our wayfarer and our captain. He moves things and throws them over his shoulder and cuts boards out of timbers on his sawmill and breaks and runs and digs and heaves and struggles. Oh, how he struggles. I have seen him look into the storm and rush right in more times than I can count. He takes on things. His family above himself, no matter the dastardly task, no matter the drain on his life. He sacrifices himself every day. He gives away his scarred hands and body, thick with the muscle of work. Bit by bit, every job, every one of life's demands, another chip from his life force offered up in service to his family.

His masculinity is powerful and humble. He is wholly authentic as a man of character and substance. Over the years I have seen him stumble and get up again. And again. He has evolved and stretched himself. He has held on to his conviction and his strong, inner code of conduct and he is more of a man today than I have ever known him to be. And isn't that what a marriage should do for each partner? Should we not be more together than individually? I didn't think so when I was young. I heard about "being codependent" and "the power of the individual." As if any of us are individuals at all. Utter nonsense. We are, on this Earth and beyond, one whole — connected and interwoven.

And it's been through our marriage that I, too, was able to slowly shed the nonsense I was taught about what it was to be a woman. I decided that for myself. I moved in the direction of what drew me, genuinely and honestly. In my love with a good man, my confidence grew in claiming parts of myself I thought were shameful in their futility. Staying home with my children, providing nourishing food for my family, making space for Troy's strength, and calming my need to exert my strengths all the time. That was probably the scariest of all, but in hindsight the most important. I am a strong woman, and I will remain one, but what that looked like then is very different from

— 90 —

MOTHERHOOD

how it looks now. Troy is my co-conspirator in this life, not one of my subjects to reign over, to shape into some ideal I have. I want him as he is, not as some manipulated plaything I've decided upon. But in order to have him as the man he is meant to be, happy and at peace with himself, I needed to focus less on what he was doing wrong and more on why I thought it was my job to take note of such things.

The more we each moved into being a curious observer of our own actions and thoughts in our relationship, the more we thrived. I became a quiet explorer, riffling through my psyche and wounds, looking for my motivations and fears. And there were a lot of those fears in there. A lot of ideas I realized were never consciously decided upon by me but somehow wormed their way into my brain. And it was in my mind where these ideas lived, not in my heart. In my heart was the hunger to love, to be loved. To be loved for who I am. And then to be known and seen and loved despite my flaws and inadequacies. And that's what I got; that's what Troy got: a love built out of what we were willing to let go of and the unknown paths we were willing to walk down together. We opened our clutched hands and whatever dropped to the earth, unusable to us, made space for us to pick up other things that we could use.

This all happened naturally, over time, with our sights set on our objective. We chose the word "steadfast" to exemplify and guide our marriage. Our touchstone to roll over in our hearts when things get hard. We grew individually and together. And somehow, in this beautiful marriage we've created, I find him more of a man than I've ever known him to be. And he finds me, his woman, more robust and fuller than ever before. He is my man, wholly and powerfully and beautifully my man. And I am his woman, wholly and powerfully and beautifully his woman. He is thick old barnwood boards hewn by life and I am old linen, woven by hand and worn soft and translucent by these shared years.

It's with this understanding and desire to continually evolve and become more of what we want to be that we entered into parenting our children as adults. It was the two of us listening to our daughter, a grown woman of thirty years, sharing with us her decision to have her baby at home without assistance. "Free birthing" I have come to hear

— 91 —

RADIANCE OF THE ORDINARY

it being called. As we listened to her, our thoughts filled with a rush of all of the things that could go wrong. Breech! Cord around the neck! Haemorrhage! But she knew what she was dealing with when she told us of her plans. She had already moved through those issues on her own, learning from other women who shared their experiences with her. We only knew what we had been told, and most of what we had been told, I've come to learn, came with an agenda all its own. I hadn't done any reading on such things, not really. I knew what I felt — fear, worry, dread — but I knew little else.

Now consider how Troy felt. He's an ER doctor, used to seeing the end result of problems, not successes. It was a big stretch for him to open himself up and listen. I overheard many conversations he had with our daughter where he tactfully brought up issues that worried him. He didn't storm or rant and rave. She didn't yell in defensiveness or hang up the phone. They spoke and they listened.

In the end, I still had my own engrained worries, but I watched the videos and read the books. I listened to other women who chose the same path and said it profoundly changed their lives and their under-standing of self and life itself. We watched videos of women educating and sharing stories around this topic. Once our daughter makes up her mind about something, that's that. So, I rejigged my worries into love and prayer, healing and sun-filled bright beliefs that all would be well. I am always aware of what I am feeding with my energy, and worry is a hungry devil. When I felt it creeping up on me, I would take that kernel of fear that lives below it, bring it out into the light of day, and fill it with luminescent, golden love. It's the only way I know to dissolve worry. We have power in there, to bring the things we focus on forward — best to saturate the things we want with our energies.

In the end, our daughter had her baby her way. I was there with her and her husband. I was there as she, thirty years after me, moved deep into her body to bring her little one into this world. She and then they. She was there in body, but in her own place, away and beyond. Untouchable. I recognized her moans and her movements. I could sense her pain and her determination. She had to make the journey alone.

And then, as the roars reached their crescendo, a baby slipped from her body and into this world. A perfectly wet, round little creature

— 92 —

MOTHERHOOD

appeared like some wondrous magic show. There were three of us there and then, with the might of a mother and the miracle of Creation, this little soul wrapped in the most perfect, soft body appeared. And this new being had all of our parts, only smaller. Fingers and toes and tiny lips tinged pink. Fingernails even! She had shoulders and kneecaps and a head covered in long hair. She could squint and cry and flail and wiggle.

I sat on the floor and watched my daughter, driven by the instinct of a mother — the collective instinct of all mothers ever — bring her child to her chest, astounded and overwhelmed. I watched in silence for a moment as the enormity of this little being filled her parents, the room, the whole world. Then I slipped away quietly to leave them there together. This new trio. This new life. I would have missed it all if I had entrenched myself in what I wanted her to do.

Of course, it might not have turned out this way; sometimes things go wrong. That's the other part of being a parent to adult children. Sometimes the decisions our adult children make have harsh consequences. Sometimes they struggle. That's important, too. It's hard to witness, and even harder not to rush in and fix things, but their lives are theirs. They need to figure out things. Where does confidence come from if not through facing obstacles and learning what it takes to move through them?

Again and again, I have been shown that what I want, what comforts me, is not necessarily what's best or what's right. I want that rightness more than I want soothing and ease. I'm getting older now. My contribution isn't as obvious. It's quieter now, but it's still there. I still have meaning. I am still a mother and, now, a grandmother. But where there was once so much of me devoted to mothering, the need has now dwindled. I am mother, but there are other things in there, too, things I have accumulated and treasures I grabbed along the way but had little time to explore back then. They've been waiting for me. But mostly, it's curiosity that remains my most steady companion. I want to see it all and learn it all. I want to know why and how. From wood turning to preserving meat, the migration pattern of snow geese to the making of herbal medicines to basic carpentry and making wild cultured cheeses — the world is endless in its offerings. I want to know God more intimately than I did yesterday. I want to know my grown

— 93 —

daughters, those beautiful young women, intimately. I always want to remember that my relationship with them as adults is worthy of my open heart and humility.

I want to live between this world and the next, in that middle space of the physical and the mystery. I want to be open to the teachings of the wisdom of spirit. I want to live in grace. I want to be grace. I want to live in love. I want to be love. I am love. I am love. These things fill me. In this nutty time on this beautiful Earth, I can be love. This is all more important than being right.

———

There's grief in there, too, witnessing my children grow from little ones into something altogether different. I liked who they were as children. I loved my role as their mother. But the mother of their world today, as they live their own lives, is not the one they needed when they were small. What do I do with that one? The one who started out so unsure and ended, with the birth of my last baby, confident. Years and experiences tucked into my bones. I figured out how to build schedules and get everyone where they needed to be on time. I learned how to discipline with structure and consistency but to leave my children knowing, no matter what their heinous offence, our love was unshakeable. Unconditional. I learned how to feed us all for weeklong camping trips and how to recognize when one of my kids needed me all to themselves. I hugged them and kissed them and listened to their worries. I protected them like a fierce mama bear. I was steady and solid. They could depend on me.

All of who I became as a mother remains within me, but little of it is drawn on these days. My children are not children. The days of little bodies casually crawling onto my lap are gone. Mostly gone. My grandchildren might come to have that type of affection for me. I hope they do. But my home, the core of my life, remains mostly quiet now. No little feet padding into a room. No teenage girl with a drama requiring my assured grounding to bring her back to a place of peace and reason. No little girls calling or looking for their mama.

I wrote the following as a reminder to myself. But, maybe, it's for more than me.

MOTHERHOOD

If you do your job right, they will grow up
To love you
But they won't need you.

They will respect you
But they won't depend on you.

They will listen
But they won't always follow.

And in the rarefied, tender moments,
They will hug you for a long time
And pull away only a few inches,
Just far enough to look you in your eyes,
To tell you that they love you.

The warmth of a chest against a chest,
Hearts beating millimetres away from the other,
As close as you will ever get to those days
When you carried them inside your womb.

They will smell you
And recognize you as mother.

You will smell them and find,
Under the layers of earthy oils and unfamiliar airs
Of adventures and lives faraway,
Your baby.

Sometimes, when there's quiet enough
And it's only you and them,
They will take hold of your hands and come close and say,
"You are my queen."
And moments later walk out the door
For lands you do not reign.

RADIANCE OF THE ORDINARY

They will go on adventures and journeys
To places you will never know.
They will share only the parts they want to,
And for those scraps you will be grateful,
And for the parts they leave out you will wonder.

Just as you once did for them,
They will grow to champion your efforts
And slay your foes.

They will take your medicine
And make it more potent.
They will take your failings
And do it better.

To love them right is to hold them
With all your might
And to let go when they wriggle.
"I got it mom! Let go!"

And that you must.

I have done it right
When the most brilliant thing I have ever done
Shines whether I see it or not.

———

I was a maiden once. A strong-bodied lass with thick black hair. I was lean and could run fast, as fast as the army boys running in formation alongside one another. I was confident and spirited, ready to overcome whatever life threw at me. I was a roaring fire, hot and fast. Boys hovered about me, and I had my pick.

Then I was a mother. The fire brought down to a slow, steady roll. The "I" opened up to the "we." What I wanted came second or third or last. What mattered was them. My life lived as devotion to others. But

MOTHERHOOD

there was still me in there. Mothering never erased me. I still explored and learned and kept me. In the fray of hockey games and rowing regattas and homework assignments that needed deciphering, I remained.

And now I'm here, with grey hair growing at my temples in wing-like streaks. I'm here, still hungry for life. Still hungry for Troy. *Who is he?* I wonder. *Who was he when I was a maiden?* What's the word for that stage in a young man's life when his pot boils over with testosterone, gumption, piss, and vinegar? When the whole world can be controlled and mastered with will and brute force? What is the name for that?

Whatever it is, it is as ambiguous as the name for the stage of life Troy is in now. "Middle age" I guess it's called. Time for a midlife crisis. A crisis of meaning solved by a red sports car. Imagine thinking the meaning of our lives, the total reason for our existence in the early years of our lives, was simply our work or to be parents or to chase pleasure or accumulate stuff. So many people follow the route on offer — go to school, get a job, have a family — only to look up in their fourth or fifth decade of following that road map and realize they don't see the point. What's the point?

And in rolls the sports car or the affair or the plastic surgery to reclaim the face from a time when they still liked what they saw in the mirror. At least that's something. We spackle and paint a house with no foundation, forever slapping on a coat or two while the joists shake beneath us.

I don't care if people want to tighten up their faces or plump up their lips. It's all a symptom of a craving culture. I don't want to fall into that world. When I look in the mirror, I'm sometimes surprised by what I see. More grey hairs, lines around my eyes and in my forehead that can't be smoothed away. I'm looking older, there's no denying it. Things aren't as perky and tight. Life has had its way with me. That's how it's supposed to be. Maybe, like with everything else, I'm supposed to be challenged by what I see in the mirror. I'm supposed to be reminded that I am changing. That death is drawing near. That the powers of my youthful beauty need be supplanted by more.

———

I spent an afternoon walking with Tyra in the forest near her home today, in the state of Virginia. Not a place I ever expected to find

RADIANCE OF THE ORDINARY

myself. There are rolling hills manicured into pleasant green fields dotted with enormous walnut and oak trees. We don't have that where we live, dangling off the tip of the vast Canadian Shield, a land formation that spreads over eight million square kilometres. It's basically a rock, a great monolithic crust of rock. On top of it, shallow soils and frigid winter temperatures meet. There are no enormous hardwoods left on our little patch of the wilds. They were all plucked away and sent to the motherland on ships. We have second-growth forests, maybe even third-growth. They are dense and impassable in many places, thick with the scrubby, spindly trees and bushes that rush in when the mother trees are yanked out.

Virginia sure is purty though. It's what our neck of the woods could be if we had milder weather and more people and less land. But that's not what we have. We have rural homes, spread far and wide. If you're willing to endure the cold, you can go farther and farther up north. As it is, most Canadians live within a place hovering just above the US border. I suppose my daughter isn't missing the snow and the cold. Not yet, anyway. But I can't imagine a life without the four distinct seasons. My body needs frosty, white winter mornings as much as it needs the summer sun soaking into my skin. Spring is joyous in its explosion of life. Autumn quietly leads us by the hand into a slower pace. I love them all.

The seasons of my life, a dance in four parts. They roll, one into the other. The sun sets and the sun rises again. The blue of the sky an ever-morphing backdrop to her glory. The blue of winter's sky bouncing off sparkling snow. The blue of a hot summer day conspiring with sunbeams to heat the shoulders of plump, ruby-red strawberries and feed the hungry, growing green of life. And in all the blues, in all the seasons, fits a life. Not linear, but over and under itself, being woven tightly on the loom. There are spots of weakness, frayed cloth, damaged cloth, but it hangs on, sometimes tethered by nothing more than a thread.

In the spring of my life, I am no different than the redbuds, exuberantly pushing out of and into whatever awaits. Rain, sunshine, winds that might topple me or rip me from my stem. They all come — it's the cost of doing business. I used to think life came as seasons do. The spring, in our youth budding and unfurling. The summer as we move

— 98 —

MOTHERHOOD

into adulthood, grow into ourselves, bountiful and fresh and sweet. Then, years later, fall comes, and we see our glory fade and slowness settle in. And then, of course, the contemplative quiet of winter, when the birds leave, trees become skeletons, lumbering bears hibernate, and we are nearing the end.

But I'm not so sure anymore. I'm not so sure of anything. Even the givens of time and space seem shaky in their explanations. Is time even linear? And if it's not, how can I move from one season to the next? Who is the "I" that's moving? Is it even the same I from season to season? I don't think it is, so it seems to me I've never been here quite like I've been here before. And if that's true, how can my journey through this life be linear at all? It's more like a tumble in a washing machine than it is some pilgrimage from point A to point B. Or, if we want to stay with the prettier analogy, we could go with life being a pilgrimage through a forest with no map. We find ourselves in deep valleys when snowstorms suddenly hit only to continue on, cold and stiff, to find the frozen lake melting below our feet. And, hey, are the geese announcing their arrival? Along the way we catch a glimpse of ourselves in the reflection of the water and we barely recognize who stares back at us.

I'm a young mother in a hospital bed giving birth to my first child, and then, just like that, I'm no longer young, but I'm still a mother, and I am in Virginia with my daughter, the first born I was just bringing into the world, and she's having her baby. I am in my bedroom, in a house far away. The blinds are closed and I'm holding my baby, any of my babies, and I'm singing the lullaby my mother sang to me. And the baby in my arms is not mine. It's my daughter's baby. I love her, but I don't know her. We are tethered to one another by some unknowable, unseeable weft. I sing to her and rock her, and I am a mother living in her summer and a grandmother living in her autumn. I am all that I've been, all the versions of me that were needed, in this blurred world where time shows its limitations. In that darkened room of lullabies, all the love of all the women whose anguish and joys form the matrix of my bones holds that fresh, sweet baby, and she is all the babies, and I am all the mothers and all the grandmothers. And there is spring and summer, fall and winter. A whole lifetime contained in those tender minutes.

Go to sleep, go to sleep, go to sleep little baby.

RADIANCE OF THE ORDINARY

She looks into my eyes. Tells me secrets of the heavens. She is so close to God.

When you wake in the morning it will be a brand-new day.

I am holding my baby. She is Tyra. She is Ella. She is Mila.

I am in my twenties with my second born, with my Ella. It's a warm afternoon in a house on a military base. I can hear kids outside screeching and laughing as they jump through a sprinkler. She is nursing as I sit on a little wooden child's chair against the wall. It's hot in her room, so I turn on the little fan to blow around the air.

All the birds in the sky are singing just for you. Listen close, my little girl, they're calling out your name.

Her head is heavy. Her little body gives way. Away from here. Away from here and into the abyss. I am holding her, and I won't let her go. She is safe.

Go to sleep, go to sleep, go to sleep little baby. Don't you cry, you know mommy's here with you.

My baby is not a baby. She's bigger and stronger, beautiful with her mane of hair and her big pouty lips. She is fading from me — she is going back. Back into the hands that brought her to us. Back to God. She can hear me singing as she leaves, and it calms her. I know this because she told me. My lullaby, my mother's lullaby, the hum and the rhythm of all the women from whom I came, ushering her from this life into the next.

"You had her, and now she must return."

I keep singing.

God

A tree says: My strength is trust. I know nothing about my fathers, I know nothing about the thousand children that every year spring out of me. I live out the secret of my seed to the very end, and I care for nothing else. I trust that God is in me. I trust that my labor is holy. Out of this trust I live.

— HERMANN HESSE,
Wandering: Notes and Sketches, trans. James Wright

Throughout the years, I've gone to great pains to avoid the word "God." I replaced "God" with words and phrases like "Creator" and "Great Spirit." Okay, I still use Creator, because what if not that? How to properly attribute the sacred and the beautiful if not to the Divine Artist? But I no longer use these words to obscure. I think credit needs be given where credit is due. Back then, though, I tiptoed around a name for the source of all that is in order to be comfortable in my words, secure in what I offered. I know the word God makes some people squirm. Maybe it's not inclusive enough. Maybe it carries the weight of perceived injustices. For me, God was a word that belonged in my younger years, in my Catholic school, in endless church masses, dull and demanding: Sit still, listen, be careful, God is watching, God knows everything you do.

One day, when I was still little, I was walking in a forest with a close family member. Overwhelmed with the wondrous smell of the pines around me and the hollow, thumping forest floor built on eons of old life, I threw my arms around a big pine tree and hugged it. "Oh, I just

RADIANCE OF THE ORDINARY

love God so much!" I said in elation. I could have squeezed that tree into slivers. It was so beautiful in that place, so close to something that made me feel something else, so unlike my everyday. I didn't know what either of those somethings was, but there was nothing else to do but smash myself up against a tree and hug it with all my might.

"What are you? A naturalist?" the adult next to me asked. I didn't know what a naturalist was (and perhaps she didn't either), but I understood the disdain in her voice.

"What's that?" I asked, my arms falling away from the tree and dropping limply to my body.

"Someone who thinks God is in a tree."

"No!" I replied in mock certainty. I felt a rush of shame and embarrassment fill me from toe to nose. Of course I didn't think that. God doesn't live in a tree! God lives in heaven, far, far away. Whatever I felt there in that forest, it certainly wasn't God, and if it wasn't God, because that's what the naturalists thought, it must be something more sinister. Something a little dangerous. Something to be wary of. I settled on the idea that it was a nice forest, but it had nothing to do with God at all. Neither did the nice beaches nor the nests filled with baby birds. They were made by Him and then, by golly, he was outta there, onto making the next thing. He had better things to do than hang around.

God was in church, and the forest was no church.

Over time, as I worked with people I loved on the wild landscapes of Creation, I began to return to that little me — the one who threw her arms around a tree as a glorious hallelujah! The blood and the soil rubbed by life and death into my skin, the stuff that became more and more me, changed me. The "something" became known to me in an intimate way. Where once there was verse quoted to me by our Catholic school teacher or a sour-faced adult making a point about my failures, there was now a growing relationship. I was connected to something sacred when I was outside, close to the source of life. When the walls and the roofs and the climate-controlled world was gone, when I was on and in and surrounded by the exorbitant beauty all from the source of . . . Well, what was I going to call it then? The source of — God? No, that was too big of a leap. So, I left it at that: "source."

— 102 —

GOD

Another euphemism that padded my delicate sensibilities. And those of the people around me, of course.

Most of the people I know appreciate words like "source" or "Creator" or "great light" or "om" or whatever else we come up with. God is too heady. Too much baggage. The new age words do the job of tying us into the spiritual without tying us into the dogma. But one fateful day, when I was deep in the forest, my shrinking away from the word "God" changed for me.

As I often do, I had wandered off the path. I like to wander off the path. I like to purposely get lost for a time, at least in the forests I know, where there's no real danger of being lost for more than an hour or two. I will eventually find a familiar marker to lead me back, but for a time, I'm out of control. I can panic and aggressively grasp for those controls, retrace my steps and get back to "safety," or I can mosey along, head to the ground, head to the sky, eyes wandering and taking it all in. An adventure.

When I'm on one of my off-the-beaten-trail adventures, I always come upon unexpected marvels. Maybe the miracles avoid the places with ruts. In any case, there's always something tucked into these wild places. Maybe a new mushroom I haven't seen before or a whole fairy ring of them. Maybe a tiny bird's nest woven into a thicket of red dogwood branches with the tiniest little eggs, small as marbles, inside. But on this day, it was a red-eared slider turtle that crossed my path, shiny and wondrous.

I squatted down beside him and introduced myself, as any properly functioning member of the forest must. He listened from inside his shell. Unlike the snapping turtle, who cannot retract into his shell and thus must "snap" in defense, the red-eared slider pulls in his tender bits by instinct. Take no offence. I didn't. I sat there looking at the markings on his shell, the intricate patterning of greens and blacks painted across each section. Yellows outlined in black around the edges by the careful hand of the artist. Thin black outlines on the tender skin around his eyes. The tiny nails on the tips of his wide, reptilian toes peeked out from their hidden shell home. He watched me with those little turtle eyes, completely vulnerable to my next move. I touched his shell with my fingertip. I couldn't resist.

— 103 —

RADIANCE OF THE ORDINARY

"You are beautiful," I gasped.

I began to cry. I couldn't help it. Moved by the sound of the birds singing in the canopy of leaves above me, the smells of the damp forest floor, and this little creature built of tender skin and a hard shell slowly moving across the earth to do what he must — be a turtle. To contribute simply by being. A moving, living, breathing, outward expression of the mad, endless, unencumbered, enthusiastic genius of . . . of God. Of course, of God. Always and forever of God!

The something that overwhelmed me was love, and God is Love. There is nothing between. It courses through every atom, into spaces unknown and universes unfathomable. Love. Me and a turtle enraptured by it. The universal connector who weaves us all together. It's through this love of God that I learned to love and continue to learn to love. Through this love I am more, but I am still just me. Elevated and humble. Grand and insignificant. I reach for the warmth and burrow into the depths wanting more, wanting to be more, and being at peace with simply being all the same. That is love and love is what I'm given in every moment of every day if I choose to open myself and receive it.

———

To me, our Creator is our Creator. He is God, whole and true, and so I call "him" God. And as I've lived, I have come to understand that drive we all have, that hunger for the sacred and the Divine. That is God speaking to our hearts. In our secular world we look to fill that God-shaped hole in our lives with reason, sports obsessions, social media, ideologies, material things, entertainment, addictions, new age ideas like "good vibes only," and whatever else comes our way that temporarily makes us feel good. They're all diversions that serve for a time, but our fuel and purpose and meaning blooms through love, and that love, as I've come to experience it, is found in God.

I want God, deeply and truly. I want to live near and under and through and connected to the source of Divine love. I want authenticity, however that may come. Relationships are not just there for us to feel good; they are there for us to learn, and they connect us to things that we cannot reach alone. Living my life with God in my centre has allowed me to live without hunger. I am at peace, deeply I am, even

GOD

when events claim it for a time. That doesn't mean God is here only for my peace; it means that I find peace because I allow him to love me.

My salvation is in the Creator of all that is, but that salvation does not await me like a carrot calling me to heaven. It is here now, in my every waking moment. I can allow myself to be saturated with love and unconfined beauty, or I can spend my time hungry while the feast goes on without me.

To that little girl, wounded and tender: Let's throw our arms together around every tree that invites us. And when we're there, you and me, cheek against bark, we'll be there together, loving God, thanking God, praising God for the pulsing life moving through us all, up into the tips of the trees — an antenna into the heavens, shooting our love right back at the same God who returns it to us through the spiraling love all around us.

Recipes

I'm not cut out for the social media age. I try to be. I share some things from around our farm — pictures of our animals, what we're building, plants and fungi I've foraged — that sort of thing. I try to be genuine and encouraging, championing real food and authentic stewardship of the land. Every now and then I even share a picture of one of our meals with a little description. Sometimes I shudder when I do this, for no matter how detailed the explanation of what and why and how we ate the beautiful food from our farm, the comments that follow will often include:

"RECIPE!"

"Recipe, please!"

"Where's the recipe?"

These are the most dreaded of all comments. I'd rather have the vegan trolls telling me I'm a "murderous assassin" when I show a steak. At least I have somewhere to go from there.

I have written endless monologues to convince people that we don't need recipes: we need to relearn, *reclaim*, the art and skills of cooking. It's not that looking through recipes for inspiration is a problem, it's that we've come to rely on recipes, both for cooking and for almost everything in our lives. And where there's a recipe, there is art and individuality lost.

Medicine used to be seen as an art. The old country doctor or local herbalist would offer different medicines and advice based on their experience; their knowledge of the local people, flora, and fauna; and the teachings they inherited from their mentors. Today, Western medicine has lost its art. Big schools designed by the Rockefellers and

RECIPES

run by pharmaceutical companies give doctors recipes and call it "standard of care." Heaven forbid a doctor follow his instincts or collaborate with a patient to try modalities outside the "standard of care." They risk a lawsuit, or maybe even the loss of their license.

Our education system trains our brains to confuse recipes with knowledge. In everything we learn, the bullet point ingredients with a little synopsis of how to put it all together. We're encouraged to stick with the recipe as it's written if we want to get it right. If you look through the comment sections of online recipes, you'll often see a little micro-battle between those exclaiming they "tweaked the recipe" by adding a half cup of raisins or a teaspoon of cumin and those proudly reporting that they "followed the recipe exactly as is and it's perfect — don't deviate!" God forbid we deviate.

I have a deep adoration for written accounts of life in the 1800s or so. Relatively speaking, it's not that long ago. Just half a wink of an eye — a flutter, really. But things were so different then, and Troy and I try to shape our lives in a similar way. I'm not a complete Luddite despite my aspirations. I will use electricity until there's no electricity to use, but I'm careful with technology, and I consistently question what's held up as normal in our culture.

We don't have Wi-Fi in our home. We never have and we never will. Our home is our sanctuary. I don't want my sanctuary buzzing with manmade electromagnetic frequencies. So, no Wi-Fi. It's early on a winter morning as I write, so it's still dark outside. I can hear the roosters calling up the sun, but it hasn't responded quite yet. I have my beeswax candles burning for light and a fire going in the woodstove. My red-light glasses are on, and so is the light filter on my laptop. So, you see, there's still technology here, but I'm respectful of it. Throwing on the electric lights and letting the EMFs zoom all around me would be "normal," but it's not how I want to live.

How I want to live is closer to how humans used to live. Back then, people had to know how to keep warm, how to chop wood and carry water, and how to determine which plants were safe to eat. They inherited knowledge about which species of wood burn hottest and which burn too fast. They learned how to cook because it was a life skill. If they didn't know how to prepare food, they wouldn't eat.

RADIANCE OF THE ORDINARY

When I first learned how to cook on a woodstove, I was overwhelmed by my lack of . . . everything. I had to learn the properties of different types of wood. Some burn fast and hot, like lightning in the stove. Other types burn slowly and produce coals that retain their heat for hours. I learned that the difference between boiling and simmering a pot came down to where I slid it along the surface of the stove, how I controlled the draft, and which wood I fed the flame. I went from being unable to boil water on that behemoth to cooking all of our meals on and in that stove, and it was a trial by fire. Literally. I relied on an elderly friend — who had never known anything but a wood cookstove — to show me the art and nuance of her knowledge. There are no recipes, no directions for such things. Not for the way I'm looking to learn. Not for the way I want to understand.

Some might say, "Oh, Tara, we evolve. We lose skills as we no longer need them. Few people know how to hitch up a pair of oxen to pull a plow or how to make a quilt from the down of their geese." I suppose that's true enough. I'm not looking to live a facsimile life of a bygone era. But I am looking to excavate down and through and all around what a sad and sick culture holds up as normal in my search for what's meaningful for me. And that includes knowing things beyond the shortcuts that get us there fast. I don't care about what got someone somewhere fast; I want to hear about the journey. I want the guts, not just the bones.

See, here's the thing. If we think that we need precise directions to learn, we soon find ourselves unable to learn at all. We lose our tolerance for failure and experimentation. And if we can't learn the lessons and develop the gifts that are uniquely ours, then we eventually become part of the collective hive mind, unable to excavate what is ours even if we try.

———

I love reading. I tend to get on a kick and suck all I can out of a topic before moving on to the next one. My latest fascination has lasted for a few years, and it's showing no sign of waning. I've been reading first-hand accounts of pioneer life. It doesn't matter the perspective; I want to hear it. But it's the ones written for children — the ones with children as the protagonists — that have captivated me the most.

RECIPES

As I read these books, I'm absolutely amazed by the tenacity and skills of even the very youngest children. Again and again, I read about what their responsibilities were in a home. How they had to milk the cows, drive them to new pastures, cook, sew, and haul water. Today we look at the contribution of our labour to the operation of our family as something distasteful. When we surrendered the work of growing and supporting a family to the corporations, the very word *work* became bitter on our tongues. But that's not the story in the pages of these books. That's not the story of my elderly friends who grew up in a time and place absent screens and entertainment.

I recently had tea with a friend, and she told me about the challenge of balancing her son's homeschooling with sports commitments. He has two hockey practices a week followed by training sessions, a game or two, and regular weekend tournaments. And then there's her other son who is also in hockey with a conflicting schedule. She is intent on exposing her children to every program or opportunity available. On Mondays they have a group "creative math" session. On Tuesdays, it's an hour drive to piano lessons. You get the idea. The whole of it is frenetic and busy and scripted. Every last minute, scheduled. She's exhausted with the hustle. It reminds me of when our own children were in competitive sports as teenagers. Rather than just playing to have fun, they became entangled in worlds of extra coaching and training and weekend tournaments. Our entire lives became consumed by something that started out as fun.

I compare that to the stories I'm so entranced by. Where children, once having completed their chores, run barefoot through grasses, risking snake bites. Where, with a glance, they recognize whether the chestnuts are prime for picking or if they need to wait a few days yet. Where they find themselves in all manner of predicaments that require them to find their way out. Challenges and hardship cannot be separated from fun and adventure in these stories. That's the honest way of learning, of growing a resilient human being. There is responsibility and a requirement to the home, to the family. And there is a wildness, an unstructured play that brings dynamic learning of the sort that cannot be replicated by the recipes of sports and classes and workshops. Children responsible for nothing other than following the dictates of their recipe.

My mind doesn't allow me to be okay with the erasure of my ancestral knowledge. I imagine my ancestors' ghosts walking among me as I learn to darn a sock, and I feel equal parts embarrassment and pride, knowing they are a forgiving lot of ghosts. At least I am trying. At least I recognize the importance of their efforts.

I don't want the limitations imposed by convenience. To take what's on offer is to take such a tiny fraction of what's possible. Imagine the frozen food aisle of the grocery store. Everything flavour-enhanced to trick the tongue so it doesn't notice the missing nutrients. The clothes in the fast-fashion store all following this season's trends. Next season? Don't worry about it, just follow along. That's not good enough for me. I want to do things my way. I want to learn about how I fit into the world as me, unique and individual me, discovering what I have to contribute.

In my old cookbook collection, books from the 1800s and early 1900s, the recipes don't have the formulaic listing of ingredients followed by precise oven temperatures and cooking times. There is an assumption, in those pages, that everyone had a modicum of cooking knowledge. The recipes are written in paragraphs that go something like this: "After plucking your pheasant, brown it over a hot fire. Add to it two good onions, three whole carrots, some bitter dried herbs of your fancy. Cover with river water, freshly fetched. Cook lowly over coals until ready." I imagine the comments section under one of my Instagram posts if I wrote such a thing!

And in those books, the offerings are never just limited to food. In some, the recipes include how to cure croup, how to make plasters for lung infections, and how to make every alcohol imaginable, from brandy to cordials. You can learn how to make hare stew and how to drain a horse's abscess in a single volume. There are tinctures for curing a bite from a mad dog and cures for "summer complaint." There are suggestions for how to make your own ink and how to dye clothing with foraged plants. It's an entire world of things we once knew. These books are records of what we had and what we've lost.

In those recipes is evidence of a time when our autonomy held strong. If you were unwell, chances were you would have to find a

RECIPES

way to get well on your own. When your colander ripped, you would need to mend it. There were no online services to deliver some cheap little thing made in China to your door. These days, we would throw up our hands in exasperation if we had to sit with a colander and pull wire through its holes or thread through an old woolen sock. "I'm too busy!" How did that ever come to be?

I should know what ironwood is. I should know how to make butter. I should know which medicines and flavours grow wild in the fields and forests around me. I should know how to butcher a deer and my cattle. I should know how to make cheeses from the cow that I milk because I like cheeses and I have milk. I should know these things because I'm a part of these things. If I don't know, if I don't participate, I can't be a part. That's the truth of it. There's no division between work and pleasure. They come together when they're the real deal. If they don't, you're getting something else altogether.

My husband asked me what I'm writing about, and I said, "How the whole fucking world is a recipe." He asked, "Am I recipe?"

"No dear, you're not a recipe."

He pulls me out of the cynical valley I sometimes stumble into. Every now and then, he joins me, and we frolic with our frustration for a bit, but by and large, one of us is able to call from the edges, "Hey, there are some beautiful little crocuses sprouting over here!" or "You have to see the new calf sprinting through the herd," and it's too much for the cynical one to resist. Who can remain a sourpuss when hope is licking their nose?

No, he's not a recipe. And I'm not a recipe. And you, dear reader, are not a recipe. And that's the whole point — remembering that. We all come from a long line of survivors who had to use ingenuity and their creative minds to solve problems and produce beauty in this world. Those things remain, coursing through our veins. To be here, now, means that we require a little navigation to find our unique expression and our connection to this world, to our bodies, to our ancestors, to our spiritual selves through and with our Creator, to the meaning of our short time on planet Earth. It doesn't come as default anymore. There are too many distractions, too many addictions wedged between who we are and how intimately that "who" is connected to the natural world. We

— 111 —

RADIANCE OF THE ORDINARY

are totally and completely dependent. And yet, we act as if buffing the illusion of independence and the convenience of modernity is worth it.

Worth it? Worth our very purpose?

And that's why I move toward what was — because it deepens my relationship to the natural world, which reveals a "me" that resonates as true. In learning old skills, in developing and creating my own art, my own way of doing things as I am taught by experience and nature, I live deeper in my meaning. We love the natural world when we are in relationship with it. We act more responsibly when the way we move and act has a direct impact on our lives rather than being hidden behind corporate logos and cellophane.

The recipe of today tells us to get a job; send our babies to daycare and our kids to school; do what the doctor says; allow administrators to decide what they will teach our children and what will be useful to them in their lives. We are told what it is we must think if we are to be upstanding citizens. We are told the food is safe. They give us four types of apples to choose from when God gave us thousands.

The recipes encourage liberal amounts of the ingredients they want you to use. Raise your children without limits. Love without discipline. Everything in moderation. Don't let them feel left out. Don't let them experience hardship. Don't say the word *no*. Say the word *no* all the time. Give them a cellphone. Let them use social media. It's normal! Heaven forbid they deviate from the recipe. When they are done with school, give them more school so they can get a job. If you can't pay for more school, let them get a student loan. When they graduate and get their minimum-wage job doing what they were told to do, congratulate them as they start their life off with a mountain of debt.

Put in the oven at 350°F and bake until crisp.

And we wonder why a third of us are on antidepressants.

———

The truth is that recipes are a crutch. Use them when you're lame, but recognize that you're lame. If you had a kink in your ankle that stopped you from walking, you would, I hope, do something about it. So, let's recognize what's missing and do something about it. Convenience is dependence. Let's at least be honest about that. And dependence is a

— 112 —

RECIPES

weakening of the muscles involved in any given pursuit. Once we stop using a muscle, it atrophies and becomes ineffectual.

I like finding my weak spots. I see it as an adventure; an attempt to discover the things I never learned or even considered. With humility, every recognized deficit can be an opportunity to move beyond who we are today and into a version of ourselves that is waiting quietly to emerge. Only I can't tell you what that is for you. And you can't tell me what that is for me. We all have a map, yes. It's made of old parchment with beautiful illustrations, but mine doesn't look like yours, and neither of us can see the destination. It just unfolds, a step or two each day, as we meander with our eyes and ears and hearts open to the sounds and stories around us.

―――――

Now, after all that, I'd like to share with you a recipe of sorts. It's how I make bone broth. We consume bone broth every day. Even if we don't sip a cup of it, we've undoubtedly used some to braise a roast or make a sauce. Bone broth is such a staple in our house that I have a whole freezer dedicated to it and shelves in my root cellar full of dried bone broth in jars.

When I was in my twenties, I couldn't have told you how to make bone broth. I might have assumed I'd just throw some bones in a pot of water for a couple of hours. I might have even pulled out a foil-wrapped bouillon cube and asked, "You mean this stuff?"

No, that's not what I mean.

The making of a good broth starts with good bones. You don't want a sack of grocery store bones if you can avoid it. If you don't have your own animals, then a local farmer who raises animals without medications, out under the sun on good pasture, is a good friend to have. Use all types of bones. A good beef bone broth includes the knuckle bones, flat bones, joints, tendons, neck bones, rib bones, whatever-bone-you-got bones. If you're making broth with chicken or rabbit, turkey or duck, use the whole frame of the animal. When I make lamb or goat broth, I include the skinned heads. You can't really do that with a beef head, but you definitely can with smaller animals, and it's well worth including for the extra nutritional boost.

RADIANCE OF THE ORDINARY

First, I roast my bones in the oven. I include a couple of onions cut in half and maybe a carrot or two in the roasting pan. I sprinkle everything with a little coarse salt. After the bones are roasted, I scoop out the marrow fat and add it to my marrow fat jar in the freezer. Once that jar is full, I make my patented (okay, not really) marrow butter, which is just half raw butter, half marrow mixed with some minced fresh herbs. It's divine, and it's a wonder on a good, thick steak.

I put all of my bones in a giant stock pot. Here's where people often go wrong. They want to stretch their bones, so they use too much water for the number of bones they have. Don't do that. It's not worth the paltry result. I fill my pot halfway with bones and the rest of the way with good, clean well water. If you are using tap water, filter it. I then add things to the pot like an old witch in a cave, only I don't add children's fingers and eye of newt. I add ingredients for extra gelatine and collagen first. That might be some duck, turkey, chicken, or goose feet and heads. If I'm making beef broth, I don't have to add anything because of the enormous amount of connective tissue in and around the bones. I then add a few generous glugs of homemade vinegar (another food passion of mine), but a raw, organic vinegar of any type works just as well.

And there it is, the base of every bone broth I make. It's from here that you can start getting wild. I like to make plain bone broths for cooking — to which I might add a few herbs, carrot slices, or dried foraged mushrooms — and medicinal bone broths for sipping, to which I add all sorts of foraged plants. From dried wild carrot heads to birch polypore mushrooms to dandelion and chicory roots, I'm always up for new flavours and expanding my dietary diversity. This is where we salvage what has been lost to us in the meagre offerings of a grocery store.

I simmer my bone broths all day long, into the night, and then again throughout the next day. Some people don't. Some people prefer a shorter time. Not me. When my broths are done, there isn't a drop of mineral or nutrient left in those bones. The liquid chills to a thick, gelatinous blob — evidence of its high gelatine and collagen content. No need for collagen powders made out of cow hides: this is real food tied to place. Our bodies know the difference.

RECIPES

If I were to put my bone broth instructions on social media, I would be bombarded with questions like, "How much water?"

"How many bones?"

"Where do I get the mushrooms?"

"Where's the recipe for vinegar?"

"How do I know how much or how long?"

And to all of that I say, there is nothing unreachable or unknowable here. I do not live in a mystical place with an enchanted forest where my magical ingredients grow. I have just learned what is here. I have developed relationship with place. And that is the calling built into this recipe. To find your relationship with Mother Earth. A relationship that waits for you and will never stop calling for you.

Live by the terroir of your home. Sip your own broth, unique and limited, accessible only to you. No two are ever exactly the same, and that's the joy in it. Learn about the wild plants and mushrooms around you. Dry them and tincture them and build your larder, one step at a time. Be still enough and slow enough to bear witness to what grows in you as you move closer to the Earth.

———

I still love cookbooks. I have many. But I read them for inspiration and almost never use them to follow a recipe. One of my favourite cookbooks of all is the enchanting *Cooking in Ten Minutes* by Édouard de Pomiane, written in 1948. Oh, what a treasure that little book is. In among the recipes, Édouard somehow managed to fit in the pursuit of pleasure in a life well lived. Here's one of my favourite passages:

> Before skinning your orange pour two cups of boiling water on the coffee which is massed in the filter of the machine. It will draw out all the aroma while you are eating the fruit.
>
> Everything is finished . . . no, it is only just beginning. Put the coffee pot back on the gas for twenty seconds. Watch it like a lynx. Whatever happens the coffee must not boil.
>
> Warm a cup by rinsing it out with boiling water. Fill it with hot coffee. Sink into your comfortable armchair; put your feet on a chair. Light a cigarette — Turkish or Virginian,

— 115 —

according to your particular weakness. Send a puff of smoke
slowly up to the ceiling. Sniff up the perfume of your coffee.
Close your eyes. Dream of the second puff, of the second sip.
You are fortunate.

At the same time your gramophone is singing very softly a
tango or a rhumba.*

I remember reading that and thinking, *How did I get this far in life
without knowing one must preheat a mug with boiling water?* I've never
skipped that step since.

---

* Édouard Pomiane, *Cooking in Ten Minutes*, trans. Bruno Cassirer
(London: Faber & Faber, 1985), 30.

Of Blood and Butterflies

A peasant becomes fond of his pig and is glad to salt away its pork. What is significant, and is so difficult for the urban stranger to understand, is that the two statements in that sentence are connected by an and not by a but.

— JOHN BERGER, "Why Look at Animals?"

In the autumn it is time to harvest our animals. They are fat and slick from a spring and summer of feasting on sweet grasses and forages. They are at their prime, thick with health and joyful with their lot in life. I walk among them, bringing pails of apples for their dining pleasure. Some of the old cows come right up to me, asking me to pop the apples right into their mouths. Others are shyer and will only take the apples if I lay them on the ground at their feet. I know who's who. Some, like my oldest milk cow, Bea, prefer a nice, deep scratch on the soft, malleable little flap of skin under their chins. She'd rather get that than an apple any day.

I walk among our herd, looking at their bodies. Looking to see who's "finished." I vividly remember how Richard taught me to do this many years earlier. We stood together, leaning over his fence on a quiet prairie afternoon. An endless blue sky, uninterrupted by forest or mountain, spread out above us. His was the land of the prairies. A red-tailed hawk perched on a fence post across the field. He could spot those hawks with ease, whether they were nearby or a tiny speck in the distance.

Richard pointed out the steers to me, one by one, explaining the differences in their bodies. "You see that one, Tara? It's not ready." I

RADIANCE OF THE ORDINARY

asked "why" again and again that day. And then, every time we worked around the cattle, I pointed out the ones I thought had a nice finish on them and waited for his expert assessment. He saw things that my lack of experience blinded me to. But I began to understand, in my feeble way. Mostly, I realized, as with everything, there is an art to being a cattleman as much as there is the skill and knowledge.

Now I walk among my herd, Chief Evaluator, deciding who lives another year and who dies. The responsibility of my decisions weighs on me. As I move through the herd, looking at their bodies, I remember each of their stories. When they were born and to whom. I look at my fat heifer whose grandmother is still here, the two of them bonded. When they chew their cud, mesmerized in peaceful pleasure, they do so together, side by side on a grassy mound before the tree line. The heifer hasn't had a calf in four years, despite the bull's best efforts. She's infertile, and her time here is coming to an end. There's no decision left to be made, only acceptance to be had.

Two fat steers, both over three years old now, are contenders as well. I walk between them, looking at their rear ends, the fat cover over their bodies, that rounded fullness still absent in their younger herdmates. And all the while, as I look at these living animals and imagine the flesh beneath their hides, all of life sings around me. Birds and sweet grasses. The cattle move about peacefully, lazily swatting at flies with their tails, staring off into parts unknown. They are hypnotized by their own chewing and burping and swallowing, their collected forages making their way through the various chambers of their ingenious digestive systems. They are a marvel, a brilliant, life-giving marvel, and I am going to eat them. Not only am I going to eat them, but to eat them, I must kill them.

In our world of wedges — great buffers to keep us comfortable — we have created all manner of devices to keep us from the grit of life. But grit remains. We just pass on our refusal of participation to the poor soul who cannot refuse. Every autumn, when it comes time to harvest our animals, I think of the person standing in the pool of shit and body fluids in a commercial abattoir. Every day, all day long, that person looks into the eyes of fearful, wild-eyed beasts and fires a captive bolt stun gun, slashes arteries, and jumps back before the blood fills their

OF BLOOD AND BUTTERFLIES

rubber boots. In a moment meant to be a sacred act, a great responsibility between eaters and that which nourishes them, it's an abomination. These beautiful animals are treated only as meat, even while their spirits still have hold. It's a separation disguised as an efficiency, but in truth, it's a robbing of our relationship with nature. A gift slapped away.

I was once told not to name my animals. "Too hard to kill them if they have a name." Every now and then someone still says something similar. I don't suppose they're ready for my standard response.

"Why would I not name an animal? One of the great joys of farming is having relationships with my animals, spending time with them and getting to know them. Is it because they're going to die that I should not name them? Every single person I know is going to die, but I don't limit myself in my relationships with them."

I'm usually met with a shrug or a concession. "I suppose."

I anticipate the fall animal harvest for weeks before. It's a busy time, and it's emotionally exhausting, too. We will harvest sheep and pigs if we have them. We will harvest some of our cattle and rabbits, chickens, turkeys, geese, and ducks. We will fill our freezers and our root cellar with the meat of our farm and that which we hunt. From the day they are born, every single one of those animals moves toward the day of their death, and that death, save an accident, will be at our hands. We are duty bound to the responsibility, the rightness of our obligation.

Harvest day is a dreaded day in my heart. It's heavy with responsibility and sadness. Sometimes I feel unworthy of participating in the day. But it's also a day of great reverence and gratitude. There is profound joy in the overwhelming magnificence of God's creations.

"Duty bound." That phrase used to mean something. It's a phrase wrapped in honour and sacrifice. To the duty, in the duty — rightness. Rightness matters to me, to us. Within our gratitude for the life-giving nourishment these animals provide us lives the duty of our hearts. Our animals, born here on this land, will know no trailer, no line to the gallows. They will remain here, under the same sky they gazed upon when they were born. They will be in their herd, peacefully lounging, when a bullet enters their brain and their life ends. Their blood will return to the same earth their bodies fell onto as they slipped from their mothers' warm bodies.

— 119 —

RADIANCE OF THE ORDINARY

In the moments after we kill an animal, we sit on the earth, hands on the animal's body, praying our prayers of thanks. I tell stories I've collected from having known the beautiful beast. We send it off with words of gratitude while all around us something profound is happening. There, in the field, a mystical transformation. The physical into the ethereal. The contained into the limitless. Not something ending. Something expanding beyond the borders of life. Under my hand, the warm body transforms from that which I have known into that which isn't mine to know. And in the wake of this alchemy, a body remains. Nourishment. Ever-giving life.

We have given our animals a good death, solemn and sacred, and now there is joy. Absolute joy. Joy in the relief of everything having gone well. Joy in the abundance of beautiful nourishment. Joy in the assuredness that life continues on. We hang the body and carefully slide our sharp knives along the inside of the hide. The thick skin slowly peels back to reveal the quality of life we have given to the animal. The fat is deep yellow from the sweet, rich forages of our land's pastures and wilds. The muscles and organs are deep red, rich with maturity and the effort of carrying this animal up hills and into valleys, through trails and wild places. The meat smells sweet and earthy and I am proud. I'm proud for the work we have done. I'm proud we have done things the hard way, moving these animals daily across our land, keeping them for years longer than they would live in a feedlot, making sure they were given all we had to offer. I am proud because the meat that's left for us is a thank you more important than any measure or gauge. Evidence better than any other of a life well lived.

The blood pooled on the grass around us attracts a lone yellow swallowtail butterfly. She comes and floats her delicate legs on the congealed blood, feeding on it. We watch in amazement. Every year we hope the hungry swallowtail butterflies will return for their blood feast. The first time we witnessed this, we were startled. Weren't butterflies meant for daisies? But nature, as nature does, laughs at our ignorance. Of course a butterfly delights in the nourishment of blood. Of course the wasps find us, landing on the flesh of the animal and pulling off little round balls to bring back to their homes. Of course we're all tied in together.

— 120 —

OF BLOOD AND BUTTERFLIES

And therein lies the wisdom of a butterfly, weighing her actions not against the opinions of her butterfly clan but with the knowledge built right into her, fed into her from antennae connecting to a mysterious ether beyond. She encourages me to be brave, too. To embrace the wildness and rawness of the parts that lie dormant inside of me, cultivated into submission by a culture that tells fairy tales in place of deeper meaning. We believe in our limitations and weaknesses because they are a comfort to us. Familiar and dependable.

But when I'm honest, I cannot deny that here in this field, there is something beyond the reach of my words or reason. There is blood on my hands, on my arms, soaking through the linen of my shirt and into the open skin that contains me. Blood from another life is absorbed into me, becoming part of me. I don't just see it there, I feel it, deep in my body, changing me, layering me, pulling me deeper and deeper into an untouchable realm. It's *beauty-full*. Full and saturated, concentrated and thick. This is a world ungovernable by man. This world cannot be manipulated with fairy tales. There is nothing here that can be marred by the misunderstandings of a lost human. This is real. This is true. The blood fades into thirsty butterflies, human skin, and the dark, cool earth. All of us connected, now, through that shared blood.

That same blood flowed from my ancestors and into me. The blood of their animals, hunted in forests and farmed in fields. From the earth into us and back to the earth again. To my descendants, a drop of my blood with all of life echoed through it.

RADIANCE OF THE ORDINARY

I wonder, how do the swallowtails drink if too many people buy meat from grocery stores? How does the blood return to the soil? How do the coyotes and the vultures feast on the entrails from the farmer and the hunter? Our wedges, our separation, spills over into all of life. A chink in the chain. We cannot divide ourselves without dividing everything.

A world of wedges. Lovers kept from lovers. The great healer kept from the ill at heart and mind. A cheap peddler's promise of easy and slick sold to the hungry while the truth is kept tucked away. It's too hard. It's too ugly. You're too feeble of mind and spirit. Look here, watch this, eat this. The real business of life, they assure us, is the business. Go to the right school. Wear the right clothes. Buy the right car. Lust after material possessions. Then lust and lust and lust again. Gerbils on a wheel staring out of their plexiglass cages on their endless pursuit to nowhere.

The bison removed the biggest wedge I had — my fear of death. A fear so strong I had unknowingly shaped my life around it. Without that day with Richard, without the many days that followed, wherein I immersed myself in what I was being taught, I don't know if I would have survived the pain of what was to come in my life.

Cutting Meat

I'm in a small butcher shop on a farm on the Canadian prairie. It's a clandestine butcher shop, but it's the best I've ever seen. It's not technically legal for farmers to butcher their own meat in this part of the world. But the customers of this farm want their meat handled by the same farmer and skilled butcher from cradle to grave; he's as committed as they are. That fine cattleman is Richard, the one who taught me about animal harvest and farming and how to live saturated in the beautiful. The one who taught me, rightly, how to look for the abundant gifts of nature and not be fooled by my personal beliefs, capped by my comfort levels.

It's a cool autumn day, made cooler still by the chilled air inside the little blue butcher shop nestled behind the farmhouse and the expansive garden that feeds this family over the winter. There's four of us today: Richard, Kathy, me, and Reuben. Reuben is from Oaxaca and has come to live with Richard and Kathy to help around the farm and hopefully earn the right to extend his temporary visa into a permanent one. He spent some time working where many other Mexicans in this area work, at the feedlots. He didn't have the stomach for it. He's here now, and he's become a good buddy to have alongside me in the long days in the "meat shed." The stainless steel tables in the shed form an L-shape. Reuben is to my right, at the end of the first table before it turns. Kathy is after the turn, the wrapper and label lady. That job is, as you will see, just as important as Richard's.

Richard is number one in the line, standing to my left. He's doing the bulk of the work, determining as per the customer's instruction sheet what cuts each piece of meat should be shaped into. Does the future

— 123 —

RADIANCE OF THE ORDINARY

eater want his steaks an inch and a half or an inch and a quarter? Do they want a roast with the blade, or did they request stew meat? He begins by retrieving the side of beef or bison from the cooler. The inside of that cooler is remarkable to me. An education beyond any of the nutrition books I've read. I've spent a good many hours in there with Richard over the years. The hanging carcasses are both from animals he's farmed and those of the farmers in his area for whom he's doing custom butchering. We can see the flesh and fat and bone of the animals raised on pasture, grasses alone, killed at their prime, and those of neighbouring farmers who farm differently. They raise their animals in smaller areas, feeding them grains and corn, raising the massive breeds of our industrialized food system — go big (and fast) or go home.

The meat hangs in the cooler to dry age. This brings it a depth of flavour and texture that the grocery store wet ageing method just can't match. Some intrepid foodies have come to purchasing that soggy, bland, wet-packed beef and dry age it themselves in their fridge. It's worth a shot, but if the quality of that animal's life is still lacking, it will never come close to this meat. In the cooler, I can see it all. I can smell it all. There is nothing to hide. Richard's animals have a bountiful cover of yellow fat, a conspiracy of grasses and age. Their meat is dark red and beautifully grained, a tell-tale sign of maturity and well-used and oxygenated muscles. That light pink meat of the grocery store from the immature, contained animals of industry is such a sadness to me. Such a telltale sign of things done wrong. Here in the meat cooler, I can stand alongside the bodies of the beasts that have moved on. I can smell the earthy sweetness of their meat. I can touch the delineation between their powerful muscles. Richard teaches me the muscles and the cuts, and it begins to make sense. Now I know why those tougher cuts, the ones from the hardest-working muscles, are so rich with the sinew and connective tissue that, when cooked right, become the meltingly tender, unctuous bits. Those wonderful steaks — I love them too — come from muscles only lightly used, and because of that they remain tender. Not so different from us. If I were a cannibal, and rest assured I have no aspirations, I wonder what I'd think of the product on offer today versus the delights of my cannibal ancestors.

A long track of railing snakes across the ceiling from the meat cooler to the corner of Richard's butcher station. He and Reuben cut out large

CUTTING MEAT

sections of meat, consult the cutting instructions, and we're on our way. I'm a novice, just learning, so I'm taught how to finesse and trim and properly cut the meat destined to be stew into proper stew meat. I've never thought much about stew meat. Stew is stew, I thought, but as with everything else, I'm being schooled. The best stew comes laced with fat and is rich with that wonderful connective tissue, fascia, and sinew that make long braised roasts so delicious. It's cut with care, uniform in its one-and-a-half to two-inch square blocks. I take care with that, finding meat in and along every cut trimmed away from the roasts and steaks. What doesn't make it as stew goes into the "ground" bins. We collect the remnants of meat from the beautiful roasts that Richard is shaping. That goes into ground, too. The bones stay in the meat unless the customer wants boneless roasts. The idea is a horror to me. It's like asking for "half the flavour and a quarter of the tenderness, please," but boneless has become a thing in this weird world of meat presented to us on Styrofoam trays wrapped in cellophane. And it's been so long that some people just don't know how to cook with the whole thing anymore. If the customer wants the bones removed, we remove them. They'll go into bags for making bone broth, a miraculous healing elixir if ever there was one.

Years later, one of our daughters came home from school annoyed with her classmates. Her art teacher had brought clean, old bones into class and laid them across a table for the students to use in their sketch class. Our daughter thought nothing of it and began to consider the project. But the other teenagers in the class began to shriek and gag. "Bones! That's so gross! I'm not staring at bones!" One gag begets a series of gags, and soon there was hysteria in the art class. The teacher removed the bones and replaced them with piled books. Our daughter was bewildered.

"How can anyone think a bone is gross? It's just part of a body. How can people be that disconnected? I don't get it."

———

Reuben is taking large slabs of meat and cutting them into roasts and steaks with the skill and experience of a man who has done this for a good long while. Both he and Richard point out where each unruly, massive slab of meat came from on the animal and the possibilities

— 125 —

RADIANCE OF THE ORDINARY

for how it will be butchered. Sometimes, they cut off thin slivers and we look closely at its grain, colour, texture, smell, and, finally, its flavour. There are flavours in that raw meat, earthy, deep, mildly sweet. Later, we compare those qualities to the carcass we are butchering for a neighbouring farmer. His steer is massive in size, one of those big breeds designed for a feedlot. Only this steer was "choice," kept back to feed the farmer's family for the year. He was fed a high-grain diet with a lot of corn. This practice creates the bland, neutral flavour so many of our tastebuds have come to associate with meat. The meat is slippery, greasy, and slick, and it smells acidic and sour. None of us taste it. We can see and smell enough to know not to.

I wish I could grab every nutrition client I've ever had and pull them into this meat shed. "See!" I would say, "This is why! This is why I'm telling you to find a farmer!"

Reuben has passed me his iPod so I can hear some of the music that fills him of longing for home. We'll be cutting meat all day and into the night. Tomorrow, bright and early, we'll start again. I watch out the window for appearances by the deeply amusing farm dog, Cheemo. He's a husky, brought to the farm by one of Richard and Kathy's sons when city life proved to be unsuitable. Everywhere we go, Cheemo follows. He is dog as dog should be. Loyal, a prankster, troublesome and adventurous.

When Cheemo joins the begging, meowing barn cats swarming outside the butcher shop, I can't help but grab a handful of trim and go outside, just a quick break, to feed it to him. Of course, if I'm feeding him some delights, it's only right to give the barn cats an offering or two as well. "Now they'll never leave!" Richard chides. But I see him dole out the goods every now and then, too.

On Kathy's station, the meat keeps growing. I am filling trays with stew meat and one- or two-pound balls of ground meat. Richard is building towers of steaks that she will wrap two, three, or four to a package depending on the cut sheet instructions. There are unwieldy roasts to wrap and endless packages of ground. Lord have mercy on the poor butcher shop wrapper who must wrap one-pound packages of beef. Standing in a butcher shop at the end of a long day forming endless tubs of ground beef into little one-pound balls and then wrapping

— 126 —

CUTTING MEAT

each of them in paper, one by one, is a task best suited to . . . maybe best suited to the requester of such a thing. To this day, I wrap our own ground beef in two-pound packages. If you have any humanity, you will ask for the same from your butcher.

How the meat is packaged is of utmost importance. Kathy taught me that. Imagine giving a gift, something rare and beautiful. A gift you want the receiver to understand is being given with thought and care. Now drop that gift in an old plastic bag from the grocery store. But before you do that, maybe throw the gift in the back seat of your car. Maybe put your muddy dog back there with it so it gets coated in a bit of dirt and the crumbs your kids left behind. Let's top it with a couple of dog hairs and some carpet lint for good measure.

It would be hard for the receiver to find, among the careless handling of that gift, the original thought and intention behind it. It's the same thing with the food we eat. Grocery stores know this. That's why they have all sorts of tricks, from spray preservatives on meat to keep them looking glossy and red under their shiny clear plastic to waxes and shellacs on produce to pretty labels on boxes. We eat with our eyes first. In the case of a little farmer with a little butcher shop, the wrapping is the final step in the presentation of the gift.

Kathy was a talented wrapper. She was the final handler of the meat — quality controller par excellence. She would unroll and rip big squares of red freezer paper from the heavy roll in front of her, just the right size for the shape of the meat that was to be wrapped. And with years of experience under her belt, she would fold and tuck and flip and turn the meat until it was time to seal the package with a piece of brown paper tape. Then she would flip it over and, in her neat, consistent handwriting, label the contents within. Every package, lined up on trays waiting for us to put them in the freezer, was beautiful. Good enough to put under a meaty Christmas tree. And inside, the beautifully, carefully cut meat of the skilled butchers alongside me.

To this day, one of my great kitchen heartbreaks is seeing what many farmers have to contend with — the shoddy and careless cutting of meat by the licensed butcher shops they are forced to use by regulators and government overseers. I have been gifted meat from farmer friends that was cut by some anonymous, rushed worker in some cold

— 127 —

butcher shop somewhere, only to open up the package and find a pork chop, paper-thin on one end, thick on the other, thrown into a package with another terribly cut piece meat. Or maybe the butcher trims all of the precious fat and debones a roast before shaping it into some obscure, Picasso-esque creation. I feel for the farmers who raise their animals with dedication and reverence, who are then forced by law to turn that animal over to a meat shop that couldn't care less.

This is one of the reasons why we decided to stop selling our meat years ago. We wanted the meat our animals left behind to be honoured to the standard we held. It may not be everyone's standard, but it is ours, and we couldn't find butchers around us who could do what we wanted them to do. It was important to us to give our animals a good death, and in so doing, we had to build the infrastructure to make it all work on a small farm. To that end, we built our own little meat cooler, not big enough to hang ten animals, but one beef or multiple sheep or pigs or waterfowl or deer. We bought meat saws and hand grinders at first. It was manual power dictated by meagre dollars. But over time and with patience, we were able to purchase those tools of ease — a meat saw and a meat grinder big enough to make a cannibal happy.

Today, Troy and I bring our dance of tasks to our own little butcher shop behind our house. Every autumn, you can find us there. Butchering and wrapping the meat that will hold us for the year. We handle every cut. We can feel and smell the life of that animal. The sadness that comes with the killing is replaced with a feeling of abundance and pride. There is no denying the results of our farming efforts on the cutting boards. We have either raised that animal right or we haven't. The good life of an animal is evidenced in the meat it leaves behind. It's tangible. I look for the tangible in everything.

There was a time when our whole family would work alongside each other in the meat shed, but now it is just us. The days are long. We have many animals to work through to keep us for a year of eating. We have five freezers to hold the lamb, ducks, geese, chickens, and turkeys. Another couple of freezers hold two whole beef and any wild game good hunting fortunes may have provided. There may be a pig if we raised pigs that year, but it's ruminant meat we prefer for health and pleasure. There's also another freezer of meat rabbits and one

CUTTING MEAT

dedicated to bones, organs, and all those precious animal fats from animals taken at their prime, after seasons of grazing on nutrient-dense pasture. All of my butter is made in the summer for the same reason. It joins the tallow, suet, lard, chicken and turkey schmaltz, duck and goose fat, and the caul fat of various ruminant animals. These are the nutrient-rich, traditional fats our ancestors ate and the ones I have raised our family on. More precious to us than any number in my bank account, these foods, along with the preserves and ferments in my root cellar, are the joy and security we move into winter with.

We've spent enough time in our little butcher shop to know who goes where and who does what. Troy has his jobs and I have mine. He manhandles the meat out of the ageing cooler and, after asking me what I want from each quarter, sets about making it so. I am the quality controller par excellence now. I take what he gives me and shave, trim, and shape it before wrapping it all up. When it's time to grind the tubs slated for ground, I fill the hopper while he shuttles tubs back and forth. He's the brute force and the brains. I'm the caulking that fills in the gaps.

And all the while, Richard, my most favourite of all the friends I have known in this lifetime, is near. I can hear him and feel him teaching me still, sharing truths that pull me ever deeper into this extraordinary world. As I write this, a red-tailed hawk *kee kee kees* overhead. His favourite bird. How could I not notice such magic?

Sometimes, when they're home, our grown daughters still join us in our makeshift meat shed. There's something primal, rewarding in its tangibility, that draws people into the task of preparing meat and preserving food. When there are ducks to pluck, there's no one I like having next to me more than my daughters. My husband does the killing and the hot water plunging. Our daughters do the plucking, and I'm the gutting gal. We stand outside under the crisp and cool autumn sky, working together. I usually work quietly. It gives my daughters space to get into their own wild and woolly conversations. Some of my favourite memories are of our family, all five, working together to fill our larders with reverence and good cheer. Just, I imagine, as our ancestors did. As natural as life itself.

Like Kathy years before me, I must slip away from the tasks outside the home to get back into my kitchen for a time so that when hungry

— 129 —

RADIANCE OF THE ORDINARY

tummies finish up with their day, there is food waiting. Good food, warm and rich. Multiple times a day, I leave my wrapping or gutting or cutting station with some of the lovely meat we're working with and retreat to my kitchen to fill a cast-iron pot with fall's vegetables, some bone broth and fresh herbs, and off-cuts of whatever's on offer. It only takes minutes, but when I return to my station, food braising in the oven, there are often piles of backlog for me to move through. Just like Kathy, who taught me that no matter what is happening on the farm, there are still humans to be fed. The nourishing of humans is something I take seriously. I've never understood the drive to raise or source good food but then not take the time to truly honour it, whether with the butchering or the cooking (or both).

Every workday on the farm ends with a feast. Sometimes the feast is small and humble. Feasts can be that, too, when we have beautiful ingredients. Afterward, there is rest. A good book or a board game or a puzzle with old country records playing. There was a time when we would head back out to work some more after supper. Not these days. We fit into a workday whatever fits into a workday, and we keep our pleasures well-tended. It's been a good day's work, and now there are stars to watch or loons to listen to. There are jars filling the root cellar shelves. There are potatoes and carrots and apples tucked away. Winter squash are lined up on the summer kitchen floor settling in for a long winter's nap.

And in our freezers is the meat that was once an animal. All of it cut and wrapped with care. The final step in the preparation of the gift. I am reminded, all year long, when I pull out a roast or some bones to simmer over our wood cookstove, of the animals whose lives nourishes our own. On each package, that animal's name. I remember them — what they looked like, their personality, what they shared with me in the moment of their death. The name is important. It tells me who to thank, along with our Creator, when we sit down to be nourished by their flesh. Life lived for death so that life lives again and evermore. I don't question the design. I live humbly in its remarkable gifts. Trying, in my feeble way, to illuminate the ordinary to its rightful glory.

— 130 —

PART THREE
Evermore

Hands of the King

We sit in silence. Fire crackling and popping intermittently in the cold room. There are candles and empty coffee cups. You, staring out the window. Snow and skeletal trees.

I hold your hand, rubbing the bones of each finger. Your big, powerful hands. Thick with life. Strengthened with trenches dug, felled trees lifted and turned, enormous loads heaved from the ground and thrown over your powerful shoulders.

These hands that could crack a nut in their palm opened and softly closed around the tender little hands of our small daughters. These hands, dense with flesh that skims across my skin like a delicate water bug. Barely even there.

These beautiful hands. Wrapped in sinew and muscle. Your skin cannot hide the toil, the effort, the sacrifice. The determination. I see it all, and soon enough there will be no more use for your flesh. Or mine. It will all fall away, leaving bone and ruddy joints. I can feel them now beneath my fingers.

My bones next to your bones. Buried deep in the earth. So similar, what we each will leave here, yours and mine. I imagine us there, bones beside bones. Threads of mycelium tying those bones back together. All the traces of this mortal life melted away.

Now I hold your hand ever tighter. I try to remember everything these hands, guided by your mind and heart, have done for your family. Have brought me. Have offered to me. My whole life in these ageing hands.

My king, my king, until my last breath, my king.

Ursula

Ursula was our dream cow. Her mother was Bea, Queen Bea if you please, and her father a mighty Brown Swiss bull. That made Ursula half Jersey and half Brown Swiss — one of the prettiest cows we ever did have. Our daughter Mila liked to regularly point out that she was the sole reason Ursula existed. She was the one who had read the Heidi book series, about a little girl who lived in the Swiss Alps among the Brown Swiss milk cows. For months, twelve-year-old Mila begged us for her own Brown Swiss cow to milk. We acquiesced, and beautiful Ursula, with her sable hair, her big, shiny black nose outlined by white hairs, and the most perfectly symmetrical little horns tipped in black, came to be. To this day, I've never seen a more beautiful dairy cow. She was practically perfect in every way.

So, it was with great excitement that we watched two-and-a-half-year-old Ursula brew a little calf within her. For nine long months we waited for that calf, surely a spectacular calf, to make his grand debut. On the morning when he had spent enough time in his mother's watery home, I found Ursula in labour. She had retreated to a small clearing in the tree line. Cows like to go off on their own when they're in labour. I took a peek, but I didn't disturb her. All looked well. I went about my chores.

After completing chores and walking dogs and eating a hearty breakfast, I went back to check on Ursula. She was still in labour, only now the little calf's front feet were poking out. Again, I slipped away to give her a little privacy. Some cows don't like humans milling about them when they're in labour. Ursula seemed to be doing well — no need for worry. But when I went back to check again, nothing had

URSULA

happened. Now I was worried. I watched for a time, and it became evident that she was struggling. I called our livestock vet, who talked me through what to do. Still nothing.

I was alone that day, nobody for miles around to help me, but these things matter little to life on the farm. It turned out I had to help pull that calf. There are breeds of cattle that often require such harrowing interventions — we don't keep those breeds. But complications still arise, all the time, and they require our interventions. I had to help Ursula get that calf out. In this situation, a farmer will often tie chains to the calf's legs. I didn't have chains. I had hands, which slid right off those wet, slippery little legs. I was too far from the barn to look for anything to assist me. I took off my shirt and wrapped it around the calf's legs for grip. I pulled when Ursula pushed. A nose came out, followed by a tongue. Ursula walked in circles, and I followed. She pushed and I pulled. Again and again, around and around we went — me pulling with everything I had and her pushing with all her might.

Having survived army boot camps, all sorts of physical competitions, and stacking hundreds and hundreds of rows of hay bales in a 45°C barn, I can tell you that helping Ursula deliver her calf remains one of the most exhausting tasks of my life. I don't know how long I pulled every time Ursula pushed, but when the little calf finally slipped into the world and landed on the earth with a wet plop, I fell backward and made my own sodden plop. My chest was covered in mosquito bites and cow shit and sweat and amniotic fluid. Lying in the mud and shit and blood, I panted, staring at the sky. I could hear Ursula making worried mommy noises reserved for the ears of her babe. She was licking her calf, cleaning him, rousing him, calling him into life. I knew I should move out of the way — an errant hoof to my belly was a definite possibility — but I was, quite literally, paralyzed in place. Whatever energy my body could generate for that cow, it had done. There was nothing left to offer. So, I stayed put and prayed that no neighbouring farmer or friend eager for a visit would appear and find me there, splayed on the ground, half naked, coated in every fluid a cow's body can produce.

When I was finally able to catch my breath and stand up, I looked over at Ursula and her new little calf. He still wasn't moving. By now he should have been. There was something wrong. I went to her, moving slowly and cautiously. What mother worth her salt would let someone, let alone a creature she didn't understand, between her and her babe? As a farmer, I need to be steady and assured, but also cognizant of the power of these animals. Ursula had just gone through a traumatic birth and now her calf was not responding. She was in a heightened state of concern, and I had to get between the two of them to see what was going on.

It never ceases to amaze me how an animal, especially a beast like a cow that has such potential for strength and destruction, knows when we are there to help. I could fill a whole book with stories of these creatures who, frantic with worry for their babies or having gotten themselves into a pickle, relinquish their power for our help. Like the time Ursula put her head through an old wooden board on the barn and couldn't get out, necessitating my careful sawing away of the board from around her horns. In such situations, animals tend to know you're their ally. It's such a quiet and delicate thing, but it's there — a type of good faith surrender. I am deeply honoured by such interactions.

Once, someone left comments all over my Instagram account, claiming, "Your cows love you unconditionally and you kill them!" That really stuck with me — it was so abjectly wrong and spoke to the infantile, Disney-esque ideas we have about animals. A cow, love me unconditionally? Ha! They wouldn't dream of such a lowering of their stock.

If we're going to anthropomorphize an animal, let's do it right, shall we? Let's start with Louis, my lovely sable-coloured Great Dane. (Now that I come to think of it, he and Ursula share the same beautiful colouring.) Louis is a sensitive fella. His great comforts in life include me, curling around a wood stove in winter and a cold toilet base in summer, food, me, meditating by the edge of a lake, and me. Also, me. He loves people. He loves me the most out of all the people. If ever we could say an animal loves unconditionally, it would be a dog. A cow is not a dog.

Cows are herd animals. They take comfort in their herd. They are their truest selves when they are functioning within their herd. They

— 136 —

URSULA

have strong hierarchies that are reinforced moment by moment. A cow on the bottom rung of the hierarchy waits while the others eat or drink. They only lie to chew their cud with others on the bottom rung. A top-rung cow slams, beats, and pushes an inferior cow that gets a little too close or a little too brazen. There are constant reminders that one must know their place. And everyone is eager to have a cow below them. Sometimes the young heifer or steer will be the most interested in a new calf, often bunting and pushing the calf around, hoping this spindly little creature will be someone they can dominate. But good mama cows put an end to that behaviour pretty quickly.

The boss cow sits atop this hierarchy. Maybe that should be Boss Cow — they've earned their reign and aren't likely to give it up. Few Boss Cows have to reinforce their rule. They walk into a group of cattle and the sea parts for them. They're given first dibs at the choice pasture full of clover and alfalfa, and they drink first on hot summer days, often standing by the cool trough for prolonged periods of time, lazily chewing their cud while the herd salivates behind them. There's a lot of that — a lot of claiming power — in a cow herd. And they all accept it. That's life in a herd. It's the language they speak, familiar and comforting even in its frustrations.

No, a cow doesn't love me unconditionally. A cow barely notices my utility. They, of the noble bovine clan; me, of the odd two-legged clan, gangly and of changing hides, moving about like a wobbly stick. I feed them and bring them things they like. I am kind to them, and they trust me to move them. They come when I call because they have faith there's something good in it for them. But that is not unconditional love.

Can a cow love at all? The scientists in the mix squirm at the idea of it. I kind of do, too, but for a different reason. I squirm because I don't understand why we think attributing human characteristics to a creature elevates it. Why do we need to make it like us to give it worth? We can't know something when we turn it into a thing it isn't; doing so diminishes its authentic self and we lose the truth. How can we protect and admire something we don't even bother getting to know? A cow's worth, any animal's worth, is not elevated by the cow's resemblance to us. A cow is sacred in its own wild uniqueness.

— 137 —

RADIANCE OF THE ORDINARY

Can we just leave it like that? When a cow has a baby, there is a connection and an instinct between the two, a touch of Creation that guides the mother to protect and nourish her baby. There is a spark imprinted on the very essence of the little being that drives it up onto its clumsy legs to search all along its mother's body, from her chin to her tail, for something it doesn't even know yet. A search for the precious colostrum it's never even tasted. Life hungry for life. Does the mother love her calf? What does it even matter what we call it? It's something, and it's tender and mysterious and worthy of our quiet awe.

There was Ursula, lowing her quiet moo to a calf who still wasn't moving. I approached slowly and deliberately, talking to Ursula calmly. The calf wasn't breathing. He had no pulse. Ursula, a big cow who would ordinarily ravage anything that came near her calf in that moment, took two steps back and watched. She couldn't do anything more. I began CPR on the wet and cool little body. I tried and I tried. Everything I could do, I tried. Ursula's attention was fixed on me and on her baby. I wanted nothing more than to give her that calf, bouncing and vibrant. He was so beautiful, so perfect in every way. But he was dead and there was no bringing him back.

After a good long while, I backed away in defeat. Ursula reclaimed her spot up against her calf. She continued to lick him with her powerful tongue, to jostle him that he might open his eyes. I slipped away and went to get the tractor. I needed to move the body. But as I loaded the heavy, wet little calf onto the sheet of plywood I had laid over the front forks of the tractor, Ursula became deeply concerned. As I backed up to the fence line, she followed with fearful eyes. I realized that I was not providing a kindness, abruptly taking away her baby. She still had hope. Reality hadn't settled into her bones. I knew her baby was dead, but she didn't.

Something told me to give back her calf. She wanted him, and maybe I didn't know what was best for her after all. Maybe she did. Maybe some instinct, something from an altogether different source did.

I drove back into the tree line and slid her dead calf onto clean grass. She went to him immediately and began to lick again. I left them there. A little dead calf and a mother whose hope and efforts would, after a

— 138 —

URSULA

time, crash up against reality. I went inside the house and stood under a scalding shower, sobbing. As the urine and shit and blood ran out of my hair and skin and down the drain, so too went my steely resolve. I was bone tired, and out in the field my lovely cow was curled up next to her dead calf, trying to warm his cold body.

She stayed there for the rest of the day and into the night. Sweet Ursula, grieving, if that's what a cow does. I think that's what a cow does. We take away their babies and tell ourselves that they moo and call them only because they want the mechanical relief of being milked. Or we say instinct is the reason they call for their calves. But they want their babies. They are maternal creatures, wholly themselves when they are with their offspring. On the morning after her calf died, Ursula stood up and went to the watering trough. Then she joined her herd in the pasture for breakfast. I removed the calf, but she returned to the spot, sniffing the grass, lying there to chew her cud.

Even years later, when I brought the cattle through that part of the pasture, Ursula would always immediately return to the spot where she had lain with her dead calf. She would stay there, smelling, looking for something that was no longer there.

––––––

It's years later from the day I spent in the tree line with Ursula and her calf. I'm sitting at a small table in a gaudily decorated room. There are sateen curtains and a plush apricot-coloured carpet beneath my feet. There's cheap wood stained in dark tones to give the illusion of oak or walnut. The man across from me is smiling; he's trying to be kind. He's handling us delicately, with kid gloves. I don't like him. He's saccharine and rehearsed and I don't know what the hell I'm doing wasting my time with this person in this place. I want to leave.

But I'm cemented in place. I can't leave. I'm held by some invisible binding to Troy next to me. He's not leaving. He's as confused by this place as I am, but he's not leaving. He's talking to the syrup man, reviewing important-looking papers and putting his initials on them before handing me the pen to do the same. There are monetary figures written down. We're paying a bill, then. There are directions for where and how the body is to be cremated. We're paying a bill for a dead

— 139 —

RADIANCE OF THE ORDINARY

body, then. Finally, there's the statement of death, that vilely named document, and on it, in the space that was formerly just a dotted line, someone has written my daughter's name: Mila Kate.

"Mila, beloved by all." That's what the book of baby names said. The book of baby names was right.

I understand then, wafting back into this house of the dead, what we're doing here. Yes, that's right, our Mila, the youngest of three wondrous daughters, is dead. I look around the room critiquing the faux everything. Faux marble. Faux gilding. Faux man pushing a tissue box toward me. I don't want his fucking tissues.

"Now for the delicate matters," he begins. He knows this is hard, he says. He understands how heartbroken we must be, but there are logistics in this logistical world that must be logisticized. Logistics wait for no one.

"Will there be a viewing?" he asks.

"No!" I snap at the very moment Troy answers "Yes." I look at him astonished. Does he know what he's saying? Does he not realize what this means?

"A private viewing, just for family."

"Troy, no!" I say in absolute horror. "We can't. I can't. I don't want to see her covered in makeup not looking like herself. I can't."

Troy stares into me, his abject misery collapsing his strong shoulders, his heartbreak hollowing out his powerful chest. He's weakened and uncertain. I have never seen him like this. He looks me in the eyes and with the resolve he has left says, "Tara, we need to see her." I don't know where this is coming from, but I understand it immediately to be true. We must see her. We need to.

We direct the saccharine man not to do anything to her body. No formaldehyde. She lived on this Earth with a strong, clean body, and we will not fill it with poisons in the end. No makeup. No pretend. She is dead, and we will see her body dead, not in some strange quasi-lifelike state to give the illusion of sleep, powdered pink cheeks that look flush with blood.

I leave that place scared. Scared of what more is being asked of me. Is it not enough that my daughter has died? Now I am asked to look upon her dead body? At what point have I reached the threshold of

— 140 —

URSULA

misery? When can I collapse into nothingness, having done what was demanded of me?

The family viewing is the next day. We arrange for a plain pine casket. I drive to the funeral home, the house of the dead, with a vintage ivory-coloured silk dress I had bought years earlier. A pretty dress with pin pleats along the front. I thought I might wear it to a summer picnic one day. Instead, it's on the back seat of my car as I drive to a strange building to give it to a strange man to dress my daughter so we can see her before they feed it all into a roaring fire.

It was a beautiful spring day and that's what I was doing. Driving with that dress.

That warm evening, we go back to the funeral home. Troy and I walk through the double doors at the head of the room. I fix my eyes on that gaudy carpet, unable to lift them. We stop and stand there together silently, our bones vibrating off each other's. I lift my eyes to see what he sees. We cling to each other with a desperate tightness. He whispers, "Oh, Mila."

At the far end of the room, that plain pine casket with our Mila inside. We are drawn to her like magnets. Maybe they have it wrong after all. Maybe there is still something to be done to right this impossible wrong. We go to her, to her body, and we see. Her beautiful face with those pouty lips, her glorious hair, thick as a horse's mane. Her little hands with the crooked baby finger that never quite found its way back straight after she broke it playing rugby the year before. It is her. It really is her. I can feel her skin and weave my fingers through her hair. It is her. Here we stay, for hours in this quiet little room, with the sobs of the people who love her most. Grief, thick and suffocating, permeates us all. It is her.

It was her and it wasn't her. Her beautiful body, her lovely face. She was not sleeping, nor was she gone. She was there with us. Her essence, her life force moving around us, sticking tight. I knew my child, could sense her feelings and emotions without her saying a word, just as most mothers can. She was there with us, there with her sisters. She was sticking close, not yet ready to leave. We prayed together. We prayed and saturated her with our love. We whispered our forgiveness and asked for hers. We chanted our adoration. We wrapped her in our most enduring gift, all we had, every last molecule of us transmuted into love.

And then we had to leave. We had to say goodbye because our time was up, and the artificial rules of the artificial place demanded logistics be honoured. In years past, her body would have stayed in our living room as friends and family came to say goodbye. That's what happened when my beloved friend Richard died. When Troy and I arrived a day after he died, Richard's wife led us to his bed, where his body lay. I resisted going into the room at first. "I just can't see him that way," I said. But when I peeked around the corner, it was that same sensation, a drawing in. There he was, my best friend. How could I not go to him?

There beside Richard's body, I had the sense he was there, too, beyond the physical body. That body was no longer living, but still, the essence of him moved through and around us. He was there in a bigger, more expansive way, in among us rather than encapsulated in the body that remained. It took time to reach this understanding. Words alone cannot fully bring us there. It's a truth we must open to so it may permeate us. An invisible, mystical whisper that makes its way into our hearts when they're cracked open and defenceless.

I don't know where Troy's conviction came from in knowing, in understanding, we needed to be there with our daughter's body. But he knew, and he was certain for me in a time when I couldn't be. I will forever be grateful to him and to what could only be the touch of God, fortifying him with resolve at a time when he was a hollowed-out shell. When it would have been easier to heed the voice whispering, "No! Don't!" he walked forward and led us into what was, ultimately, a profound and necessary part of our grieving.

———

I understand why Ursula goes to that same spot in the pasture every spring. Why she sniffs the earth and searches the tree line. Maybe, just maybe . . . Hope remains. Something she will never know again has left his scent, his imprint, on those pasture grasses. She can sense something, some feeling of closeness or a memory or an echo in her bones, imperceivable to the rest. It's the same reason I replay those last moments with our daughter, when, one last time, I wove her hair through my fingers. It's why I noticed each golden strand, every hair in her eyebrows, the perfection of her beautiful lips. I would remember because I had to. My chances to notice such things had ended.

The Death
of Our Daughter

What do you want me to say?
What can I say to such a thing.

There was a little girl once. She was round and sweet with cheeks so soft I had to brush my lips and my nose against them all day long. Little hands and golden-brown hair with thick waves washing through it. She was my last child. The baby of three daughters. I always liked that number: three. Three daughters. Each as different as the patterns in the bark of the three birch trees that grow from the same clump in our back woods. They come from the same place and yet their branches reach and spread with their own ideas and motivations. Their scars uniquely theirs.

Every mother worth her salt will tell you tales about her wonderful child if you ask. We were proud of our daughter, the only one left at home as her sisters grew up and moved out. She started playing hockey when she was only three years old. I remember buying her hockey gear that year, marvelling at the smallness of those little black skates and laughing at the shoulder pads made for a body that barely had shoulders.

She loved hockey and we loved watching her play. She grew into a beautiful skater — the part I loved watching most of all. Oh, the hours we sat on those concrete bleachers in the frigid hockey rink, teeth chattering while we cheered her on. In the moments when play stopped and the players stood around a circle for a face-off, I watched as her teenage body reverted to that little girl form: chin tucked, hips

THE DEATH OF OUR DAUGHTER

forward. She never stood like that anymore except there, on the ice, in the moment before the puck drop. I watched for it every time. It was all that was left of her little round self.

From a young age, Mila had a sensitivity to things beyond most people's awareness. Everywhere she went on our farm, a herd of barn cats would follow. Our most high Shepherdess of Barn Cats. Once, one of her cats went missing. On the fifth day of his absence, Mila woke up long before the sun and left us a note on the breakfast table: "I think I know where Toque is. I'm going to find him. Don't worry, I ate breakfast." She was ten years old.

Sure enough, she came home as we were eating our breakfast and told her tale. She had awoken that morning with the realization that Toque was in the deep, dark cedar woods and couldn't get home. She didn't know why. Maybe he was lost. Maybe there were coyotes or fishers hungrily awaiting him around a corner. Mila knew she needed to go into those woods, and she did, alone save her conviction. She found her cat. Of course she found her cat. Toque was at the very top of a cedar tree, meowing for salvation.

Things were like that with Mila. From the time she was just able to walk, standing in front of a wild rosebush watching bumblebees land before her nose with a focus much greater than a child that size should be able to muster, I knew there was a depth, a knowing that was somehow different. As she grew, I came to realize that this depth of knowing, of feeling, can be both a gift and a cross to bear.

Mila could not understand cruelty. It was simply beyond her comprehension. She couldn't chalk up such things to human nature because, to her, human nature was not cruel. When she started having tummy aches every morning before school, I understood. Her teacher had chastised her, and us, for exploring her fascination with rocks and geology. "Now is not the time for geology. That comes in grade three," the teacher said.

There were also problems in the classroom with a clique of little grade two girls — imagine! They wrote something cruel about Mila on a sticky note and put it on her back. Her recess playmates were limited. When her one friend decided she wanted to play with the cool girls, Mila was bereft. She wasn't welcome to join.

— 145 —

RADIANCE OF THE ORDINARY

We decided our instinct to homeschool was worth exploring. Mila was bright and curious. She was hungry for knowledge and always eager to learn new things. Homeschool was a perfect fit. She blossomed. We followed her lead and opened our worlds to wolves and frogs, bats and cats. We visited retired geologists in small towns and joined old ladies in their rug hooking meetups. Mila was always a hit with elderly people; they enjoyed her curiosity, good manners, and authentic interest. She could talk to anyone, but she refused to talk about herself. She was always more interested in the other. Always a skilled conversationalist, willing to listen, there for real interactions of depth and meaning.

Mila returned to school in grade eight. She had heard about a liberal arts–focused school and wanted to give it a try. I didn't want her to give it a try, but her enthusiasm and desire were powerful opponents to my wishes. The school required an audition as part of the admission process. The guitar players could play a song or two. The singers could sing a jaunty tune. Mila wrote up a little skit she agonized over for weeks. It was a one-woman play about her morning routine of milking a cow. Surely not many of the eighth graders would be starring in productions about milking a cow, right? Of course, unable to bring her cow, Anja, onto the school stage, Mila had to mime the milking part — the part she was mortified by. "They're going to think I'm weird squeezing an air udder," she groaned. She tried to make that part as quick as possible before she stood up from her pretend stool and leaned on pretend Anja and delighted her audience with a wonderful tale of what it meant to be trusted by a cow. She was accepted to the school. Of course she was. She was brilliant, and everyone knows brilliance when it flashes before their eyes.

She spent her summers training to be a nature guide. Kayak and canoe expeditions. Mountain climbing and hiking. She was steady and dependable, as responsible as they come. She did what she said she would do, and she excelled. She was a powerful rugby player, strong and fast. When no-contact hockey with girls saw her spending too much time in the penalty box, she switched to playing hockey with boys. I remember watching her on the ice with those teenage "boys"

— 146 —

THE DEATH OF OUR DAUGHTER

(more men than boys judging by size alone), amazed at how well she held her own.

During an especially tough game against a team known for their dirty play, Mila got into a shoving match trying to guard the net. She was up against a boy twice her size, but it didn't matter. She dug in her skates and returned his shoves and tricks with her own. An elderly man sitting in front of me turned around and, with a sparkle in his eye, asked, "That your daughter there?"

"Yes, that's my girl."

"She a farm girl?"

"Yes! How do you know?"

"Oh, you can always tell a farm girl!"

She was so proud when I told her that on the car ride home. She threw her head back and laughed that delighted laugh. "What? He said that? Tell me again!" Grit. She had grit. Grit wrapped around the softest heart I knew.

I loved how that man saw the grit in her, because she was such a hard worker. She would come home from school and, seeing her beloved papa outside working on a project, quickly change her clothes, pick up a hammer, and join him. Whenever she found someone working, she would offer a hand. That's who she was. Others over self.

There were things she saw, things she could touch, that were out of reach for most of us. Some cosmic stream of truth coursed through her veins. I never quite knew it fully. I don't think I was supposed to. Knowing it was there, that alone is what was for me to know. I wonder if she knew what it was. Maybe it came as a hunger or an ache. Maybe she came into this world with instincts about things the rest of us struggle mightily to decipher. In her diaries — seven of them, spanning from when she was eight years old to the day of her death — her perceptions and observations are beyond her years.

I know this because when she died, she left us those diaries. All of them. Including the last one. The one covered in red velvet that I gave her the Christmas before. The one that held the story of her last days on Earth. She gave it all to us — the truth, raw and unabridged, that she couldn't say in life. That diary, too, was shrouded in mystery.

— 147 —

RADIANCE OF THE ORDINARY

Tucked into the back fold of her passenger-side car seat. The police who recovered her car and looked it over didn't find it. It was only after her sisters had driven the car home from the police station, down the dusty gravel roads to our farm, that we discovered it. Tyra went into the car searching for something that called to her, a message from the ether. She came out with the diary. And in that diary, Mila's undoing, captured in her own words.

How did Mila, our youngest born, built of grit and a tender, loving heart, die by suicide? Our honour roll student. Our athlete and farm girl. Our talented artist and writer. Our giving, funny girl, still so much a girl. At eighteen, she would still delight in a turtle crossing her path — in sitting in the screened-in porch on a hot summer day, rocking in her hammock and playing her ukulele with a cat on her lap. For hours she would practice. Hours and hours and hours . . .

How can such a thing be? How could such a beautiful soul die because she chose to die? She was so much to so many people. She was the bounty of life encapsulated in one young girl. So large in every conceivable way. There was no hole in her absence. There was an unending pit that swallowed all light, all sound, our very footing. It's impossible to this day, yet it is more real than anything in my life.

The policemen with hats under their arms told us.

"Are you the parents of Mila?"

And down we fell. Tumbling over and under. Our bodies battered against rock. A beast snatching our ankles and pulling us down, down, down into the black. Thick and cold and black and endless.

———

I stopped writing here.

I was in the kitchen when Ella found me. "How's the writing going?" she asked.

"Frustrating," I said. "Too much time writing about the details of Mila's death and never getting it quite right. Too much background without getting to where I am now, to what I've come to know as truth."

"Well then skip that part. Don't put in the details. Just write about where you are."

— 148 —

THE DEATH OF OUR DAUGHTER

But that's wrong, too.

How do I bring you with me to this terra incognita without showing you the way? I'm not sure. Maybe it's not a map. Maybe it's a meandering story in which one sentence, one idea, finds its resonate frequency in another person.

Why do I share this story at all?

Maybe I share it in a quest for redemption. Redemption for Mila. Redemption for me. Maybe it's because I understand that the shame, burrowed deep in my bones, is only excised through sunlight. I was fiercely proud of my daughter, of who she was. I was fiercely proud when her teachers told me they never knew anyone quite like her — a girl who asked them about their families and then remembered to ask again about their children's recital or their wife's trip. I was fiercely proud of what mattered to her. Of her writing talents, her way of seeing the world. Shame had no place in my love for her. How she died is not indicative of how she lived.

What, then, does it say?

The lunacy of the Covid-19 lockdowns enveloped us then. Mila's school was shut down. Her social life, too. She was seventeen, in her final year of high school. In her journal, she wrote of her frustration with her boyfriend and friends who, in the limited times they could get together, were always smoking pot. They would laugh and act ridiculous, and Mila would sit there, bored and annoyed. Eventually she tried it, too. That was in the last autumn of her life. She would be dead by the coming spring.

How it all unfolded remains surreal to us all. Mila was strong and vibrantly healthy from the get-go. Born ten-and-a-half pounds, my plump Christmas turkey. But she was always sensitive biochemically. Even the red dye in candy caused her to react — a lesson we learned at a friend's birthday party — and so she lived only eating the nourishing foods from our farm. Maybe that was how she became instantly addicted to that seemingly innocuous substance called "pot."

Whatever caused her addiction, it was hard and fast. Within a couple of weeks of writing in her diary, "I tried it! And I like it!" she was vaping potent pot almost every day. This is not the pot that old

— 149 —

RADIANCE OF THE ORDINARY

hippie Uncle Larry grows in his backyard. She and her friends were using black-market vaping pens sold openly here in Canada, even to minors, from our First Nations reservations, where pot shops can be found one after another down the main drags. In a few short months she went from trying marijuana to smoking it just to fall back to sleep.

Her diary, and her friends, told us the rest after she died. She started seeing and hearing things. "Marijuana-induced psychosis," it's called. I never even knew such a thing was possible. She stopped sleeping, which didn't help the damage being done to her brain. She decided to move out of our house, and in the few short weeks after, her alcohol and marijuana use exploded.

I last saw her on Mother's Day. She came home, and I worried about how much weight she had lost, how tired she seemed. We hugged a good long while, and I cried. Her eyes filled with tears at the sight of mine, and she asked what was wrong. "I just miss you," I said.

"Aww, I miss you, too. Wanna have a girls' day this week?"

I remember giving her a look — the kind you give when you don't believe what someone is saying. She was surprised. "No?" she asked.

"Yes," I said, but for whatever reason I didn't believe it was going to happen.

We told each other we loved each other, and she left. She promised Troy she would come home again soon and the two of them could go for a ride in the car she had just bought herself.

Once the police released her car to us, he and I made that trip together, but without her.

———

I had no need, no desire, to learn that the headstones of today are mostly carved with lasers. Little nozzles dancing over the surface of polished granite, etching shapes and letters from a selected catalogue of preprogrammed images. The roses grandma liked. Maybe the bowling pins to represent old Sam's favourite hobby.

I abhorred them all. I was offended by the idea of my daughter's name being etched into stone by a machine. What right did a lifeless piece of metal have to proclaim her dead, to set her name into stone? I didn't want

— 150 —

THE DEATH OF OUR DAUGHTER

to see that. I didn't want to look at it. It wasn't who she was. She was not a lifeless machine. She was talent and artistry and real. No, I wouldn't have it. I would find a stone carver, a person with hands and hand tools to form the words and the image we wanted to honour the life of our daughter.

Find one I did, and on our very first phone call we spoke for close to an hour. He found a way to gently ask how our daughter died, and he shared that his daughter had died by suicide, too. He and his wife came to the farm for our first meeting. We had worked on the design of the headstone, and now we walked and talked. We sat on the bench at the top of the granite ridge — the same place we had held our daughter's memorial. The place where a small, clandestine gathering of people converged to listen to a memorial I had somehow written, while a lone dragonfly flew around us.

It was other grieving mothers, the ones who knew the agony of where we were, who helped me in those early days. They understood. They stood as beacons of hope. In both the grief groups I attended and there, on that rocky ridge. These women didn't lie to me. They didn't offer false promises about the pain disappearing one happy day. They assured me that, eventually, the pain would soften. The jagged shards would dull. Always the hole, forever the ache, but there stood those women before me, nine years, ten years, eleven years later and still living. Some maybe just surviving. But my friend on the ridge, the stone carver's wife, she was living. Her marriage was strong, an undefinable, quiet bond between them. Like the forging of metal through hellfire. They were hope for us.

When I saw her recently, I asked, "Do you ever feel shame?"

"Oh, yes," she said. "I do."

It's shame that sticks like a thorn in my side. It pokes me and calls for my attention. Who calls for my shame? For what do I feel shame? Is my child's life a failure because of how it ended? Am I a failure for her final decisions? And how did she even die? We have all manner of words to use when someone kills another person. Perhaps it was manslaughter or murder in the first, second, or third degree. When someone dies by suicide, there are no categories. They killed themselves. But who, I wonder, is the "they" we're referring to? Who is the "she" I speak of when I say, "She took her own life"?

— 151 —

Is it the she that was *her*? That tender consciousness, that kind being who lived with such grounded common sense and an intolerance for cruelty? Is it she who wrote beautiful stories of waking early in the morning to milk her cow in the heavy silence of a slumbering barn? The girl who could connect to the ethereal beauty of Creation through the paws of a barn kitten? Is that the "she" who took her own life? Or is it the possessed brain, damaged by poison, that hijacked the girl lost and scrambling in the woods?

How do I share that with the people who ask, "How did your daughter die?"

I think, buried in these feelings, lives grace. So I allow them to wash over me without need to erase or run from them. They are there in the silence. They are here now, as I write these words, sitting on my porch with the rain falling all around. Grace.

———

"Are you the parents of Mila?"

I don't know what else. I was on the floor then. Crumpled and wailing. All I remember is Troy with his arms wrapped around me asking the police to leave us.

What happened from there is important to share. Not because I want to let anyone into that open wound, but because it's not just my wound. Because we all have wounds, open and bleeding. Because, maybe, if we can find the words and the ways to be there together in the pain, however it may come, then we can better be in this life together.

That's what happened to us. We sat with our other two daughters that afternoon, all of us weeping, wrapped around each other, asking why and how, dazed by bewilderment, but also vowing that Mila's death would never harden our hearts to ourselves, to each other, to this life.

Early the next morning, Troy and I sat on our darkened porch, sipping coffee and listening to the haunting sound of the loon on the nearby lake. Loons were a consistent presence then. The most lonesome cry for a most lonesome heart — our escort into anguish. If my broken heart could call to the heavens, it would make that sound, echoing off endless, motionless waters. My heart couldn't but the loon did it for me.

THE DEATH OF OUR DAUGHTER

That morning, Troy and I made a promise to each other: We wouldn't look away. We wouldn't drink wine to blunt our pain. We wouldn't fill our lives with busyness and distraction. We would remain in those dark, icy, tumultuous waters together, for as long as we needed to. We would meet grief and go wherever it brought us. It was our sacred vow, proclaimed through panic in an endless forest. We were lost. We couldn't find our way out, but something deep, deep inside told us we had to be here. We had to be lost. We had to struggle. There was no rescue, only surrender.

In those early days, there was a pain in me so exquisitely and endlessly raw that I was panicked by it. I knew nothing of what to do or how to live with such pain. I found myself on the floor of my bedroom, imagining how I could use my fingers to peel away the floorboards beneath my body. If only I could shave the wood with my fingernails, shard by shard, until I made a hole big enough for me to slither into. And then, like a snake, I would melt into it. I would live there, in the dark, between the world of my bedroom and the kitchen below. It was a constant thought, my deepest wish. To live in a dark place of in-between.

I couldn't escape the pain. It hung on to me, pushed down on me. It pulled at my hair and chewed on my stomach. It fell on me, tripped me, curled up next to me in my bed. It was exhausting and caused me to wretch at the sight of food. It was my most loyal of companions. I looked at Troy, watched as his strong body drooped in abject misery, and knew that pain, even when you think it cannot hurt you more, always can.

We moved like that through the days, shuffling with pain's arms around our necks, dragging its feet behind us. There was nothing to do, nothing real to say. Only unanswered questions. Only "Why?" Pleas into nothingness.

Mila came to me then, into my world. She came to me not in a dream but in reality. She came silently but confidently. There were no words, but she told me things, relayed messages without needing words. It was an effort for her to come, I could see that. Or maybe I could just feel it. It was me and her alone in a space. Dark, but not scary. It was peaceful and still.

— 153 —

RADIANCE OF THE ORDINARY

She walked up to me, our eyes locked. She hugged me. We held each other. I felt her body as I knew it. I buried my face in her hair, "as thick as a horse's mane," I used to tell her when I played with it. I held her and she held me. She needed me to know, she came to tell me, she was okay. She was at peace. She was held in love. Love moved through her and into me and then back from me into her. A great, swirling, boundless love. There was no division between us, and we needed no words. That was to be our real last hug. She wouldn't be able to return for another. It was enough.

She left then, walked away. Walked from me and into somewhere else. I don't know how long we hugged. Maybe it was an eternity. Maybe it was mere minutes. But that hug was so saturated with her love, her essence, that even today I can sit quietly with my eyes closed and allow it to flood over me again. She gave me that. Of course she did. That's who she was and who she remains.

From then on, the most wondrous things began to happen. There was a day, early on, when Troy and I were outside in the early morning. The sun was shining, but that's all I really remember. We were moving about the farm, thick with misery, numb and dumb. We went from one task to another. We let the ducks onto the pond with barely any notice of them. We brought the dairy cows into the orchard like programmed machines, shutting the gate behind us. I didn't even care to stop and listen to one of my favourite sounds in all the world — a cow tearing grass from the soil beneath her hooves. It didn't matter. I couldn't care less.

We bumped into each other as I headed down our gravel pathway to the house. Troy was walking in the opposite direction. We looked into each other's faces, something we've always done, performing that instinctual, instantaneous assessment developed through time together. We wrapped our arms around each other, and I shoved my face into his neck. We stood like that, crying, for a good long while. Just crying. Just still. Just us. Then I heard a soft noise, a coming and going, fading and growing. I opened my eyes and saw a few dragonflies flitting around us, their iridescent wings shimmering in the sunlight. And then I saw another and another. We pulled our heads away from each other and looked around. More and more dragonflies came. Soon

THE DEATH OF OUR DAUGHTER

there were hundreds of dragonflies, all of them encircling our little spot on the gravel path. They were moving around us like a tornado, maybe thousands of them now, the sounds of their wings drowning out our voices. We were the eye of their storm! We stood in astonishment.

"What's happening?" I had to raise my voice to be heard.

We started to laugh and cry in disbelief, in *joy*. The dragonflies continued, flying around and around us, creating a vortex filled with a love so full and wondrous all we could do was laugh and gasp and cry some more. It was an elation beyond anything I had ever felt. It was Divinity itself. There, from within our pool of anguish, came the opening. Those dragonflies held us in the mysterious, sacred unknown. There was intelligence and a brilliance, a great offering of love. It's humbling to be touched by such magnificence.

On another day, Troy and I rode our ATV down the country roads and along a lake. We did that sometimes, a way to blow things out of our minds through our streaming hair. We came upon a small old cemetery on the corner of a farm. For whatever reason, Troy pulled over and said, "I want to go look." We walked through the cemetery, mostly silent save the sound of my voice reading aloud the names on the headstones. I think that, after I die, it might be nice to hear my name from the lips of a human on Earth every now and then, so I do that now. After a few minutes of walking and reading names, I heard a faint meow coming from the forest behind us. I stopped and listened. I must have been hearing things. The forest was surrounded by a lake; no kitty would be roaming here. But there it was again, a sad, drawn-out, unmistakable meow.

I called, "Kitty, *ts ts ts!*" Another meow.

A week earlier, Theo, one of Mila's beloved barn cats had gone missing. Her cats were so important to her. She cared for them and adored them. I used to tease her that she clenched her jaw every time she petted them — a clenched jaw was better than squeezing them to death. She hated that she did it, but she couldn't help it.

There was no way this could be Theo. We thought he had surely fallen victim to a fisher or a coyote, or that he had been picked up by a cottager who thought him too adorable to release. There was simply

— 155 —

no possibility of that lost cat showing up here, at this precise moment, in a graveyard so far from home.

Then Theo emerged from the forest, meowing as he trotted briskly toward me. I picked him up in astonishment, and he purred and kneaded me wildly. How we came to be in that cemetery at that moment is beyond me. I leave it beyond me. Mila had taken care of it.

There were so many stories like this, still so many. A hug between my little sister and I, our soft underbellies pressed against each other. Crying from the ache of the Mila-shaped hole in our hearts when we both became aware of someone else. A third person wrapped around and between us. "Did you feel that?" she asked later, as we peeled ourselves away from each other. "Yes, I felt it." Was it Mila? Was it God? No matter. They are both of the ever-streaming love that moves around and within us.

There were other things, too. A large "M" written in elegant script on my dining room table, by the carbon of a burnt wick from my bees-wax candles. Pileated woodpeckers following me through the forest. Huge flocks of chittering, chattering goldfinches moving around me like my own personal cloud. They were never on our farm before she died, but that summer they came in droves, and they return to this day.

One day, Troy and I met for lunch in the house after a long morning of farm chores. We ate quietly and sat at the table afterward, our heads in our hands. Two souls sitting at a table sobbing on a beautiful summer day. Suddenly, a small noise came from a corner of the room. At first, I thought it was a mouse. But it happened again, and the sound came from closer than behind a wall or in a closet. Again, another noise. I looked at our woodstove, decommissioned during those hot summer months, and inside I saw a swirling cloud of dusty ash. Something was in there. I sat on the floor in front of the fireplace and looked through the glass. As the cloud settled, a perfect little bluebird appeared, filthy and confused, in the centre of the woodstove.

Years earlier, my dear friend Richard had told me bluebirds are good luck. I never saw bluebirds where we lived, regardless of how mightily I searched for them. But I saw blue jays. So, I told Richard that blue jays would have to be my good luck. When he died, I couldn't go anywhere without finding blue jay feathers on my path. I would laugh every

THE DEATH OF OUR DAUGHTER

time, laugh and cry, and tell Richard how much I missed him and loved him. But this wasn't a blue jay in my woodstove; this was a bluebird, perfectly round with an ochre tummy, staring back at me.

It took a gallon glass jar and some creative finagling to get that little bird out of the woodstove and back into the wild. When we opened the lid of the jar outside, the bird burst straight out, flying directly to a tall tree in our pasture. Before it even reached the tree, another bluebird came from an adjacent tree. The two met at precisely the same time on the same branch. United.

Troy and I turned to each other and hugged. That little bird, a sacred being of Creation, carried a message on its wings. And we never would have been there for it if we had been distracting ourselves from our pain. For as much as we wanted to run from our anguish, we came to understand, more deeply every day, that it would only bring us further from the gifts in the rubble. We needed those tender little moments. We needed the balm of the Divine. It was the only thing that could touch the ferocity of the agony.

I'd like to stay there, in the memory of those tender moments, writing these stories to leave in the realm of the unknowable and mysterious. There were many. And in each one, such gifts. We began looking for them. We began finding moments of solace in the living expressions of life eternal. The material world became unsatisfactory with its linear offerings and sharp corners. There was too much left unsaid, too much glossing over where substance was needed. God moves through life, and that is where we found Mila, by continuing to participate in life.

I knew death wasn't the end. I knew that with more certainty than I understood most things, but I didn't know how to have a living relationship with someone I couldn't see or feel or hear. But I did have our final visit. I had that last physical hug. There were clues there, a way of communicating by evoking the energy or space between and within two people. Words can't be used simply because words belong here, to this realm of the Earthly creatures.

I am closest to my daughter when we're sitting cross-legged on the floor, facing each other, holding hands and looking into each other's eyes. There is energy and light and a love so great moving around us that, even now, it makes me catch my breath. It is real, living in joy and pain. Both at once, one never taking the place of the other.

———

In the last pages of her diary, the letter she left for us. A letter written moments before her life here ended. To each of us she wrote of a memory we shared, our own private ones, just each of us and her. She wrote of moonlit sleeps in the desert and thunderous lightning storms watched from the safety of our porch with a loyal dog at our side. She wrote of her love for us and of her seeming brokenness. She wrote of the little brown bunny hopping in front of her as she wrote. She was in there, our tender and beautiful soul. She was still there, seeing beauty, allowing it to touch her, even in her darkest moment. She was still there, thinking of us, giving to us that which was so precious to her and making sure for us to know.

As a mother, all I want is to find her in that moment. My fantasies for the first year or two after her death were of me rescuing her in myriad ways. Or of us given a second chance. So many people "attempt suicide." There are clues or warnings. That wouldn't be Mila. If she was going to do it, she would do it. But why couldn't we have received a call from the hospital, "Your daughter has attempted suicide"? Then we could have had our chance. Scooped her up and gone to the ends of the Earth for help. We would stop at nothing. That's who we are! We, like her, born with bones built of determination.

Maybe that's why we didn't get a second chance. There are things we will never know. Not here anyway. Not now. We have to live with not knowing, live with acceptance and surrender. That doesn't mean there aren't moments when pain overwhelms me even still. I know those moments will never go away entirely. Sometimes I think of my Bapka, my Slovak grandmother, who even in her nineties would weep when I asked about her children, Frantiska and Antony, who died when they were young.

"Oh, my Frantiska," she would say, holding her cupped hands up in the air as if she were cradling a little round face.

— 158 —

THE DEATH OF OUR DAUGHTER

A mother's hands never forget the shape of their child. I can still feel the weight of Mila, my baby even at eighteen years old, hugging me. And I know she can feel it, too.

———

I inherited my Bapka's handwritten cookbooks when she died a few years ago. I was recently reading through them when a receipt for "Green Acres Cemetery" floated out from between the pages. It was an installment receipt for five dollars. My grandmother had been prepaying her burial plot. That's how things were done back then. Headstones were purchased and inscribed with a blank space after the hyphen following their date of birth. The great mystery of when they would die on display. But die they most certainly would. That was assured. And they didn't want to leave their loved ones with the burden of paying for a burial and a headstone.

In a culture that pushes away the idea of death, it can be exquisitely uncomfortable to face it with such blunt candor. Not many people buy their burial plots or their headstones in advance anymore, I'm told. If they do, it's usually because someone else has gone before them and they want to be buried nearby.

The little country cemetery just a kilometre or two from our home is divided into an older section and a newer one. In the older section there are headstones from the 1800s, rows of crumbling stone carved by human hands. Some have more than one name on them, the ages ranging from a few months to a couple of years, and I think of the families with multiple children dead so young. There are crumbling crosses marking the graves of soldiers and sections where the bones of entire families have been buried.

That was where we wanted our daughter buried. Below the old, arching trees reaching over the rusty woven-wire fencing from a neighbouring farm's land surrounding it. In the newer section, shiny granite headstones are covered in plastic flowers and surrounded by solar garden lights. We wanted her in the quiet of the ruin and the real. And that's where we'll be buried, too, right next to her. Our headstone carved in the same font as her name, by the hands of the same talented

RADIANCE OF THE ORDINARY

stone carver. The stone of our graves pulled from the same earth as hers. One day, they will lay my body in a plain pine box and bury me in the earth. Another stone carver will come and kneel at my headstone to chip in those four digits after the hyphen. I wonder if I'll see him do it or if I will be a tad preoccupied with other things. I don't know.

Every Sunday we go to the cemetery to sit on the earth and be with our daughter. It's not where she is, and it's not the only place we find her, but it's a ritual, and rituals bring peace and comfort. Sometimes we bring beautiful pieces of music to play for all the departed souls buried there. Sometimes we pray. Sometimes we talk to her. We light a candle in the winter and leave it burning in a lantern, nestled in the snow around her stone. In the summer I roam the farm, picking wildflowers and others I've planted, and we bring her lush bouquets. Soon, when we go, I will see my name and my husband's name on the stone beside hers. A reminder, an awareness, upfront and consistent. Life is fleeting. Love as mightily as you can.

Our headstone will stand now, during our lives, solid in its promise. For now, life. But soon enough, death. We keep that promise close, and in it, our open, vulnerable love for this gorgeous life and the humans we get to share it with.

––––

There was a time when I held a contract with God. He could have it all; do as he deemed necessary, put me through the trials and tribulations he thought fit. But there were things I was not capable of. Things I could never live through. God knew that, and so God, loving as He is, would never give me what I could not survive. God would never take one of my children from me.

Then the knock at our door in the middle of a spring night. Policemen.

"Are you the parents of Mila?"

All of life stops. The birds fall silent. Colours morph into greys. The pain is so wretched, so vile and endless, I contemplate peeling up the floorboards in my closet just to squeeze my lifeless body into the pocket of space between them – neither upstairs nor down. Neither

THE DEATH OF OUR DAUGHTER

here nor there. Oblivion. Some darkened netherworld of nowhere allowing the rot to eat me away, piece by piece.

There is nothing else we need, not a thing in the world that matters beyond willing our child back to life. That's it. Only that one thing. Every last bit of life energy poured into the reversal of a serious wrong, a most impossible mistake. We sob and shake and collapse. We vomit with heartbreak and curl ourselves into tight balls, protecting our gushing guts and bleeding hearts from the predators. And then, in brief spurts, a realization: "Oh wait, it was a dream! This isn't real!" And euphoria rides in on a gallant, prancing steed, decorated in ribbons of shimmering golds and reds. A celebration! It lasts for less than a blink of an eye before grief thunders in, all-powerful, all-consuming, and shouts in our faces, "There is no glossy steed coming – ever!"

Never, ever, ever, ever, ever, ever . . .

Ever, never, never, never . . .

Months before she died, Mila brought me to the sofa and played me a video. "It's so sad," she said. She had watched it before but still she looked at me with tears running down her cheeks. It was a narrated video of Edgar Allan Poe's poem, "The Raven," and we watched as the raven called "nevermore" to Poe's heartbroken protagonist. When would he know again the touch of his beloved? "Nevermore," insisted the raven.

Our daughter is dead. Our daughter is dead. Look at it and see it. Don't look away. Look back and read those words again.

The raven swears it.

———

Someone said to us, "Why you? Why you?" And it shook me. Why *not* me?

To whom do tragedies happen? To me – I see it now. To me, of course; to me and me again and me again. I am nothing special. There is no contract. I had it wrong all along.

Carved into Mila's headstone, below the date of her death, are the words, "loved evermore." The ravens come, but somewhere in the forest, somewhere in that unmarked, lonely place, their taunting call

RADIANCE OF THE ORDINARY

morphs. "Nevermore" is a lie. It's a torturous falsity and I see that through the clarity of love's endurance. It's "evermore" that our ravens sing. "Evermore" falls from their wings and reaches with them to the heavens. Evermore. Forever and ever, untouchable, eternal love.

Evermore my girl. Evermore until I hold you again.

Leo's Lookout

Spring is a temptress, impossible to resist. She flies into us in sweet warming winds, laughing as she tickles the trees and makes them flush with buds. She dances across the skin of the Earth, her toes on the sleeping underworld, rousing the yawning, slumbering life. When she comes, she brings singing birds and legions of frogs. She shakes squirrels and bears from their warm dens. She jostles languishing bees and dormant roots. She touches the feathers of migrating birds so they cannot resist the itch any longer; they must, for some unknown reason, fly to the lands from which they were born.

Every spring, long before the temperatures prompt me, I open our bedroom windows so the calls of spring peepers, the small frogs with the big songs, can serenade me all night long. They are relentless in their calls. From dawn to dusk they sing the thawing ice into submission. Soon, the bullfrogs and the leopard frogs will join in. Then the geese, my beloved Canada geese, will come home.

On the day of the first flush of returning geese, I go to the tip-top of a huge granite outcropping in our forest. I'm told some iceberg in some ice age decided this was the place to leave a little mountain of stone. Creatures have made homes in its caves and beavers have built houses along its base, which juts out into a wetland below. It's a special place to me. On windy days, I can lie on a wooden bench Troy built on the top of that cliff and look up at the ravens that come here to play in the wind currents swirling up from the water below and crashing against the winds thrown up from the forest behind. They call to each other and soar for hours, barely flapping their wings at all.

— 163 —

RADIANCE OF THE ORDINARY

We call this place "Leo's Lookout." Well, Troy, knowing how much I love this spot, named it that, given that I am a Leo according to the constellation that governed my entrance into the world, and because he needed a name for the little restaurant he and my daughters built me up there one Mother's Day. That day, they cut out hearts from cream-coloured construction paper and wrote little messages on them, dozens and dozens of them. On each heart, a sentence describing something my daughters loved about me. They tied those hearts to branches in the forest around our farm — a trail of love to Leo's Lookout. I kept those hearts, each one. They say things like, "Mila loves how brave you are," and "Tyra loves how imaginative and creative and fun you are," and "Ella loves your loving ways." What a thing, to be seen with such generosity by the people you love most in the world.

When I got to the top of the ridge, I found little benches that Troy had built and hauled up there. Sitting on those benches were my daughters with a beautiful meal for us all. When Mila and Ella were young, they created a restaurant called "Miel" (French for "honey" and also, brilliantly, the first two letters of each of their names). They put great care into creating menus, complete with various appetizer, entree, drink, and dessert options. Troy and I would place our order early in the day, and then they spent the entire day clanging away in the kitchen, nattering with each other and causing general mayhem.

When it came time to eat, they put on their aprons and sat us down to a candlelit meal for two, with the most impeccable service to boot! They served their creations, truly delicious and impressive right from the beginning, course by course, ensuring our table was always clean and their customers happy. They sported faux English accents (because who is not more civilized with an English accent?) and paid great attention to detail. To this day, Miel is the most wonderful restaurant we have ever eaten at.

So, when I found myself on the ridge with handfuls of hearts, it was not to have a picnic of sandwiches, but a feast worthy of a queen. We sat there together, on that cool Mother's Day, devouring homemade empanadas and stuffed mushrooms and steamy cups of chai made from the milk of our sweet cow, Bea. They had even prepared my favourite of all, a Queen Elizabeth cake, made just how I like it, sweetened with dates and finished

LEO'S LOOKOUT

with a crackly butter topping. I remember sitting on a bench, looking at the "Leo's Lookout" sign Troy had made out of old barnyard wood and a rusty chain he used to spell out the words in cursive — rusty-chain cursive. Looking at my daughters — how big they seemed to me then, more young women than children — reminded me of how soon such moments would be gone. They would be moving on with their lives, into the great unknown. Our job of parenting little sprouts, over.

What I didn't know, never could have known, is that only a year later, we would be walking to that granite ridge with a procession of family and friends behind us. In Troy's hands would be a fine wooden box. A wooden box he had spent the last few days making with a dear friend of his. Inside the oak box he had inlaid ash, a wood said to contain the energetic properties of strength. In Norse mythology, the ash tree is known as the "Tree of the World," connecting the physical world to the spiritual. Inside that box were the ashes of the body of our youngest child. Our Mila, once powerful and strong. "This one has bones like lead," exclaimed anyone who dared pick her up as a little one, now light as dust in our arms.

We went to the ridge together. I walked in silence beside Troy, hanging on to him for dear life. The tree branches a blur. I couldn't tell you if a bird sang that day. I wouldn't know if there were frogs. We walked to our destination and that's all I knew of what I was doing. Behind us, our two older daughters, linked tightly together. Behind them, smudges of people, but not too many. Our gathering was illegal because of Covid restrictions. Our funeral, our youngest daughter's funeral, held one week earlier was only open to ten of us. We had to sit apart in the wide-open church with masks on. That can never be forgiven.

There, at the top, I read the eulogy I had written for my dead child. I don't remember writing it. I don't know how I knew what to say. So many pieces were still missing and so much of my mind unstable. And yet, I wrote it and I read it. All the while, I looked around and wondered why these people were here, on our secret ridge, watching me as a lone dragonfly circled overhead, landing in front of us for a moment before beginning its circling again.

Places can hold us when people can't. I can return to that ridge and sit with the ghosts of my daughters serving up their beautiful meal

— 165 —

made just for me. And then, on this Mother's Day, I can return in anguish, remembering that last day I saw my baby — a Mother's Day, too. She had recently moved out and came home to make me a meal with her sisters. Troy and I had gone canoeing. I remember leaning over the edge of the canoe, looking to the bottom of the little lake to see what the small, plump fish were doing. My fingers skimmed over the water's surface as Troy paddled in the warm spring sun. The blue herons had returned, and we went from nest to nest, looking up to see if we might spot those dinosaur-like creatures glaring down at us. When we got home, we ate the wonderful food our daughters had made for us. The next morning, Mila gave me a hug, and we shared our last words. And then she was gone.

Those ghosts live on the ridge, too. I bring them all with me on the day those first geese proclaim their return home. "We're here! We're here!" Life returns. They return, but not as they left. Their families will be different. Some will have been hunted; some will have died. For some, this will be their first year with their mate. For some, this will be their first year without their lifelong partner. Will they merely swim and eat, or will they be confused by their instincts and experiences? Will they try to claim the eggs of others as their own because they don't know what to do with themselves otherwise? Do the antics of geese pairing up with mates or the hatching of little round goslings bring them an ache so lonely they don't know what to do with it?

Or maybe that's just me.

Last autumn, Troy and I went for a walk in the forest. We traipsed through leaves of umbers and maroons, soft buttery yellows and deep chocolate browns, as high as our knees in some places. Evidence of industrious squirrels feasting on beech nuts and acorns lay all around us. We ended up on the ridge and, with nothing else to do, decided to stay awhile. I found a big stash of hedgehog mushrooms that we collected to add to our dinner that night. We walked around on top of that giant rock and spoke of our daughter, of the magic of that place. There's something mysterious there, attractive to animals of every ilk, but unknowable, too. The feeling of the ridge transcends the logical "glacier dropped it off" explanation. If someone told me it was a stone dropped from a dragon's mouth many eons ago, I would be more likely

LEO'S LOOKOUT

to believe them. But it's mystery that fills our days and our hearts now and mystery that we have become comfortable with.

Sitting up there on the ridge, we decided it was for the best to move up there for a time. Not forever, but certainly for a while. We'll bring our canvas tent and some timbers and see what we come up with. We'll walk back to the house to do farm chores and get food, but the ridge seems a place worth knowing more. And it seems a place capable of holding us and showing us, even in the smallest degree, what lies beyond the veil that blurs our eyes.

We're heading up to Leo's Lookout soon. We're bringing some beams Troy has milled from our trees. Maybe one day we'll build a little cabin. Maybe not. There are no ambitions beyond being there more.

The ridge remains. The ravens tell their children and their children tell their children that this is a place to come when the winds are high. They come to play. We come to heal.

Little Pig in a Hut

When I was a little girl, I fantasized about a miniature world I could tuck myself into. More than anything, I wanted to go to school and find a box around every desk in my classroom. It didn't even have to be a wooden box — a sturdy cardboard box, enough to enclose me, would be fine. There would be slits cut in the box and little flaps I could open with the pull of a string to answer my teacher's questions, but otherwise, it would just be me in there (let everyone else find their own box), tucked safely within those walls, unexposed.

I also fantasized about having miniature friends who would love me and whom I could keep in my pockets. When I took off my school clothes at the end of the day, I would pluck my friends from my pockets and gently place them on the headboard of my bed. They had been cooped up all day long, and they would stretch their little legs and play with their little dog and his tiny ball. I could tell them secrets, tell them when I was mad and sad. I could tell them about my mean grade one teacher, the one whose presence I prayed and prayed might be mitigated by my imaginary box.

I walked into that classroom every morning hoping my prayers had been answered overnight. Surely — okay, maybe — each desk would have a box around it. Of course, they never did. The onslaught of the surly teacher continued, and so, too, my prayers.

Years later, Mila came home from kindergarten with a drawing of a little brown pig with red spots. A large brown arch had been painted over the pig. The teacher had transcribed the talented artist's words on the bottom of the page: "I wish I was a little pig living in a hut." I

— 168 —

thought, "You, too, huh?" I hung that picture on our kitchen wall — the perfect encapsulation of my childhood heart. It made me wonder about what we pass down to our children. Beyond my brown eyes and my height, are there things like a lonesome heart and a burrowing instinct that echo through the blood we share?

As I grew older, whenever things got to be too much in my life, my adolescent self would fantasize about doing what I had to do — school, mostly — but from the safety of the small and secluded. It wasn't necessarily the box that drew me in anymore, but in times of angst, I would still bring little me forward and remember how much peace she found in her little people in their little world, lined up on her desk in her own little microcosm of life.

I suppose little has changed. I'm here, in this expansive world, but I'm still most comfortable with the small and quiet. Once, on a springtime visit to Virginia to see my daughter and her family, I was walking through a vast, rolling field with bees buzzing and strange birds making strange calls to my foreign ear. It was a beautiful day, and I was grateful to be in it, feet in the grass, head warming in the sun. I had my granddaughter in my arms. She's big enough to reach and point to what interests her but not big enough to know the names. What freedom in that. As adults, we confuse knowing the name of something with actually knowing it. She's under no such illusion. Everything is a wonder. Everything worthy of her investigation.

She pointed to the redbud tree and so we went. She wrapped her chubby little hand, dimples where knuckles will one day be, around the opening magenta flowers and ripped them toward her. She wanted to feel those flowers, smell them, put them in her mouth. Me, too! I brought us deeper into the tree, this secret redbud world for her and me. Nobody else anywhere. Tiny flowers falling from her hands.

Later, we were on our bellies on a grassy knoll by a pond. She ripped grass from the earth and opened her hand to examine the verdant green against her skin. She looked up at me, smiling with astonishment. *How did that stuff get there?* I noticed a plant growing among the grasses and clovers. It looked an awful lot like a green onion. I picked it and smelled it. It smelled an awful lot like an onion. I tasted it. It tasted like an onion! We don't have wild onions where I live, but there, in that

RADIANCE OF THE ORDINARY

tiny little world of grandma and babe on their tummies, a new friend appeared. A wild onion introduction.

We picked redbud flowers into a jar and filled our pockets with wild onions. I made a wild cordial with the redbuds and a friend's honey. The wild onions were added to that night's dinner. Everything from near and close, found because there was time to find it.

I am awed by vastness, but it's not an enduring call for me. Bring me to a field and I will sit on the ground and watch the earthworms around me. Plunk me in my garden and I'll spend an exorbitant amount of time "weeding" because I found the bees sleeping in the closed squash blossoms and wanted to see what happened when the flower opened to the sun and woke them up. Bring me to an endless ocean and I will drop my head to search the shoreline for the life I can touch and examine. I am more entranced with the designs in the tree bark than with the heights of the branches.

Give me a room full of people, and I will find the one who wants to turn over those treasures with me. I hunger for the intimate. I don't want to know everything. I don't need to fill myself with superficial generalities. Give me bits and crumbs and tiny spaces. Little worlds to explore and get to know. My one and only man. My handful of friends. The beautiful young women I am blessed to call daughters. The eyelashes of my cow. The shape and intoxicating smell of a milkweed flower.

Our culture tells us that glory comes to the big. Everything a calling to expansion. Take up space with our big houses and big pay cheques and big lives captured on screens. The whole thing a digital popularity contest wherein people are transformed into numbers, into "followers," and the more those numbers grow, the "bigger" we are. Our big accounts somehow make us into big people with big influence. We can touch millions of lives. Only, I wonder what that touch feels like. Can anyone say? Is it warm and sincere or is it a one-dimensional dopamine hit — a cheap simulacrum for what we truly hunger for?

Like I have found with so much of what's on offer in this culture, the closer I get to being in alignment with its tips and tricks, the more hollowed out I feel. The more the gnawing hunger for . . . What is it for? It's hard to tell when we're on the one-way track to "success." Sometimes we even confuse the hunger with being on the right track

LITTLE PIG IN A HUT

and just needing *more*! Push more! Love the grind! I have found myself there many times, pushing to accomplish what I needed to do, but my motivation was never dollars — it was always to bring myself into alignment with meaning in my life. Sometimes we can have both.

I realize now that I don't need a box around me to find what calls to my heart. I am already held, already endlessly loved in those small moments I can enter into anytime I like. Me and a barn cat on my lap, sitting under an old apple tree with all the time in the world. Walls made of love instead of cardboard. My little friends purring and buzzing and chirping instead of playing with pocket-size dogs. Close. Small. Tight. Held. Holding.

———

When I was around eleven years old, I remember having a conversation with an older woman about being a kid and being an adult. She assured me that my round face would indeed not be so round one day — that as I got older, I would have beautiful cheekbones and grow into my adult, womanly face. This was a big relief for young me, convinced as I was that I would hit my twenties with a taller body but the same face, same haircut even. Then she told me a secret about getting older: While people would see me as older — as Tara at twenty or Tara at forty or Tara at sixty — on the inside I would remain the same person I had always been. To young me, that was a stunning revelation.

I started to look at people, especially older people, differently. Up until then, I had seen my grandmothers as my grandmothers. They were somehow different because they were old women who were my parents' mothers. They loved me and I loved them, but our relationship was centred around me. As kids, there's a time when the whole world centres around us, or so we think, but as we grow up that illusion fades. It had never occurred to me that inside my old Bapka was a woman — the same woman who lived before she was ever a grandmother or a mother, who might still have some similarities with a girl like me. Somehow, I had always assumed that part of her was gone and forgotten.

I have lived through decades now. It's more than some people get, but it cannot be a mistake. I will have just as much time as I'm meant

— 171 —

to have. It's strange how we determine the tragedy of a death or the fullness of a life by how old someone is when they die. We come for different things, we contribute and hold meaning outside of measured time. I've always thought it a paltry gauge, this idea of years lived as a stand-in for life lived. Sometimes a life is short, but in that life there is profundity, and in that death lives change. We are called into depths impossible to reach with a guarded heart. I used to think that and now I know that. The death of our child continues to pull me to new places, helps me to touch and be touched by the mysteries unknowable to the girded spirit.

That's me in my fifties — a woman living with anguish reassembling into something still unknown. Every day, another step, and every day an unfolding of a path unfamiliar to me. I know so much more than I did as a young woman, and because of that I know that I know nothing at all. I only know that when I am right, living in a right heart, I am open and courageous. When the next portion of my path is illuminated by the Creator's love, I take my steps in faith that it will lead wherever it is I am meant to be. I believe in the rightness of our design and in our calling and I try to move in alignment with the larger forces of this world. That is me in my fifties. Humbled and clear.

In my twenties it wasn't that way. I try to put myself there, in that twenty-something-year-old mind of mine, but it's tough. Parts of who I am were more exaggerated, and other parts barely a whisper. I was on autopilot much of the time, determined and pragmatic. Things had to be done. Brick by brick, a foundation was being built, but I doubt I was even cognizant of that. I was raising babies, three of them by the time I was thirty-one. I was running and playing and trying to figure out how to feed and clothe a family on meagre funds. I was figuring out how to be a mother, what type of mother I wanted to be. It was a time of coming into my own. How much I really thought about that I don't know. I was doing. I was stubbornly figuring out what I really believed from the tangle of what I was told to believe. Mostly, the two were in opposition. But there was a path, offering itself into the unknown if I took a chance. And when I did, it showed me truths I had never anticipated, so I stayed on that path for a while, soaking up whatever came my way.

LITTLE PIG IN A HUT

I suppose getting pregnant at the age of twenty changed the direction of my life. I used to think I would end up in prison someday; it seemed a reasonable prospect for someone as wild and impulsive as I had been as a teenager. I was a whirlwind of destruction in my relationships, including the one with myself. I was a wounded soul, but I understood that pain as the manifestation of being a "fucked up" girl. It never occurred to me that maybe the things I had lived through had hurt me, that the people around me could do me wrong. They were adults, so they were right; ergo, I was the problem.

When I got "unexpectedly" pregnant, my whole world imploded. I always thought if I got pregnant, I would simply have an abortion. It was a reasonable solution offered by the culture around me. Besides, that's what the people I knew did. My best friend had multiple abortions. One time, when she got pregnant and didn't want to have an abortion, her mother bribed her with a puppy as a replacement for the child she wanted to keep. It was instilled in me through the movies, books, and sex ed classes we had. It was an easy solution.

Only, when I got pregnant, I knew instantly there was no way I could do it. I was in the army then. My pregnancy test came via an army doctor who, when I went to them for my terrible cramps, thought they were likely more than what I thought for certain was food poisoning. A positive pregnancy test delivered in a prefabricated metal hut with a grey army blanket slung between two metal lockers to create the illusion of a private room. My mind raced like a trapped wildcat. I needed out of there. If I could just get out of there, it wouldn't be true.

But the medical staff had different ideas. I was loaded into a field ambulance and sent two hours up the highway to the nearest town. Before I left, they made me drink two litres of water and told me for the ultrasound to work — they were worried about an ectopic pregnancy due to the severity of my cramps — I had to drink one more litre of water on the drive. That morning, I had just been me with some cramps, but there I was that afternoon, in the back of an army field ambulance, barreling down the highway with a bladder about to explode. (Though somewhere during the ride, absolutely unable to contain myself, I opened the back door of that ambulance enough to squat down and pee.)

— 173 —

RADIANCE OF THE ORDINARY

I soon found myself on a cold table in a tiny hospital with a doctor pointing to a little shape on a screen. There was a flashing white bit in the centre of it. That bit, he said, was its heart. Its heart. It. A baby. There was a baby in there. I was looking at its beating heart. There were two of us on that table. That baby and me.

When I returned to the base that evening, I went to the discount department store in the nearby town. My friend needed to buy some underwear. I bought a pair of baby booties.

And that was that. I stopped smoking, I stopped partying, I stopped drinking. I filled my plate with chicken and beef and milk and fruit at the mess hall. I was moved out of the field and sent back to my unit. I left the military. I left my friends. And that's how I entered into my twenties. Absolutely untethered and unknowing, but full of gumption and determination to take on things. Maybe that's what's needed at that time of your life? Maybe we're not supposed to be as contemplative, to have things all figured out? There was bravado, I had that. I would do things my way. It started with that baby — with people telling me I was too young, I shouldn't keep her. They told me to have an abortion or put her up for adoption. Not one person told me to keep my baby. I understand why now. They thought they knew what was best for me. But they were all wrong.

Every life has its pivot points, its befores and afters. The first one for me was the fire in our country house, followed by the move to the city and my parents' divorce. Then, as an adult, it was the birth of my first daughter. Into this world, through my body, came this nine-pound, black-haired baby. I didn't know my body was capable of such things. I remember feeling those contractions, sure I was about to die, only for them to recede like wild waves pulled back into the unseeable depths of the ocean, then rush forward again. I was in there, experiencing this transformation, witnessing something beyond myself — this superpower that illuminated the tether to the Divine. My body was bringing forward that little flickering heart. My baby. They said I wasn't ready, but here was my body powerfully telling me otherwise.

Into my arms they put that little jewel, glowing and round. She was here and I was here. Together, we were something altogether different

— 174 —

LITTLE PIG IN A HUT

than we had been only seconds earlier. I was instantly transformed, a mother lion defending, and dedicated to, my sweet, mewing little cub.

And so began the journey of my twenties. Having made that monumental decision, all of my nonconformist choices thereafter seemed easy. This little being, the greatest decision of my life, reminded me every day that I was right. It was so hard, those first many years, but it was right — there was no debate. In that, my first understanding of how what is right for me often comes with what is hard. And often, it's all the sweeter because of it.

My thirties brought in a crisis of meaning. All around me, suggestions and pushes to "find my purpose." What was my purpose? I had no idea. And what is a person without a purpose? I became almost obsessed with finding my purpose. There I was, raising three beautiful girls and supporting a wonderful man who was working so hard for our family, and I was concerned because I didn't know what my purpose was. As if there was one thing, one singular key to unlock everything else in my life. I took classes and became a nutritionist. I joined different recreation clubs. I read books and books and books. And in all that, I still didn't know my purpose. It never occurred to me that living as I was living, raising our children, being there for them and Troy, was purpose. Surely there was more. Surely, I was supposed to be more. I needed to grow into a bigger version of myself. I needed to expand into . . . something.

The teachings of my youth rang loudly in my being. To be a mother was not enough. To feed and care for my children and Troy was in some way a diminishment of what was expected of me. I carried on, following the callings of my heart, but oh, the time and energy I wasted in trying to be more.

I imagine how much more peace I could have had in my heart back then if only this fascination with purpose and meaning we're sold had been tempered by some sage advice from the women who had come before me. I didn't have anyone like that around. The women I knew, even the older women, seemed as stuck on that ride as everyone else. They still didn't know their purpose; they were still searching for something, though they didn't know what. If I could tell that hungry young woman something now, it would be this: Those moments when

— 175 —

you find peace, when you're reading a book at bedtime with your little girls or sitting in the grass for a picnic? Those moments, that life, is your purpose. And what purpose could be more profound and beautiful than that?

Purpose, I've come to understand, is not a static, physical thing. It's fluid and ever-changing. My purpose, as it turns out, can be to fling my arms around Troy when he walks in the door, all breathless and wild with joy to see him. I can plant a big, passionate kiss on his lips. "I'm so happy you're home!" The next day, my purpose might be to tell one of my daughters how proud I am of the woman she's become. Maybe that afternoon my purpose is to scoop up the little half robin's egg on the trail I walk and make up a story about the little snail I found living in it.

My purpose is love, and finding it in all of its manifestations. To be love, in all my manifestations. It's why, as my path unfolds, I am there noticing that unfolding, willing to take another step into the abyss with faith. I'm not afraid of the unknown because I understand that whatever awaits, there will always be the opportunity for love. That is my purpose. To be courageous and to have faith in whatever I am called to do next. My forties taught me that.

My fourth decade of life was one of refinement. I began to live with deeper discernment. As the powers that be continued to show their cards, I became more aware of how I'd been manipulated. Just as I did when I was a child, I once again found solace in the small. I pulled myself back from the neon and loudspeakers, into the silence and honesty of the tangible. Things I could touch and taste and listen to. Opinions and judgements that had muddled my mind for most of my life dissolved in the clarity of truth. Truth that I found in a forest where I used my fingernails to scrape away soil from trout lily bulbs. Mila and I collected each tiny one and put them in the makeshift baskets of our shirts. Then we ate them all at once, sitting in a sunbeam that pierced through the forest canopy and landed precisely on an overturned beech tree that became our bench. These are the moments, pure and true and connected with the humans I love so deeply, that stood, one after another, as great clarifiers in my life. Just being there completely — mind on nothing else, heart tuned to the moment — allowed

LITTLE PIG IN A HUT

the breath of God to blow away the chaff. Purification through the small and miraculous.

Now I know that, if we get the gift of many years in a life, it just keeps getting better. The angst of trying to figure it all out as a young woman has been replaced with calm. There's nothing to figure out. I have given that away, surrendered into life. I can be driven and determined without needing to control. I can be stubborn and impatient but choose to act with patience and generosity. I stand in the warm, gentle current of God's love and I recognize it as home. I want to be there, to be part of that eternal warmth. And I get to make that choice. I determine whether my heart is peaceful or pacing. I determine the love that comes to me by the love that I give. That's it. That's all there is. It's so perfect and so silly and so outrageously wonderful that we think it too simple, too naive. But it's a superpower at each of our disposal if we're brave enough to shake off our cloaks of cynicism.

Cynicism is just a guard for a wounded heart. It stands all strong and steely, pretending to be our friend. I can be as cynical as the next gal but I catch it more quickly now. I hear the sentence coming out of my mouth and before it even ends, I've changed my mind. No, I don't have to think that. No, that's no longer true in my heart. The older I get, the more I choose to replace the cynicism with a childlike naivety, a soft vulnerability. I don't care to know everything; I care to learn as much as I can. I like to ask questions. Sometimes those questions lead to conversations about topics I've never much thought about and, almost always, those conversations lead to something deeper. Like a recent conversation I had with a local fella about gravel. There we were, having a wonderful conversation about how he clears lots and lays driveways, but eventually we landed on his brother, who had passed away years ago. He teared up talking about him, and I wondered how often, in his rough-and-tumble life, he gets to talk about how much he misses his brother. It was a simple moment, leaning up against a red truck with a man so different than me, but in that moment we found our humanity and something else entirely, something mysterious and profoundly meaningful.

There are gifts that come to us and gifts we can give. As I get older, I realize the difference between the giving and the receiving has become

— 177 —

RADIANCE OF THE ORDINARY

more blurred. I don't even know if I believe there's a difference. We live in a constant flow of love. I was going to write that there's an exchange, but that's not altogether correct. It's not tit for tat, not a "you give me this and I give you that." That was how I understood things to be in my twenties and for part of my thirties. If I wanted something, I paid. If you wanted something, you paid. Even if we leave out the paying and the barter, it's still this for that, an expectation of something in return. But it's here, in this place of freely offering what's mine to offer without conditions or expectations, that I have come to better understand how there is no delineation in the ever-flowing stream. We can take off our shoes and step in, giving our time, our compassion, our good words and deeds, our sweetness, our talents, our laughter, our protection, our lightness, our imaginations — all of our unique gifts out of, and through, love.

To me, that's loving myself. Truly loving myself.

Back in the third decade of my life, when I was hunting for my purpose like a rabid she-wolf, I remember the constant insistence from the books and gurus in my midst that I must love myself. I didn't even know what that meant, so, clearly, I wasn't doing a great job of it. Loving myself, said the wise ones, was all about taking care of myself. And yet, self-care can become yet another task on a never-ending list of tasks. We can become another project, another thing to tackle, to *do*.

I tried to find some peace there, in that loving myself place, but it didn't work for me. How the heck was I supposed to go about loving myself? I read the books and tried the things, thinking that once I figured it out, I'd feel better about the whole purpose thing not happening, but that love was elusive. I didn't hate myself. I didn't condemn myself or criticize myself at every turn, though I certainly did at some turns.

Over time, and with practice, I got better at listening to the voices running through my head. I noticed some of those voices weren't mine at all, but replays of old wounds. I started countering those, again and again, and recognizing their invalidity. But try as I might, I never did fall passionately in love with myself by practicing the ritual of self-care or affirmations. It never rang true for me. It was only through the living of my life, smaller and smaller, closer to the ground, that the

— 178 —

LITTLE PIG IN A HUT

eternal spring of love washed over me and brought me closer to the centre — that brilliant, untouchable centre — of all things, including myself. The more I opened to love, the more love I felt within myself, moving into and out of and through me the same as it did through the world around me. And there in that endless, roaring waterfall was love for me. Not because I am a special, wondrous creature, but because I am tied into and fed by and feeding all that is. My love for myself is not a separate puddle, it's part of that all-encompassing deluge, and still, it is only a drop. A sweet, eternal, limitless drop. I am a child of God. I am a child of God! In me lives the soft kiss of Creation. I recognize that and I can't help but love it.

I'm in my fifties now. This decade of life has brought me anguish beyond comprehension with the death of Mila. And she has brought me to depths that stretch me into worlds I've never known. I have no fear here, in this time of my life. I am at peace with not knowing. I'm not threatened by my failings or my inadequacies. They are bountiful, and I see them with clear, sharp vision. They don't scare me anymore. And that brings me an authentic, unshakable confidence. I can sit up and sniff the air, take a look at the lost marauders charging across the plains, intent on doom and destruction, and I have no urge to run. They're an illusion. Their world, the world of governments and corporations and Wall Street is an illusion. They create problems and then sell us the solutions. But the problems are fictions. They ask us to enter into the lie of the machine. When we understand that, we have no need for their false solutions. If the problems are not real, how can the solutions be?

We can be drawn into the minutia and the muck, but at the least, we should do so understanding our participation in propping up the machine. We must recognize our contribution to their cause. The machine cares not on what fuel it runs — fear is as good as desire. But I care. I have this one life. I know this intimately because I keep death close. I walk with death every day. As my usher to my eternal home, it's welcomed here. Welcomed with respect and honest eyes. Death reminds me that fear and worry rot me from the inside, and life offers,

— 179 —

RADIANCE OF THE ORDINARY

at any moment, her open invitation to get close and small, tight into the truth of what is real.

I like it here. It brings me excitement to imagine life in my sixties and my seventies and maybe even beyond. Maybe it all ends tomorrow. That's okay, too, but I would go still enraptured by this life. Still hungry for more. It's not, it turns out, a dark, dank life in the shadows on this side of the hill I've gone over. It is, in fact, beyond lovely. I dropped my ego somewhere on the way up. It was a cumbersome, heavy thing that weighed me down. I sat it down on a rock somewhere and told it to take a rest. It finds me every now and then, but I just find another rock and tell it again, "Rest, my friend, you've done your job." And how lovely it is to experience this world without it! I can risk being silly. I can take the chance of looking like a fool. It's worth it, to me, to learn something or find something I have never known before. Because the truth of it, the deep, burning, wonderful truth, is that I don't mind what people think of me. I am okay with your disdain. I understand your displeasure. I am willing to be the object of your anger. It's okay. I will deal with that however it's warranted, but none of that can touch the most precious thing in me, the core of me that lives and breathes in the light of love.

I like it here. I like this me, closer to my real me than I've ever been. I like the me that spends less time focusing on the things my loved ones aren't doing right for me and more on how I might do and be more for them. I like what that creates in my life. I take care of myself because it feels good to have a body free of pain and a mind clear and sharp. I want to be a mother who my daughters admire and are admired by, even now. I want to be the woman of my man's dreams. His steadfast confidante, his soft touch, his adoring and loyal friend, his steadfast life partner, and his ravenous vixen. I am those things and I want those things and he wants those things and he is those things. We are standing together here in this life, two wanting for each more than they want for themselves. I can do that. I can be that.

I move onto this side of the mountain, or "over the hill," if you will, understanding I'm not moving downhill at all. This body needed me to arrive in this place of authentic desire to care for myself. Not because I want to fit into a tight pair of jeans and look like I'm twenty

LITTLE PIG IN A HUT

again, but because I want health and vitality for the body that carries me in my life now. Gravity and the years wear on my skeleton and crinkle my skin. I no longer look like I did. The jet-black hair of my youth has faded to brown, and now, bit by bit, into grey. The tight and buoyant bits exhale into a relaxed recline. There is no disguising it; my body is ageing. I don't mind. I have no war with my body. It has served me well. But I need it to continue on as long as I'm here to continue on. For all those years, my body ran fast and lifted heavy things; it outgunned and outmaneuvered boys twice my size, it brought my beautiful babies into this world, each of them as big as a Christmas turkey. What a marvel, this body! And now, time and wear and tear are catching up to it.

My maniacal workout regimes of the 1990s no longer fit. Now, I lift weights to preserve the muscle I need to carry me through the life I want. Now, I dream of scaling slippery mountain peaks on adventures with Troy rather than looking hot in my latest outfit. I eat nourishing foods our ancestors would recognize, not because I'm afraid of what will happen if I don't, but because there is deep pleasure in nourishing oneself, in the clarity that comes when I'm free of the foggy mind and sluggishness that processed foods deliver. The execution of how I take care of myself is similar to what it always has been, but the motivations are altogether different. And that makes a profound difference. I'm not another task. This is just what it is to live life in harmony with my design as I know it. Authentically me, excavated with diligence and determination in the darkest of caves and the most luscious of meadows.

Now, imagine what's to come in my eighties! If we're both around, I see me and Troy still grabbing at each other's little wrinkly bums. How grand that will be!

———

I came to the land not knowing how it would change me. Early on, the call of the catbird pulled me into a gorge, hunting for the wounded, hungry cat that never was. Really? That was the call of a bird? I was clueless that such a bird existed and astounded by nature's sense of humour. Sometimes I go to the cows in the pasture and hang out with them for a while. I try to make friends with the shy ones if they're up

— 181 —

for it. My favourite cow, my old gal Bea, often squeezes out the others and comes to me for scratches. We'll stay there for a good long time, and I'll wonder what she might know that I don't. It's something. It's there. She knows and understands something beyond my reach. I can be in that mystery with her. I just don't get the answers. And that's enough for me now. I don't want the answers to everything. I don't need to know. I'm dissatisfied with concrete proclamations because they all tend to be dishonest in the end. We don't know everything. We'll never know. What is said today changes tomorrow. My security doesn't hinge on another's statements of fact. My peace is tied into bigger little things.

I'd still like to be a little pig in a hut. Maybe not the pig part, but the hut seems swell. My sister recently asked me what I got out of setting up a winter tent and sleeping out there in the forest with Troy for parts of the winter. We already live a good distance from civilization, surrounded by forest. We're already secluded. But it's not seclusion I'm after as much as connection to the simple and the sacred. In our winter tent, our bodies lie on furs over snow. We are in communion with the earth, its energies harmonizing with our own. The coyotes come near, closer than they realize, and call to one another. Imagine that — being at the centre of such a symphony, lonesome howls bouncing off the trees all around you, finding their way from the throat of a coyote and into your ears. Or the calls of a puffed-up barred owl travelling over and around rock cliffs and skimming over the feathers of sleeping ravens to nestle into your tent alongside you. It brings us close to truth, sleeping close to Creation. It brings us into alignment with ourselves. It saturates us with the love of God. That's what I get out of it.

There's a spot along an open meadow in our forest that rises up into a copse of paper birch trees. There are always rabbits there, hiding beneath the junipers. The deer come in the winter and melt oval-shaped patches in the snow with their overnight beds. And the pièce de résistance is the beaver family that lives in there. It's the perfect spot to build a little hovel in the earth. A sweet little hobbit house of my own. I still dream of it. I am still comforted by the idea. I read books about monks in monasteries and nuns in convents, and I'm drawn to the smallness of their lives, the simplicity and the focus on details rather

LITTLE PIG IN A HUT

than sweeping generalities. It calls to my heart. But those buildings, those vast stone structures, opulent and extravagant, leave me cold. I had a few different nuns as teachers. One in particular, Sister Kelly, was the focus of my adoration. She was kind and warm and encouraged me to write. She told me once about what her bedroom looked like: a simple metal bed, a small desk, a candle, a crucifix, a dresser, a closet. Small and simple. Looking at her shining face with no makeup, her thick black hair, her clear brown eyes, her strong, tall frame, and the calm and joy she exuded, I figured she had it all figured out. Sister Kelly knew how to live.

I mostly forgot about her over the years. I never had enough money to get too materialistic, but I wasted enough time pining for things. Once I had this thing or that thing, or once we lived here or there, or once this job was done and that one started, or once my kids started doing this or that and I could do this or that, or once we replaced our old truck, or ... You get the idea. I remember sitting with Troy on the couch of some old home on some old army base. He said, "Do you realize how much we always look to the future? We do it all the time. Like, things will be good when ..." There wasn't much to argue about there. He was right. We did it all the time. We didn't even know how not to do it.

That awareness was the necessary first step. How could we ever hope to have peace and satisfaction in any given moment when we were constantly running to the future? Could we be okay even when things weren't perfect around us? That was a big one to untangle. It took continuous monitoring by the both of us. At our weekly meetings, a practice we developed years ago to address the scheduling of our days and review how well we were doing with the objectives of our lives, we started to reflect on how well we were doing with our desire to stop living in the future. It took a good long while, but how sweet the spoils of victory! We still look forward to what is to come, but it's not in anticipation of escaping what's here now.

It's worth it, the sifting through the debris of our lives. To crouch down on the earth and pick through what we want to keep and what we no longer need. It's worth our time and attention. It requires quiet and focus and a soft, careful hand. There is nothing to whip into shape.

— 183 —

RADIANCE OF THE ORDINARY

There is nothing we need to better ourselves for the job. We don't need grandiose gestures or extravagant programs led by strangers who promise to bring you to a self only you can really know. We just need to be willing to be small and still, to connect to the tether that is always there if we care to feel around for it. We are all safe. We are all held in little warm huts, cocooned in endless, unstoppable, uncontainable love. A love that is accessible and waiting on us to remember.

Frogs

It was a particularly dark evening, no moon to be seen, the roads slick with rain. It wasn't raining hard, a soft drizzle, but the weather was odd, like a two-layered cake. Hot up to my knees, the cold nipping at my nose. Mila had just turned thirteen. We were about to make the long journey home from a hockey practice. We couldn't put a finger on it, but we both felt unsettled as we packed her gear into the trunk and headed off into the foggy night. I needed to turn my high beams on against the black of the night, but the thick fog bounced the illumination back into our eyes, so we had to rely on the low beams and were left squinting.

As we drove along the county roads, we caught movement in our headlights. I slowed down, realizing the shining concrete was slick. I brought the car to a crawl, and the movement became clearer and more horrifying. Frogs, hundreds and hundreds of frogs, were hopping out of the roadside ditches and onto the warmth of the concrete. Hopping to their deaths.

As we rolled along, we realized it wasn't hundreds of frogs in one spot. It was tens of thousands of frogs. They just kept on coming. We could feel the bigger bullfrogs hit the undercarriage of our car. We screamed in horror. Mila started directing me to try and avoid the amphibian kamikazes. "To your right!" she shouted. "That one's coming right at you!" "Mom! To your left!" I was picking my way through them in a metal box on wheels. Not exactly nimble. We couldn't understand it. What was it about the road conditions, slimed over by frog carcasses now, that enticed the frogs to leave their warm little ditch houses and sacrifice themselves to the bright-eyed machines?

— 185 —

RADIANCE OF THE ORDINARY

Even after we had long left the concrete roads and turned down the winding gravel roads that would take us home, the frogs coalesced. It was as if they had held a meeting and collectively decided this was the evening they would meet up for their great froggy jamboree, come rain or shine!

I don't know how long that drive lasted, but I remember how we screamed and laughed like hysterical chimpanzees. It was the kind of shrieking laughter that only comes from horror — from a frantic situation where you know you're not in any real danger, but it's not good either. Like the moment when you're at the top of a roller coaster, just before you drop. Or like that time when a bat landed in my hair out in our barn. Oh yes, I know, they tell you it's an urban myth that bats don't want to land in your hair. My barn bat didn't get that memo. Here's a tip for you: If a bat lands in your hair, don't frantically swat at it with your hands. You'll merely create a web of hair to hold the terrified bat in place. It will struggle mightily. You will hear it up close, directly in your eardrum, as it thwaps its wings in an attempt to escape. I screamed as I danced around, maniacally trying to get the bat out of my hair, while my daughters screamed and laughed, too. It was the same with the frogs. That same scream. That same laugh.

We drove and drove and still the frogs came. We lifted our feet when they banged on the undercarriage of our car. I weaved and bobbed as Mila watched the edges of the roads and shouted directions. For each one I avoided, I got a "Good job, Mom." Again and again, Mila said, "Good job, Mom." For every "good job," another scream and another flattened frog. Drivers passed us in the opposite lane, leaving skids of slimy frog guts in their wake.

By the time we got home, we were spent. I shut off the car and we sat panting in the darkness, rain pattering against the metal roof. Our hearts were still pounding.

"That was apocalyptic," Mila said.

"It really was."

"Nobody will ever believe how bad it was."

"No, they won't."

"Mom! Why were they doing that all at once, all that way?"

"I have no idea."

— 186 —

FROGS

"There must have been tens of thousands of frogs."

"Probably more."

We eventually went inside. Troy and Ella greeted us by the door. We tried to explain, tried to share the enormity of what we had just experienced, but we might as well have been telling them about locusts eating the siding off houses. Unless you see it, you just don't get it. But Mila got it. And I got it. And when the weather and the season and the smell in the air was just right, and some animal instinct conjured that day in our memories, we'd say, "Remember the frogs?" And we'd both shudder.

———

Five years have passed, and I'm driving down country roads not unlike those we travelled on the "night of the frogs." I'm alone. I've just left a grief support group for parents whose children have died. I still haven't figured out how I'm part of such a group. It seems preposterous. I'm oblivious to weather. I'm oblivious to the cold or the warmth or the rain on my skin. Maybe I'm hungry. Maybe I'm exhausted. Maybe I'm not even here.

I've been to a few of these meetings now. A group of women, mostly, although men are welcome. But I can understand why men, for the most part, avoid such things. Men work out their stuff in different ways. Maybe I do, too. I don't know. I'm going because it seems the right thing to do. It seems like it might be helpful to talk to other moms who know the pain I'm feeling. I'm going out of desperation, in hopes of finding evidence that a mother can live through this agony.

And now I'm here. In this silent car, driving through the dark night to get home. A frog appears on the road. I do my best to avoid it, but before I even return to my lane, I see another. And another. I slow down and quickly realize the frogs are back. Hundreds of them. Tire track marks on their flattened bodies. I have a long way to go before I get home. An hour, maybe two if I drive this slowly. I'm trying to see each of them, their bodies hopping in front of my rolling tires, but there are too many. The more I drive, the more frogs appear. I inch along, hearing my daughter's laughter and screams. "To your left! Mom, right in front! Ahhhh! There, Mom!"

— 187 —

RADIANCE OF THE ORDINARY

Suddenly I notice the rain, just enough to erase the dividing lines on the road. I notice how dark it is, how the air is sweet and sour. And I am back in the car with Mila, only there is an empty seat. It will always be an empty seat now. The frogs continue to thump below my feet. They keep coming. Keep dying. Their carcasses a smear of carpet on the road.

Out of the depths I feel something crack, and I hear a scream. Not a mirthful scream. Not a playful shriek, but a rumbling, frothy wave that explodes from my guts and fills the car with thick tar. I am driving and I am screaming and the frogs keep coming.

I've never heard such a sound emanate from my body, and it scares me. I want to make it stop. But there is no stopping it. No stopping anything. I have no control. I am rolling down the road, sobbing and screaming at the horrors of this life. Trying to save as many frogs as I can.

I don't understand. I can't understand. I want no explanations. I don't want to go home and google "Why do frogs throttle themselves onto the road to die?" It doesn't matter. It makes no difference. They do. And I can't do anything to stop it.

———

As a little girl, I prided myself on my ability to catch frogs. I left the jumbo bullfrogs to the boys, who seemed to equate frog size with status. I didn't like the big ones. I liked the nimble tree frogs and the iridescent leopard frogs. I liked the ones I could hold in my hand and admire for a time before letting them go. When Mila was still a little girl, a budding naturalist even then, she told me that touching frogs hurt them. "It's like rubbing powdered glass in your skin," she said. It made me feel guilty. I stopped catching frogs.

Now I just admire them. Every spring they appear. The spring peepers come first with their rambunctious symphonies, night after night. We open all of our windows wide, even though it's still too frosty. What choice is there? The peepers are broadcasting live on the airwaves! Every night they serenade us with their calls of awakening life. The long winter slumber is over. Life continues anew.

Have you heard the song of the spring peeper? If it's a broken heart you have, you need to. Find them. Drive out to them if you must. On

FROGS

an early spring evening, find the wet ditches or the shallow wetlands dotted with cattails and dogwood. If you've driven, get out of your car and wait. If you're inside, go outside. Sit with them. Be their audience. Everything beautiful must be witnessed.

In return, those tiny little frogs come with the offering of hope. Winter is over. For now. It will come again, and we will survive again. For now, there is melt. The sap runs through the veins of the maples again. The smell of firewood and bubbling syrup fills the air. Great plumes of sweetness sending smoke signals to the Canada geese: "Come home, come home!" And they do, flying through the syrup-scented clouds, anointing their feathers with droplets of sugar. They honk their arrival, and I stand underneath them, arms lifted in exultation. "Welcome home! Welcome home! We missed you! Welcome home!"

How would any of that happen, how would spring know it's time to return, had the spring peepers not sung it all into existence? If they had not shimmied out of their warm hibernation, risked the cold, and joined their choir, would the buds of the lilac still have swelled? Would the ice have softened? Would the songbirds have known it was time to return?

And if a tiny frog, just one in millions, has that kind of hope, who am I not to?

———

We are at the cemetery, Troy and I. We're doing what we always do — the ritual of the visit. I come with wildflowers. He comes with a jar of water to fill the vase. He cleans off her headstone; I pull the weeds from the flowers we've planted. Sometimes we sit on the ground. Sometimes we stand and look to the sky. Sometimes there are dragonflies that come to rest on the headstone for a time. Sometimes there are birds singing to us from the tree canopy overhead.

As I'm plucking weeds from the front of the headstone, a small brown frog appears. His bottom is round and his body compact. A young frog with camouflage meant for fallen leaves and tree bark. I watch him take one hop and disappear. I ask Troy if he can see the frog in the scattered bits overlaying the grass. He looks for a good long time and admits defeat.

— 189 —

RADIANCE OF THE ORDINARY

"Where is he?"

"Right there," I tell him, and point to a spot right in front of his shoe. When you see him, you see him, but it's near impossible without help.

Troy stares at our daughter's name carved into that stone.

"God, I miss her."

And the little frog says, "I'm still here, even if you can't see me."

Salvation on Eight Hooves

On a recent summer morning, my daughter Ella and I woke early and made the annual trek to my friend Henry's farm. He had called the night before to let me know that his magnificent strawberry patch was "just right." And everyone knows that on that "just right" day in a summer strawberry's life, all previous plans must be dropped, for what can be more important than that berry? Furthermore, how could I refuse the invitation when my fine strawberry-picking partner was even more eager than I?

By the time we arrived, the sun had already claimed the day as her own. We took off our shoes and let our toes sink into the rich humus while we marvelled at the ocean of berries all around us. We each plucked a berry from its cluster of green leaves and stood facing each other as we popped them into our mouths. Our eyes snapped open wide from the burst of sweetness, and we laughed. We were ready to set forth to the task at hand: pick as many berries as we needed to preserve to get us through the year.

After his morning farm chores were finished, Henry came and found us in "the patch." I stood up to give him a hug, and he asked how the berries were looking. I could see him puff up a little bit when I told him they were heavenly. Different varieties grew in every row, each more delicious than the next, thriving in the organic, rich soils worked by Henry's team of powerful Percheron horses. Little red gems with rounded shoulders warmed by sunbeams. Henry never begrudged the picker who was also an eater. He understood that the temptation to nibble was beyond the mere mortal's capacity to resist.

Henry has been my friend for many years now. He's an old-school farmer — one who is passionate about the health of his soil and animals. His tractors are older than me; he needs them little. Everything he does, he does with draft horses and conviction. He is experience and skill all wrapped up in devotion and kindness. The best of things.

That morning, in among those beautiful strawberries, Henry and I spoke about loss and heartache. What better to speak about in such a sacred place? A year before my rummage through his strawberry patch, Henry's wife of thirty-four years died. Janet was his co-conspirator; his partner in the endless tasks of a farm. Whenever we visited, she poured us tall glasses of chilled milk and offered her baked goods made from farm ingredients. One of my favourite visits was on a perfect summer morning many years ago. Mila and I woke up early and took the farm truck up to their place. Mila was nine or ten that year and a big fan of Henry's strawberries. We picked berries, flat after flat, all morning. I do believe Mila's eat-to-pick ratio approached 2:1.

When we finally finished, we tucked our berry flats safely into the shade of a large oak tree, and Janet insisted we sit with her and Henry under a large weeping willow. She had made ice cream from the luscious cream of their grass-fed, heritage breed Canadienne cows. We shared stories while we ate that rich ice cream dotted with perfect little berries, an explosion of zingy, sweet juice in every bite. I began to worry about Mila, who, despite her careful berry-eating ratio, had not expected such an irrefutable offering of berries *and* homemade ice cream.

On the long drive home, Mila sprawled across the back seat of the farm truck, moaning and groaning in tummy-pain misery. "Who ever knew a strawberry could cause so much trouble!?" she wailed. By the grace of all that is good, she was able to keep those strawberries where they were.

Henry and I reminisced about that day. We spoke about his beloved wife and her kindness, her work ethic. His entire life deeply woven into hers and hers into his. How does it feel to be with someone for so long — your life partner, your loyal sidekick in every decision and every intimate secret — and then, one day, to lose them? I wanted to know. I wanted to

SALVATION ON EIGHT HOOVES

open the space for Henry to speak of those things if he wanted to. Since Mila's death, I have learned, if nothing else, that most of us are woefully inept at meeting others in their misery. Instead, we offer pep talks, "give them space," or sometimes act as though nothing ever happened.

Troy and I experienced all of these things. Our culture, if we even have one here in North America, is abysmal when it comes to healing rituals and traditions, but this shortcoming is felt most acutely when someone precious to you dies. In the earlier days of our grief, I read a book that spoke of an Indigenous tribe that wrapped grieving spouses and parents in warm furs and sat them by a fire in the centre of the community. When they were hungry, they would be fed. They stayed there with no expectations but to grieve, kept in the heart of the community so they could be seen and heard, so everyone would be reminded that all was not well, the living embodiment of grief saturating them all. Nothing to look away from, nobody to push away, until those in mourning were "well."

We ached when we read that. Imagine such a thing. . . . I barely can, but oh, how much we would have given to have people so willing to be with us in that raw, gushing place. But life is busy and impersonal today. Words and emotions must be compartmentalized. At our daughter's memorial, someone left immediately after the service, unable to share a single word, because they couldn't bear to face us. In the days after, one of my best friends disappeared altogether. People who knew our daughter, who were close to her and had even loved her, faded away. Even family members didn't know what to do.

There was no warming fire with our people around us, sobbing with us, sharing our grief. It was me and Troy alone on our porch, alone in our woods, beside other bereaved parents, shaking our heads in disbelief. It was lonely and isolating, and in among our grief was a simmering fury over the abandonment. It has made us acutely aware of how willingly our culture leaves people to grieve alone under the self-protective guise of "giving them time." It is a failing, our inability to be in that place with others — not for an hour on a phone call, but for days or weeks or months. To be loyal and willing. To not pretend, a few weeks later, that nothing ever happened at all.

— 193 —

RADIANCE OF THE ORDINARY

Months after Mila died, friends and family would intermittently invite us to spend time with them. There would be hustle and bustle — people about, a shared meal, conversation about work and life; all of it bone-crushingly exhausting. Into the weakened corners of our hearts, we had to tuck away our pain just to partake in a few hours of exchange with others. Sometimes, in an attempt to connect, someone would shuffle over to us as we were dishing up food, lower their eyes, and ask, "How are you — really?" Ah, yes, do allow me to rip off the girders that are keeping me together enough to put this duck on a plate, and tell you how I am — *really*.

But that's what stands for connection today, at least in some circles. Over time, we had to figure out our own way to solace. For me and Troy, it was each other. It was books on grief written by other parents who knew. It was our connection to and faith in a loving God, even still. It was hours sitting in meditative silence. It was sharing the same stories again and again. It was the enchanted visits and messages nature delivered on buzzing wings and sweet winds. It was sobbing wildly when we needed to.

Through that pain of isolation in our grief, we have come to a desire and willingness to be there for others in their pain. I'm not afraid of it. It's impossible to be afraid of something that has so intimately become a part of oneself. Pain cannot hurt me any more than it has. That which I most feared has woven itself into my very being. I accept it. In place of Mila's life, there will be no untouchable, ignored realm because of fear. There is a hole, yes, but it isn't black and cold. It's alive and whirling with life. There are dragonflies flying in its depths and fireflies sparkling in its heavens. There is space, endless space, filled with streams of iridescent, golden love that pulses and throbs. Everything is mystical and unknowable and yet completely and deeply known. Love lives on, unstoppable. It's not a lost memory remembered again and again. I don't keep my daughter alive through my memories. My daughter is alive in ways my little raisin brain can hardly comprehend.

I brought this collection of thoughts and feelings with me to the strawberry patch. I brought them because they are me, living within me, but I certainly didn't offer Henry a sermon. Instead, I offered him my ear and my heart. I asked him questions and I quietly treaded

SALVATION ON EIGHT HOOVES

beside him as he brought us both into the cavernous depths of his grief. I didn't stop him when he showed me what was raw and bleeding. I asked for more when he spoke of his loneliness. I listened and listened, and he talked. He is alone now. Maybe his friends and family don't want to bring it up when they stop by. As if anyone can ever forget the loss of a great love, their peace contingent on people "not bringing it up."

Henry told me that after his wife died, he sold his beloved horses. "Nothing seemed worth it," he said. I understood that feeling completely. Days after Mila died, in the warmth of a burgeoning spring, we, too, decided nothing was worth it. We couldn't fathom taking care of our farm. I didn't want my garden. I couldn't stand my cows, my favourite animals on all the Earth. I didn't want to fence them; I didn't want to move them. I didn't care about anything. I didn't want to care for anything. There was nothing to give. We were hollowed out.

Friends from our farming community worked out who could take what. They seemed to have the sense we just didn't. They would take our cows for as long as we needed, and one day, whenever that day might be, they would return them to us. They showed up with their trucks and trailers and decided who would take the heifers and the steers, the bull and the cows. I remember little about that day. It was warm. I remember crying and being held by a friend who had come with her husband to load the cows. My friend Andrea had urged me to keep the three dairy cows. She knew how much I loved my cows, and dairy cows are always special animals on a farm. We work with them so closely and get to know their personalities intimately. But I didn't want to keep them. I didn't care. She offered to come and get them at any time if I decided against it after all. With great hesitation, I kept them.

I'm so glad Andrea had that wisdom and forethought. She was right. I needed my milk cows even if I didn't yet know it.

Every day I led that quiet trio into a new pasture. The orchard, always a favourite spot among the grazing cattle, also happens to be my favourite place to put them. It's beautiful, with lovely heartnut, apple, cherry, pear, and mulberry trees dotting its landscape. My garden, fenced in of course, also blooms and grows in the orchard. When

— 195 —

RADIANCE OF THE ORDINARY

my cows are there, I can see them from my bathtub. Sitting in the cool waters of a bathtub, looking out an open window at an orchard where three beautiful beasts eat grasses as the evening birds sing their evening sounds, is some of the most powerful medicine this heart has ever known.

Two weeks after our daughter's death, we woke in the middle of the night to a less peaceful scenario: the sound of a cow bellowing like a great raging elephant. I jumped out of bed and threw on some clothes.

"Troy! Hurry, something's wrong!"

I ran outside thinking she must have had her calf. We knew she was expecting soon, but we should have had a week or two yet. When I got close enough to make out shapes in the darkness, I was confronted with a horrible scene. Our cow Olive was rearing up on her hind legs and smashing the front of her body down on a little mound on the earth. She was bellowing, snarfing, huffing, and flinging her head wildly from side to side.

"Holy shit! She's killing her calf!" I yelled to Troy.

She was wild with rage. I had never seen a cow react to her calf like that. It was against all order and instinct. But there she was, using her powerful head to fling the calf's soft, lifeless body into the air. Wherever it landed, she would follow and drop down on it with her front hooves. We jumped over the fence, keenly aware of the danger. Even the most docile animal remains unpredictable. We needed to get between Olive and the source of her rage — that limp little calf.

There was no pulling her or pushing her away. She was consumed with murderous revenge. We quickly grabbed a reel of electric fencing and pulled the thin white string in front of her. There was no electricity flowing through the line, but she reared back at the sight of it, giving Troy a second or two to scoop up the helpless little calf and run for the real fence. Olive, contained only by the string I had stretched out between my open arms, quickly ducked me and ran after Troy.

"Run!" I yelled at him. "She's coming!"

He made it over the fence just in time, Olive's thundering body inches behind him. She was hellbent on murder. We left Olive with her rage and brought the little calf into the barn, laying her on a lofty bed of warm wood shavings. The calf was alive, but we were certain she

SALVATION ON EIGHT HOOVES

would die soon. Surely her body was full of broken bones; maybe she was even bleeding internally.

I couldn't stand it. Why was this happening? Hadn't I endured enough? My own daughter dead only two weeks ago. . . . I didn't need this shit. I couldn't take any more. I was angry, so violently angry with Olive. Her baby was so perfect and beautiful, and she was trying to kill it! What a stupid, vile asshole of a mother! I wiped her little calf with towel after towel, doing the job that Olive should have been doing, but no — she was out there fuming that we had stopped her from finishing the job.

And then we heard it. Olive started up again with those noises — those rabid, raging elephant noises that had awakened me less than an hour before. I snapped my head up and looked at Troy in alarm. He had just returned with a kerosene lantern so we could better assess the condition of the beat-up little calf.

"Why is she starting with those noises again?"

"Maybe she's still mad," he said.

But something about that didn't sit right with me.

"Maybe she's having twins," I whispered in return.

We left the traumatized calf wrapped in a blanket and headed back to the field. Sure enough, another small calf lay sprawled on the ground. Her mother, now proficient in the act of hurling her young through the air, wedged her nose between the calf and the ground below, then flung it with all her fury. This time we were quick. I grabbed the reel with the pretend electric fencing while Troy used his powerful muscles to pick up that slippery, heavy, awkward bundle and run. We brought the second doomed creature into the barn with the first and frantically worked to dry her, too.

An inspection by lantern didn't reveal any obvious injuries on either calf. There were no protruding bones nor any that felt broken. We built up more bedding around the dry calves and wrapped them up tightly in a blanket, bound together as they had been in the warm, peaceful home they inhabited moments earlier, just before their violent introduction to the world.

The morning songbirds were singing by the time we were done; the darkness of night transforming into the hint of day. We checked on the

— 197 —

dairy cows as we walked toward the house. They were peacefully eating their breakfast of pasture grasses and wildflowers. Olive ate with her friends, lazily swinging her tail. She pulled a mound of sweet grass from the earth and looked up at me as she chewed.

"Oh, hi," she seemed to say. "Lovely morning, isn't it?"

"Asshole," was all I could muster in reply.

Once inside, I pulled some frozen colostrum from our freezer to thaw. I still doubted the calves would live. Twins, heifer twins, was so special, and they looked so healthy, but their "special" welcome from mama must surely have caused some damage to their delicate little bodies. Could they survive them? In the meantime, it was imperative that I get the life-giving colostrum into their bodies. Colostrum is critically important to mammals — humans included. If we don't get colostrum into our calves shortly after they're born, it will impact their future size, vitality, and immunity. Most farmers with cattle know to keep some frozen colostrum tucked away for misfortunes such as ours.

I warmed the colostrum to room temperature while anger and frustration coursed through me. I was in the depths of despair. I was absolutely saturated with grief. There was no space, not a single atom open to anything else. I couldn't care for calves. I could barely care for myself! And there was something else there, too. How could a mother cow, such a maternal creature, reject her own with such vehemence? How could she? When I would give it all, every last drop, to have my child again.

In hindsight, my reasoning was nonsensical, but I was not in my mind in those days. I was bobbing around among the debris of my life, consciousness in a body. Trying to remember to breathe and blink while the whole world rumbled along, demanding my participation. I didn't want to participate.

I spent the entire day with those calves. I fed them colostrum from a bottle. I rubbed them down with warm, dry towels — poor substitutes for the rough, powerful tongue of their mother. I spoke to them in hushed, soothing tones, telling them in my human language, mysterious to them, how beautiful they were. They accepted the milk eagerly. They tried to stand again and again, collapsing each time. I imagined the broken and bruised bones beneath their caramel-coloured hair. I

SALVATION ON EIGHT HOOVES

didn't know if they would ever be able to stand. Outside, less than a hundred metres from the barn, Olive carried on nonplussed, relieved to be free of those demons that caused her so much pain. She didn't call for them. Not even once.

I stayed in that barn out of obligation. I had to keep those animals alive. The sun streamed through the slats of the wooden door and in through the hole where a window used to be, before our Guernsey, Daisy, broke it with a swing of her mighty head. Barn cats hopped in and out of the paneless window, surveying the situation, sensing warm, fresh milk was near. Every now and then a mother hen popped through the hole, looking for a place to hide her eggs, but she quickly left in a huff at the sight of a human.

I sat on an overturned pail in the corner, my head in my hands, watching the calves sleep against each other. It was cute, sure. Those little hooves, still soft and clean. Their black noses and impossibly long eyelashes. Yes, they were supremely beautiful, but I was numb with grief. I only saw work and responsibility ahead of me. I saw the likelihood of more death, and the monumental task of milking their mother twice a day so we could feed the calves and process the rest into cheese, butter, kefir, and yoghurt. I wanted none of it. I was exhausted; absolutely incapable of giving anything more. I cried all afternoon, listening to the faraway, disembodied voice of my daughter calling for her barn cats, the sweet sound bouncing off the trembling rafters above my head.

But the calves didn't die. They stood up, one wobbly leg after another. Then they jumped their little jumps and raced each other around their pen. I gave them more colostrum, then milk, and then more milk. There wasn't a single thing wrong with them. No bones askew, no malfunction in the works. They were whole and vibrant and eager for life. I don't know how many hours I spent sitting in the barn with them while they eagerly drank from the bottle, filling themselves to the brim with that wondrous elixir of life. I don't know how many hours I spent watching them play. They came to me with their plump, wet noses, eye to eye with me as I sat on my pail, and they breathed their sweet, milky calf breath onto my face. Their breath into mine. An impossible innocence with the power to weave itself into my grief. The grief was not replaced or edged out. It was there to stay. But for a second, just a second, I could hold wonder alongside my grief, and that felt an awful lot like hope.

We tried to reintroduce Olive to her calves. First it was through the wooden gate — a sniff to remind her of what she lost. Maybe the sight of her calves would shock her into maternal desire, and she would clamour to reach them in ecstatic reunion. That didn't happen. Instead, she throttled her body against the gate, determined to break it down and get rid of those dastardly little creatures once and for all. At the sight of them, Olive started her bellowing anew, and the wild, white-eyed fear returned. We took her away.

But we were determined. Every day we brought her back. We put the calves in an outdoor pen where she could see them but not pulverize them. She watched from the fence line, running back and forth as the calves chased each other on the opposite side. She was confused; we could see it. Something within her drew her to the calves, but she didn't quite get it. When the curious calves came near, she let them get close enough to sniff her, stretching out her own neck to push her shiny black nose through the wood slats of the fence, only to ram her head against the boards before the calves could touch her.

This went on for days and then weeks. Finally, a searching black nose received a lick from Olive through the fence slats. She became consumed with coming up to the barn and watching the calves frolic in their pen. She seemed to want to get to them, and we were certainly eager to stop being their milk source multiple times a day. We put a harness on her, and Troy brought her into the calf pen. She ran after them a little too aggressively in her desire. The calves were frightened. They ran from her to the safety of me. When I tried to get out of the way, they ran into the barn. It went like this for days, Troy hanging on for dear life while Olive, having decided there was something to these little creatures after all, ran after them with too much enthusiasm. Over time, she got close enough to give them a lick here and there, but she didn't understand that the calves were her babies, meant to suck at her udder. And they didn't understand that her udder was the source of endless delights.

We had to train the calves to her udder, and we had to train Olive to let them nurse. It was all-consuming. Our patience was depleted,

SALVATION ON EIGHT HOOVES

and still, the animals demanded more. I was numb. I couldn't care less about such things. But if it were true that I couldn't care less, then why was I out there taking care of them? Those little calves, in that sun-drenched room smelling of sweet baby breath and clean hay, were a tether to something I didn't even know I needed tethering to.

One of Mila's barn cats, Theo, became a big fan of the twin calves. He visited daily, weaving himself around their spindly legs, purring wildly as they nudged him with their big black noses. They were friends of the highest order. How do you sit on the damp earth on a beautiful summer day with a sweet barn cat and two twin calves playing next to you, chewing on your hair, bumping up against your shoulders, and not feel a thing? Even the darkest hole cannot keep out a glimmer of light.

I've learned that salvation comes not at once, but in drips. It can't come if we're running from something; it's too quiet, too slow, for that. Salvation comes when we sit, head in hands, open and aware. It comes in tandem with misery, hand in hand with anguish. There is no miraculous opening of the sky, no mighty angel rushing forth to rid us of that which we think unendurable. Instead, we must endure.

There is no magical healing in a pair of twin calves. Or maybe the honest way to say it is that there is as much healing in a pair of twin calves as there is in the glowing light of the full moon or the fragrance of milkweed coaxed open by the warming sun. In our deepest grief, perhaps there is more space within us than we realize. We have capacity beyond our familiarity. The moment you shift your gaze, you see there are things you hadn't noticed. Even in misery, there is wonder.

I'm grateful now for that time with those beautiful animals that came to anchor me to this place. They were my medicine, whether I wanted it or not.

———

On that day in Henry's strawberry patch, these were the things we spoke of. Maybe not quite like this, but buried in our words, transmuted through the space between us, it was all said. We made space for our grief. We shared what was real in each of us. The sun shone on his straw hat, and with tears in his eyes, he reached down to pluck a

RADIANCE OF THE ORDINARY

strawberry, plump and sweet, from the ground. Pain and strawberries. Friends and loss.

It is cold now, the snow thick and persistent under the blue winter sky. I visited Henry again recently. He had called me a few weeks earlier to tell me he had welcomed a new team of horses to his farm. A beautiful brother-sister duo of Percheron/Canadian horses. After Janet died, Henry had considered selling the entire farm in addition to his horses. But where would he go? Still, it seemed impossible that he could stay there without her, on that farm they had built together.

Standing there on his land, I could hear again the thumping of its heart. Henry would keep that farm alive, at least in body if not in spirit, with his new team. He wept for Janet as he reached up to place his open hand on the neck of his beautiful, shining horse. Still reaching. Still open. Finding peace.

Apple Trees

Have you healed?
Is there healing in that for you?
You seem like you are healing.
May you heal.

I hear these words, each of them spoken to me over the last few years, as I reach for the apples around me. Every tree here bowed and heavy with her apples. Trees that were strategically planted, over a hundred years ago, by humans long gone. Other trees planted by us, young and flexible with flushes of fruit. They have grown for years with perhaps a blossom here and there, but the fruit is new to them. I wonder if they are marvelling at their own newly awoken superpower. From them, beautiful, rosy orbs to tempt the seed carriers.

I grew up not knowing that there were "good apple years" and "no apple years." But there always was a red delicious apple in my paper lunch bag. So ubiquitous, it was no more special than the brown paper it came in. I hated red delicious apples. They tasted like chalky, overly sweet potatoes to me. I traded mine or threw them away without a thought. Some anonymous tree, in some anonymous land, picked by some anonymous person who took that apple and waxed it and polished it so it was as perfect as the plastic fruit on my auntie's dining room table.

These apples, the ones all about me, are not those apples. These apples I have come to know. These trees I have come to understand. In front of our house, the most magnificent of all. An apple tree so full and robust and heavy with apples that she encircles more than half of our screened-in porch. She is the one who scratches along the metal

RADIANCE OF THE ORDINARY

gables of our bedroom on windy nights. She is the one who grows apples, striped light green and pale red, that grow in clusters like grapes. Tens of thousands of apples, and she holds them all. Her trunk is as mighty as an oak. Her limbs stretch far and hold strong. She is our great privacy screen when we sit on our porch early in the morning and I read stories to Troy. She celebrates with us when we retire to our little porch with something cold at the end of a sweaty summer day. I wonder if she dreams of the brown thrashers that pick worms from her skin while she hibernates through our long, cold winters.

There are other apple trees, too. The tree behind our house offers the old-fashioned McIntosh. The one from the time "before." Before storage and transportation and the changing desire for sweetness over the delights of complexity messed around with the trees. These Macs, my favourite of all apples, are perfection. A crunch so hard, a taste so piquant and sharp, and a juice so explosive they snap you into the now. There is no way to eat these apples mindlessly. They will stop you in your tracks. They will make you look at them while you eat. There is no room for mindless consumption when tastebuds meet Creation.

We have trees that offer apples you won't find on store shelves. Small green apples with pink polka dots. Ruddy green apples with rust-coloured stripes that, I am certain, are the mothers of "Granny Smith," only infinitely more delicious. There are oblong apples and medium-size apples and perfect, dark ruby crab apples. Some are for cider making. Some for fresh eating or storage. Others are perfect for apple butter, and others shine as preserves.

For each apple, a tree that grew it. For each tree, a different story — a different time in her life. Our young trees are simple. Their bark smooth. Their limbs can bend in great arches under the weight of their fruit. Some break. Some splinter. Too ambitious in their growth. They're full throttle, and then they burn themselves out. There is something uncomplicated about a tree like that. I pick her apples with gratitude, but her limbs are sparse. She is lean and open wide. She's still taking it all in.

There are a handful of old apple trees in among the younger ones in our orchard. Over the decades, they've had big limbs cut back or

— 204 —

APPLE TREES

broken off. The chickens dust bathe under the shade of one on hot summer days. We had a watering trough under that tree once, years ago. Troy and Mila used to fill it up with icy well water and then sit in it and play chess under the tree's arching canopy on sweltering summer days. They were cooled by the shade of her limbs covered in leaves and wee baby apples. They would take a kombucha with them and stay there for hours. I remember standing by the fence post watching them there, with the tree framing them as they laughed at each other. I thought there was no moment between a father and his daughter more perfect than that one. I took a picture. I'm so glad I took that picture.

———

I spent Sunday morning inside the world of our most luscious apple tree — the one I already mentioned, Ms. Bountiful and Bodacious. I had to separate her limbs to walk into her. I would take one step in and stop to pluck her apples and drop them in my bushel basket. Then, once I had reached every last apple within my grasp, I would take another step in. In less than three steps, I would have my full bushel and start another. There were leaves winding through my hair, encircling my body. Apples dropped on my head and then onto the ground as a single pluck loosened five more apples from her branches. One of our more playful barn cats, Lucy, came to pounce on the dropped fruit. The tree laughed and shook. I could feel her vibration through every leaf that touched me.

She is such a beautiful apple tree. So unencumbered by scarcity. She is a tree of faith! The tent caterpillars came a few years ago. She must have known it before we did after all of those decades living through cycles of tent caterpillars and their dastardly descendants. She must have known, as they floated down from the skies on their translucent wisps, that her winter dreams were to end in destruction. She was stripped bare of her plump little buds and newly opening sweet green leaves. They ate everything. And when she was a skeleton, they moved on to her neighbouring trees. In the forest, even the human ear could hear those caterpillars munching, their poop hitting the forest floor.

— 205 —

RADIANCE OF THE ORDINARY

She could do nothing but wait for the ravaging to end. And when it did, she took what she had, as did all of her apple siblings, and tried again that very same year. It was either that or enter into winter depleted. A hard winter would be enough to kill her. Her second round of leaflets were puny and shriveled but they gave her enough of the sun's nourishment to get by. There were no apples that next year or the one after that. She needed everything she could muster just to survive.

She is an old tree, but she is full. She is exuberant. Life has given her a choice spot to live. Her roots are nourished by nutrients that another apple tree, further down in the corner of the yard, cannot reach. That tree had to grow tall and thin to live within the dense trees surrounding her. I need a ladder to pluck the few apples she can grow.

But it's another tree in our backyard, the one framed by the big picture window in our living room, that calls to my heart now.

She's a quiet, unassuming tree, maybe even a bit ugly. A craggy apple tree. People before us cut off limbs that died when she was no longer able to supply her blood to their tips. We, too, have taken out our saw and cut back lifeless limbs that threatened to splinter what's left of her. It's only served to exaggerate her odd shape. One long limb branching from a trunk full of scars. There was life there, behind those scars, once. She throws up vertical branches every year, an attempt to increase her leaves to absorb the life of the sun, but it's not enough. There are too few leaves. There are too few branches and limbs. Life is dwindling for her. I look at her in the winter from the warmth of my sofa in front of a chugging woodstove and wonder what she is doing behind that snow-encrusted, skeletal form.

She is everything Ms. Bountiful and Bodacious is not. A ladder under her two main branches and a little shake and her tiny apples all succumb to gravity. Her apples are small, tiny even. But they are layered and sweet and tart and zesty and they remind you that an apple is not just an apple, and that nature is a marvel. In her apples, a reminder of our unique gifts. The endless, imaginative genius that will meet us if we open ourselves to it.

In this time of waning life, who would blame this tree if she simply decided to stop offering apples? If she simply went off into retirement,

APPLE TREES

having given over a hundred years of apples to thousands of creatures, wouldn't we all agree on the fairness of her preserving what's left? "Forget the apples, old girl, just take care of yourself!" But she continues to blossom year after year. She continues to grow her wondrous little apples. The new generations of deer that come here every fall, the shy mothers showing their fawns all of the choice apple trees on the land just as their mothers showed them, always go to her first. They will eat every last ground apple before moving on to another. Last year I watched as a plump doe stood on her rear legs and stretched herself to pluck apples off the tree's branches with her mouth. What apple tree wouldn't be flattered?

Maybe she knows that. Maybe she does it for them.

She will die soon. She will die with the last of her apples dangling from her limbs. The last of her energy devoted to life beyond her own. She will give it all away, every last drop of her for a seed. She teaches me, and I am a witness to her devotion. There is joy and abundance in the perfection of her apple tree counterparts, but she is wisdom and selfless determination. She, like all the other trees, like all forms of life that live and serve, will one day be absorbed fully back into the fold. The trunk that remains will crumble and feed the universes that live amongst her roots. She is perpetual.

Recently, our new mulberry trees brought the cedar waxwings here for the very first time. Six of them came and landed in the branches of the craggy apple tree to wait for those mulberries to hit the peak of perfection before their feast. A new type of bird with a new song and a different grasp on her skin. She would have noticed that. Does she delight in the touch of their little claws curling around her? Life that depends on her, even when she can no longer offer the plump and the shiny. The deer still come. The goldfinches still land. The human still picks her fruit. And she still endures. She offers everything she has, until the last drop of life courses through her and she is nothing more than a skeleton of wood.

They ask me, now, if I "have found healing." They ask me if what I do "brings healing." People want there to be "closure." People want us to be okay. But the truth is, there is no end. There is no finish line. All of life is the opening and closing of wounds and love and peace

— 207 —

RADIANCE OF THE ORDINARY

and pain. It doesn't end. Not here, anyway. I don't look for healing. I don't want courses or gurus or weekend retreats to fix me. I want old apple trees anointed by the touch of God. Trees that wrap themselves around me and laugh at their abundance and trees that gasp the last of their life force into a lovely little apple, round and perfect, that I may eat. A resurrection of a weary heart in every bite.

When I Die

Some days I go outside to be still upon the earth. Sometimes my bed is rich pasture grasses with cows grazing around me. Sometimes it's the frozen ground I lie on, crystalline snow wrapping around the curves of my body. I like to lie still enough that nature forgets I'm there. My heartbeat just another thump on her skin. My breath confused with the breath of foxes. My softness mistaken for the porcupine watching from a tree.

If I do it right, if I can untether myself from the superficial and the insincere, beauty brings me home. The bumblebees, fighting for territory before I plunked myself among them, resume their noisy rumble. The salamander hiding under the rotting woodpile peeks out his head and, sensing not a lick of danger, comes forth and goes about his day. The barn swallows fly back into the butternut tree beside me and start again with their calls to one another.

Soon, the vultures arrive, darkening the light beneath my eyelids with their enormous, circling shadows as they take my pulse from the air. I am a potential candidate. When that happens, I know I've got it right.

Not yet, good birds, not yet. But soon enough, my day will come.

When I do die, I bequeath my body to you. This body will have given me all that it could, and to it I bestow the great honour of feeding the earth just as the earth has fed me. I will not need this devoted carrier of my soul where I'm going.

When I die, the warm hands of God will lift me away.

I am unconfined and small, light as a filament of a thought. He places me on the earth in an endless glowing field. And here in this

— 209 —

sacred place, swaying walls of golden wheat sing their songs to my little girl. Mila is soft and sleepy, reaching for me. "Listen to our lullaby, Mama." *Hush, hush, hush.* I am beside her watching all of life above us. The endless blue sky, filled with fat, round clouds, our touchable ceiling. She reaches for my hand, and I am in her world now.

I can move again.

I turn my head toward her and we smile. I can feel her smile rush through me in great, pulsating waves of elation. We are together. Tears and laughter for the pain and the love, the anguish and the beauty of life. Grief and exaltation for those we wait for and those we hold again. There is nothing here and there is everything. Love and joy, home and us. Together. Together.

We stay there for a lifetime. Maybe longer. There is no need or want for anything else. We are warmed by the reflection of sunlight on the golden shafts of wheat planted by my grandfather long ago. Her hand in mine. I can feel it exactly as it was. Exactly as it will be.

And now my Bapka arrives, carried by the sounds of a laughing brook. My dearest friend, Richard, comes, soaring high in the sky on the feathers of a red-tailed hawk. He's enticing us to follow. Up and into and ever expanding. *Come, come. We are here and it is time.*

When the rest of our loves arrive, we will go to them. But not now. Now is opening before me through her loving eyes.

I am home.

ACKNOWLEDGMENTS

This book was made possible because of the support and encouragement of so many people. Surely I will leave some of you out, but I shall endeavour to do my best nonetheless.

To my three beautiful daughters, loyal and true. Thank you, Tyra and Ella, for your endless support, encouragement, and unencumbered joy for my work and my passions. Being your mama has been the great honour of my life. If only everyone could have such gorgeous, brilliant, loving, and fun young women cheering them on. I am so proud of the women you have become.

To Mila, my angel and my teacher, thank you for your wisdom and your compassion. You taught me so much about love and softness while you were here and continue to teach me and pull me into new understandings from your heavenly home. Your life with us is mysterious and profoundly beautiful. There are things I will never quite know, not here, but there are so many things that I know for certain because you have shown them to me. I know you rest in peace in God's loving arms. I also know we will hold each other again. Thank you for showing me that. You have left in your wake an unshakable faith in my soul. I thank you for such an extravagant gift. Evermore, sweet soul.

I'd also like to express my eternal gratitude to Richard, my best friend and mentor. Richard taught me what life was by his grounded acceptance and reverence of the natural world. It's impossible to fully express how his example shaped my understanding of life and death. I was, and will forever remain, in awe of him. I would be remiss in not also thanking his lovely bride, Kathleen, who welcomed me into their home and lives, feeding me farm feasts along the way. Thank you for letting me be a small part in your beautiful world.

To my granddaughter, Analuiza, who fills our lives with effervescent joy. May you find something in these pages that means something to you one day. And to all of the grandchildren and great-grandchildren to come, know that you were loved long before you ever made your appearance.

To my parents, Renny and Jenny, my God-appointed teachers and guides, who outfitted me to become who I was meant to be and to show me what's important in life. I am grateful for all you have given me. Also, my indebted gratitude to my little sister and her beautiful family and my many aunts, uncles, cousins, grandparents, and my stepmother, Heather, who showed little me what big families, elaborate feasts, strong communities, and good, foot-stomping music was all about. To Josephine, my beloved Bapka, whose selfless love and dedication to family impressed upon my heart — thank you. I will never be as good a cook, as skilled or as talented as you, but I will never stop trying. I hope you were proud of the pierogies we made at Christmas.

To all of my readers on Substack and those who came before on various blogs and on my Instagram account, I thank you. It's a rare and wonderful thing to connect with people in such meaningful and vulnerable ways on our little corner of the internet. How blessed I am that you think me worthy of your time and support. It is no small thing, and I hope that our meanderings through our lives results in

ACKNOWLEDGMENTS

us bumping into one another every now and then. Maybe we'll even find ourselves sharing a tea and a quiet chat by a fire or under some overzealous sunbeam making its way through the tree limbs. How lovely that would be.

To Maria Pace, the wildly talented and beautiful human being behind the wonderful images in this book. I am deeply honoured to have these pages christened by your hand.

To Brian Sanders and his crew at Peak Human. Thank you for finding me among the many people you could have highlighted and thinking my message worthy of your documentary. To Justin Rhodes and his crew at Abundance Plus, I thank you for showing our lives in your documentary series, *Divergence*, in such a sensitive and intimate way. I am honoured.

To my editor, Natalie, and all of the good people at Chelsea Green, I thank you for your skill and patience, and for finding something in my words that you thought worth promoting and sharing. You have all been a delight to work with. I'm so lucky to have had this opportunity.

I am so blessed to have a small handful of intimate friendships in my life. Each of these women brings such unique talents and passions, interests and intelligence. I thank all of you (I hope you know who you are) for our long chats on our forest walks or while sitting beside the fire sipping a good cup of coffee with great dollops of raw cream melting into it. Life is preciously short and being able to spend moments with humans like you is truly an embarrassment of riches.

Of course, always in my heart, is my thanks to God for the beauty saturated into everything. What a force and a wild, powerful imagination to offer to us, such a thing as a bird's feather or a summer wildflower to sit with and ponder for hours. How do you do that? Forgive me for the moments when I don't notice your masterpieces surrounding me. I love you. Thank you.

And while I'm speaking of the Creator, I will add my thanks for the wondrous creations I get to live with. I am indebted to my cows who fill my soul with peace and my frantic moments with the offering of rest. Specifically, to Bea, our senior citizen Jersey who owns the strings to my heart: Thank you for being a friend. To all of the animals on our farm, wild and domesticated, if I ever stop being awed

— 213 —

RADIANCE OF THE ORDINARY

by you, pack up and move away. You deserve better. But I will never do that, I swear it.

With gratitude always to Sister Kelly, my grade six teacher who told me I could write and whose kindness and attention fed my ambitions to do so.

There are endless friends and extended family who have touched me, taught me, and shown me parts of what it is to live in this world at this time that I never could have known without them. I'm grateful to all of you sharing this place at this time with me. We are a collective, a whole deeply interwoven and connected with one another. Thank you for your gifts and your talents. We need them more than ever.

Lastly, but never last, to my husband, Troy. Nothing written here would be possible without you. You are the very embodiment of a good man. Your steady nature, your good humour, your strength and drive, loyalty and love, power and gentleness have been the very stuff of my life. My pain is endured because you share it. My love grows because you feed it. I am able to bloom because of your care. When I was little, I dreamed of you. It took a good many years to find you, but you came. I will live out my days in service to this life we have worked so hard to create together. I am your woman. You are my man. Find me wherever we go from here.

ABOUT THE AUTHOR

SUZY LAMONT

Tara Couture is a writer and homesteader with a background in nutrition. She and her husband live on Slowdown Farmstead in Ontario, Canada, where they raise the cows, rabbits, ducks, geese, chickens, fruit trees, and vegetable gardens that provide them with most of the food they consume throughout the year. Tara writes about ancestral nutrition, family, homemaking, nature, sovereignty and autonomy, grief and loss, and authenticity on her Substack, Slowdown Farmstead.

the politics and practice of sustainable living
CHELSEA GREEN PUBLISHING

Chelsea Green Publishing sees books as tools for effecting cultural change and seeks to empower citizens to participate in reclaiming our global commons and become its impassioned stewards. If you enjoyed *Radiance of the Ordinary*, please consider these other great books related to nature, memoir, and farming.

GHOSTS OF THE FARM
Two Women's Journeys Through Time, Land and Community
NICOLA CHESTER
9781915294678
Hardcover

HEDGELANDS
A Wild Wander Around Britain's Greatest Habitat
CHRISTOPHER HART
9781915294470 (US)
9781915294722 (UK)
Paperback

FEATHER TRAILS
A Journey of Discovery Among Endangered Birds
SOPHIE A. H. OSBORN
9781645022428
Hardcover

GETTING HEALTHY IN TOXIC TIMES
An Ecological Doctor's Prescription for Healing Your Body and the Planet
DR JENNY GOODMAN
9781915294333
Paperback

For more information,
visit www.chelseagreen.com.